Dillard's Presents

Southern Living®
Christmas COOKBOOK
cooking • entertaining • giving

benefiting Ronald McDonald House Charities

RONALD MCDONALD
HOUSE CHARITIES

Merry Christmas

from all your friends at Dillard's.
We are proud to support the

Ronald McDonald House.

The purchase of this book helps families of seriously ill
children have a comfortable haven near their child.

Thank you for your generosity.
May your family have a wonderful holiday season
and a healthy and prosperous 2012.

ISBN-13: 978-0-8487-3480-0
ISBN-10: 0-8487-3480-7

Printed in the United States of America
First Printing 2011

Oxmoor House

VP, Publishing Director: Jim Childs
Editorial Director: Susan Payne Dobbs
Senior Brand Manager: Daniel Fagan
Senior Editor: Rebecca Brennan
Managing Editor: Laurie S. Herr

Southern Living Christmas Cookbook

Project Editors: Emily Chappell, Diane Rose
Assistant Designer: Allison L. Sperando
Director, Test Kitchens: Elizabeth Tyler Austin
Assistant Directors, Test Kitchens:
  Julie Christopher, Julie Gunter
Test Kitchens Professionals: Wendy Ball,
  Allison E. Cox, Victoria E. Cox, Margaret
  Monroe Dickey, Alyson Moreland Haynes,
  Stefanie Maloney, Callie Nash,
  Catherine Crowell Steele, Leah Van Deren
Photography Director: Jim Bathie
Senior Photo Stylist: Kay E. Clarke
Associate Photo Stylist: Katherine Eckert Coyne
Assistant Photo Stylist: Mary Louise Menendez
Production Manager: Theresa Beste-Farley

Contributors

Copy Editor: Dolores Hydock
Proofreaders: Donna Baldone,
  Catherine C. Fowler
Indexer: Nanette Cardon
Interns: Sarah H. Doss, Alison Loughman,
  Lindsay A. Rozier, Caitlin Watzke
Test Kitchens Professional:
  Kathleen Royal Phillips
Photographer: Mary Britton Senseney

Southern Living

Editor: M. Lindsay Bierman
Executive Editors: Rachel Hardage,
Jessica S. Thuston
Food Director: Shannon Sliter Satterwhite
Test Kitchen Director: Rebecca Kracke Gordon
Senior Writer: Donna Florio
Senior Food Editors: Shirley Harrington,
  Mary Allen Perry
Recipe Editor: JoAnn Weatherly
Assistant Recipe Editor: Ashley Arthur
Test Kitchen Specialists/Food Styling:
  Marian Cooper Cairns, Vanessa McNeil Rocchio
Test Kitchen Professionals: Norman King,
  Pam Lolley, Angela Sellers
Senior Photographers: Ralph Anderson,
  Gary Clark, Jennifer Davick, Art Meripol
Photographers: Robbie Caponetto,
  Laurey W. Glenn
Photo Research Coordinator: Ginny P. Allen
Senior Photo Stylist: Buffy Hargett
Editorial Assistant: Pat York

Time Home Entertainment Inc.

Publisher: Richard Fraiman
VP, Strategy & Business Development:
  Steven Sandonato
Executive Director, Marketing Services:
  Carol Pittard
Executive Director, Retail & Special Sales:
  Tom Mifsud
Director, New Product Development:
  Peter Harper
Director, Bookazine Development & Marketing:
  Laura Adam
Assistant Director, Brand Marketing: Joy Butts
Assistant Director, Special Sales: Ilene Schreider
Associate Counsel: Helen Wan

For more books to enrich your life,
visit **oxmoorhouse.com**

To search, savor, and share thousands
of recipes, visit **myrecipes.com**

Cover: Chocolate Extreme Cupcakes (page 78)
Page 1: Toffee-Tiramisù Layer Cake (page 91)

Contents

festive FARE

WHETHER YOU'RE LOOKING FOR A TRADITIONAL HOLIDAY
DISH OR SOMETHING FRESH AND NEW, A WIDE ARRAY OF
TASTY OPTIONS AWAITS YOU ON THESE PAGES.

breakfast & brunch
FAVORITES

Select from these recipes to plan a hearty early morning feast to enjoy while unwrapping gifts on Christmas day.

Eggs Benedict Casserole

Eggs Benedict Casserole

MAKES 6 SERVINGS
PREP: 8 MIN.   COOK: 55 MIN.   OTHER: 8 HR., 10 MIN.

  1 (12-oz.) package English muffins, cut into 1" pieces
  2 (6-oz.) packages Canadian bacon, cut into 1" pieces
  6 large eggs
2½ cups milk
 ½ tsp. dry mustard
 ½ tsp. salt
 ¼ tsp. freshly ground black pepper
     Quick Hollandaise
     Paprika
     Chopped fresh chives

1. Combine muffin pieces and Canadian bacon in a lightly greased 11" x 7" baking dish.
2. Whisk eggs and next 4 ingredients in a medium bowl. Pour egg mixture over muffin mixture. Cover and chill 8 hours.
3. Preheat oven to 375°. Bake casserole at 375° for 30 minutes. Uncover and bake 25 more minutes or until golden brown and set. Let stand 10 minutes. Cut into 6 squares. Drizzle squares with Quick Hollandaise sauce; sprinkle with paprika and chives. Serve immediately.

quick & easy

Quick Hollandaise

MAKES 1 CUP
PREP: 5 MIN.   COOK: 1 MIN.

  3 pasteurized egg yolks*
  1 Tbsp. fresh lemon juice
 ¼ tsp. salt
     Dash of ground red pepper
 ¾ cup butter

1. Process first 4 ingredients and 2 Tbsp. water in a blender until smooth.
2. Cook butter in a small saucepan over medium-high heat until melted and bubbly. (Do not brown.) Turn blender on high (with blender lid on and center cap open), and immediately add hot butter in a slow steady stream, pouring through center cap opening. Process until thickened.

*Using pasteurized eggs for this recipe eliminates the need to heat them to 160° for food safety.

Asiago, Mushroom, and Sausage Strata

(pictured on page 10)

Asiago cheese, portobello mushrooms, and sourdough bread add an upscale twist to traditional cheese strata.

MAKES 8 SERVINGS
PREP: 21 MIN.   COOK: 1 HR., 2 MIN.   OTHER: 8 HR., 35 MIN.

  1 lb. ground pork sausage
  2 Tbsp. butter
  1 (8-oz.) package sliced baby portobello mushrooms
  1 medium shallot, minced
  1 Tbsp. minced fresh thyme
  1 (16-oz.) loaf sourdough bread, cubed
1½ cups (6 oz.) shredded Asiago cheese, divided
  4 large eggs, lightly beaten
3½ cups half-and-half
 ½ tsp. salt
 ½ tsp. freshly ground pepper

1. Brown sausage in a large skillet over medium-high heat, stirring often, 6 to 7 minutes or until meat crumbles and is no longer pink; drain. Melt butter in pan over medium heat; add mushrooms and shallot, and sauté until tender. Stir in sausage and thyme.
2. Place bread in a lightly greased 13" x 9" baking dish. Sprinkle mushroom mixture and ½ cup cheese over bread. Whisk together eggs and remaining 3 ingredients; pour over mushrooms and bread. Sprinkle with remaining cheese. Cover and chill at least 8 hours.
3. Let stand at room temperature 30 minutes.
4. Meanwhile, preheat oven to 350°. Bake at 350° for 25 minutes. Uncover and bake 30 more minutes or until set and lightly browned. Let stand 5 minutes before serving.

Asiago, Mushroom, and Sausage Strata, page 9

Breakfast Soufflés Lorraine

Christmas Morning Baked Cheese Grits, page 12

Cinnamon Apple-Stuffed French Toast with Caramel Syrup, page 12

editor's favorite

Breakfast Soufflés Lorraine

Serve your choice of flavor of these soufflés inspired by a famous bakery specialty.

MAKES 6 SERVINGS
PREP: 20 MIN.   COOK: 35 MIN.   OTHER: 10 MIN.

    3 bacon slices
    ¾ cup chopped onion
    2 large eggs
    1¼ cups half-and-half
    ⅛ tsp. salt
    ⅛ tsp. freshly ground nutmeg
    ¼ tsp. freshly ground pepper
       Butter-flavored cooking spray
       Parchment paper
    1 (8-oz.) can crescent roll dough (we tested with
       Pillsbury)
    1 cup (4 oz.) shredded Gruyère cheese

1. Preheat oven to 375°. Cook bacon in a large nonstick skillet over medium-high heat 5 to 7 minutes or until crisp; remove bacon, and drain on paper towels, reserving drippings in skillet. Crumble bacon. Add onion to drippings in skillet; sauté over medium-high heat 5 to 7 minutes or until tender.
2. While onion cooks, whisk eggs until frothy in a bowl; whisk in half-and-half and next 3 ingredients.
3. Set 6 (4½") quiche dishes coated with cooking spray on a large parchment paper-lined baking sheet. Unroll dough on work surface; roll into a 14" x 12" rectangle, sealing perforations. Cut dough into 6 (6" x 4¾") rectangles; press 1 rectangle in bottom and up sides of each prepared dish, letting corners of dough extend over edges. Sprinkle dough with bacon, onion, and cheese. Ladle egg mixture over onion mixture. Carefully fold corners of dough in toward centers over filling, creating an X pattern. (Some egg mixture may seep around edges of dough.) Coat tops with cooking spray.
4. Bake at 375° on bottom shelf for 25 minutes or just until custard is puffed and crust is browned. (Do not overbake.) Let stand 10 minutes before serving.

Fiesta Breakfast Soufflés: Bake 18 frozen crisp potato tot crowns (we tested with Ore-Ida Crispy Crowns) according to package directions. Cook and crumble bacon as directed in recipe, discarding drippings. Omit onion. Prepare egg mixture and crusts as directed, omitting pepper and nutmeg, and adding ½ tsp. adobo sauce from canned chipotle chiles in adobo sauce and ¼ tsp. ground cumin to egg mixture. Omit Gruyère cheese. Divide tots, bacon, 3 Tbsp. thinly sliced green onions, 1 (4-oz.) can drained chopped green chiles, and 1 cup (4 oz.) shredded Mexican four-cheese blend among prepared crusts. Ladle egg mixture over cheese. Fold corners of dough over custard. Coat tops with cooking spray; bake and let stand as directed. Top with salsa, sour cream, and chopped fresh cilantro.

Florentine Breakfast Soufflés: Omit bacon and onion. Sauté 2 garlic cloves, minced, in 2 tsp. olive oil in a large nonstick skillet over medium-high heat 30 seconds. Add 3 Tbsp. drained, chopped bottled roasted red peppers; sauté 30 seconds. Add ¼ cup dry white wine and ¼ cup sliced green onions; cook 1 minute or until wine is almost evaporated. Add 1½ cups coarsely chopped fresh baby spinach; sauté 1 minute or just until spinach wilts. Remove from heat. Prepare egg mixture and crusts as directed, adding ½ tsp. Italian seasoning to egg mixture. Divide spinach mixture among prepared crusts. Omit Gruyère cheese. Ladle egg mixture over spinach mixture; sprinkle tops with ⅓ cup grated Parmesan cheese. Fold corners of dough over custard. Coat tops with cooking spray; bake and let stand as directed. Serve with warm marinara sauce, if desired.

editor's favorite • make ahead

Christmas Morning Baked Cheese Grits

(pictured on page 10)

This rich casserole has a light and airy texture that melts in your mouth.

MAKES 8 SERVINGS
PREP: 20 MIN.   COOK: 45 MIN.   OTHER: 8 HR., 35 MIN.

- 1½ cups whipping cream
- ½ tsp. salt
- 1 cup uncooked quick-cooking grits
- 3 large eggs, lightly beaten
- 1½ cups (6 oz.) shredded sharp Cheddar cheese
- 2 Tbsp. butter
- ⅛ tsp. garlic powder

1. Combine 1½ cups water, whipping cream, and salt in a large saucepan; bring to a boil. Gradually stir in grits. Cover, reduce heat, and simmer 5 minutes, stirring occasionally. Stir in eggs and remaining ingredients.

2. Pour grits mixture into a lightly greased 11" x 7" baking dish. Cover and chill at least 8 hours.

3. Remove casserole from refrigerator, and let stand 30 minutes.

4. Meanwhile, preheat oven to 350°. Bake at 350° for 40 minutes or until set and lightly browned. Let stand 5 minutes before serving.

fix it faster

Preheat oven to 350°. Prepare casserole, but do not chill. Bake at 350° for 40 to 45 minutes or until lightly browned.

editor's favorite • quick & easy

Cinnamon Apple-Stuffed French Toast with Caramel Syrup

(pictured on page 10)

For superior results, we purchased unsliced bread from the bakery for this recipe and sliced it ourselves. We gave the recipe our highest rating.

MAKES 8 SERVINGS
PREP: 20 MIN.   COOK: 10 MIN.

- 6 oz. cream cheese, softened
- ¼ cup granulated sugar
- ½ tsp. ground cinnamon
- 8 (1½") slices challah or French bread
- 1 (12-oz.) package frozen baked apples with cinnamon (we tested with Stouffer's Harvest Apples)
- 1 Tbsp. butter, melted
- 1 Tbsp. vegetable oil
- 1½ Tbsp. granulated sugar
- ½ tsp. ground cinnamon
- 5 large eggs
- ¾ cup half-and-half
- ¼ cup packed light brown sugar
- 1 tsp. vanilla extract
- Caramel Syrup (see Caramel-Mocha Syrup variation on facing page)

1. Preheat oven to 400°. Beat first 3 ingredients at medium speed with an electric mixer until smooth.

2. Cut a pocket through top crust of each bread slice, cutting to but not through bottom crust, to form a pocket. Stuff each pocket with about 2 Tbsp. each cream cheese mixture and apple chunks.

3. Stir together butter and oil. Set aside.

4. Stir together 1½ Tbsp. granulated sugar and cinnamon until blended.

5. Whisk together eggs and next 3 ingredients in a shallow dish until well blended. Dip stuffed bread slices in egg mixture 5 seconds on each side. Cook on a hot griddle brushed with oil mixture over medium heat 2 minutes on each side or until golden. Transfer to a baking sheet.

6. Bake at 400° for 6 minutes or until thoroughly heated. Sprinkle with cinnamon-sugar mixture. Serve with Caramel Syrup.

Overnight Yeast Waffles with Caramel-Mocha Syrup and Cinnamon Butter

Baking these rich waffles in a Belgian waffle iron creates deep pockets to hold the luscious syrup and spiced butter.

MAKES 6 SERVINGS
PREP: 18 MIN.   COOK: 10 MIN.   OTHER: 8 HR., 5 MIN.

- 1 (¼-oz.) envelope active dry yeast
- ½ cup warm water (100° to 110°)
- 2 cups warm milk (100° to 110°)
- ½ cup butter, melted
- 1 tsp. sugar
- ½ tsp. salt
- 2 cups all-purpose flour
- 2 large eggs
- ¼ tsp. baking soda
- Caramel-Mocha Syrup
- Cinnamon Butter

1. Combine yeast and warm water (100° to 110°) in a 1-cup glass measuring cup; let stand 5 minutes. Combine yeast mixture, milk, and next 3 ingredients in a large bowl. Add flour, stirring until smooth. Cover and chill 8 hours.

2. Whisk eggs and baking soda into batter. Cook in a preheated, oiled waffle iron until crisp. Serve waffles with Caramel-Mocha Syrup and Cinnamon Butter.

Caramel-Mocha Syrup

MAKES 1⅓ CUPS
PREP: 2 MIN.   COOK: 19 MIN.

- 1 (14-oz.) package caramels
- ½ cup evaporated milk
- 1¼ tsp. instant espresso
- ¼ cup maple syrup

1. Place caramels in a medium saucepan. Stir together evaporated milk and espresso; add to pan. Cook, stirring constantly, over medium heat until caramels melt and mixture is smooth. Stir in maple syrup. Serve warm.

Caramel Syrup: Prepare recipe as directed, omitting espresso.

Cinnamon Butter

MAKES ½ CUP
PREP: 3 MIN.

- ½ cup butter, softened
- 1 Tbsp. cinnamon sugar

1. Stir together butter and cinnamon sugar until smooth.

editor's favorite

Brown Sugar-Cinnamon Coffee Cake with Spiced Streusel Topping

Serve this breakfast favorite warm with mugs of hot coffee.

MAKES 9 SERVINGS
PREP: 10 MIN. COOK: 50 MIN. OTHER: 4 MIN.

- ½ cup butter, softened
- 1 cup firmly packed light brown sugar
- 2 large eggs
- 1 cup sour cream
- 1 tsp. vanilla extract
- 1¾ cups all-purpose flour
- 1 Tbsp. baking powder
- 1 tsp. ground cinnamon
- ½ tsp. salt
- ½ tsp. baking soda
- ¼ tsp. ground mace
- 1 cup finely chopped pecans, toasted
  Spiced Streusel

1. Preheat oven to 350°. Beat butter and sugar at medium speed with an electric mixer until fluffy. Add eggs, 1 at a time, beating until blended after each addition. Beat in sour cream and vanilla.
2. Whisk together flour, baking powder, and next 4 ingredients. Add to butter mixture; beat at low speed until blended. Stir in pecans. Spread batter into a greased 9" square pan. Sprinkle with Spiced Streusel.
3. Bake at 350° for 50 minutes or until a wooden pick inserted in center comes out clean. Cool in pan on a wire rack.

Spiced Streusel

MAKES ABOUT 3 CUPS
PREP: 4 MIN.

- 1 cup all-purpose flour
- 1 cup firmly packed light brown sugar
- 1 tsp. ground cinnamon
- ¼ tsp. ground mace
- ½ cup butter, cut into cubes
- 1 cup coarsely chopped pecans

1. Whisk together flour, brown sugar, and next 2 ingredients in a medium bowl; cut in butter with a pastry blender until crumbly. Stir in pecans.

editor's favorite

Sugar-Crusted Pumpkin Bread

Studded with dried cranberries and walnuts, this tender, flavorful bread with its crunchy top is cholesterol-free and boasts healthful fiber, antioxidants, and omega-3s.

MAKES 1 LOAF
PREP: 12 MIN. COOK: 1 HR., 10 MIN. OTHER: 10 MIN.

- 2¼ cups all-purpose flour
- ½ cup whole wheat flour
- 1 Tbsp. ground flax seed
- 1 Tbsp. toasted wheat germ
- 1 Tbsp. baking powder
- 1 tsp. baking soda
- 1 tsp. ground cinnamon
- ¾ tsp. ground cloves
- ½ tsp. salt
- 1 cup granulated sugar
- 2 large egg whites
- 1 cup canned pumpkin
- ¼ cup canola oil
- 1¼ cups light vanilla soy milk
- ⅓ cup chopped sweetened dried cranberries
- ⅓ cup chopped walnuts
  Butter-flavored cooking spray
- 2 Tbsp. turbinado sugar

1. Preheat oven to 350°. Combine first 10 ingredients in a large bowl. Whisk egg whites until frothy in a separate bowl; whisk in pumpkin, oil, and soy milk. Add pumpkin mixture to flour mixture, stirring just until dry ingredients are moistened. Fold in cranberries and walnuts.
2. Pour batter into a 9" x 5" loaf pan coated with cooking spray; sprinkle with turbinado sugar. Bake at 350° for 1 hour and 10 minutes or until a wooden pick inserted in center comes out clean. Cool in pan 10 minutes. Remove from pan. Cool completely on a wire rack.

Colossal Apple-Walnut-Browned Butter Muffins

Apple and cinnamon, the wonderful aromas of the season, will fill your kitchen on Christmas morning as a batch of these rich, tender muffins bakes, but you can re-create the experience any day of the year.

MAKES 10 MUFFINS
PREP: 20 MIN. COOK: 37 MIN. OTHER: 5 MIN.

Colossal Apple-Walnut-Browned Butter Muffins

10	Texas-size paper baking cups
1	cup butter
3	cups all-purpose flour
2	tsp. baking powder
½	tsp. salt
¼	tsp. ground cinnamon
1¼	cups packed light brown sugar
3	large eggs
¾	cup sour cream
¼	cup milk
2	tsp. vanilla extract
2½	cups chopped peeled Gala or Fuji apple
1½	cups chopped walnuts, toasted
10	thin unpeeled Gala or Fuji apple slices

1. Preheat oven to 375°. Place paper baking cups in 2 (6-cup) Texas-size muffin pans.

2. Melt butter in a large skillet over medium-low heat. Cook 5 minutes or until butter just begins to brown and develop a nutty aroma. (Watch carefully so as not to burn.) Remove from heat; let cool.

3. Combine flour and next 4 ingredients in a large bowl; make a well in center of mixture. Stir together eggs, sour cream, milk, and vanilla; slowly whisk in butter. Add to dry mixture, stirring just until moistened. Fold in chopped apple and walnuts. Spoon into prepared muffin pans, filling almost full. Insert an apple slice at a 45° angle into each portion of batter to a depth of half the apple slice.

4. Bake at 375° for 32 minutes or until muffins spring back when lightly touched. Cool in pans on wire racks 5 minutes. Remove muffins from pans to wire racks; cool slightly. Serve warm.

Hot Curried Fruit Bake

Just a hint of curry, almost unidentifiable in this recipe, adds a delightful, unique flavor to this warm fruit. Serve it alongside a savory breakfast casserole or with ham and biscuits.

MAKES 8 TO 10 SERVINGS
PREP: 13 MIN. COOK: 55 MIN.

1	(20-oz.) can pineapple chunks in juice, undrained
1	(15-oz.) can sliced peaches in extra-light syrup, drained
1	(15-oz.) can apricot halves in extra-light syrup, drained
1	(15¼-oz.) can pear halves in heavy syrup, drained and halved
2	small Granny Smith apples, peeled and coarsely chopped
½	cup drained maraschino cherries
2	tsp. lemon juice
½	cup packed light brown sugar
1	Tbsp. cornstarch
½	tsp. curry powder
⅛	tsp. ground cinnamon
2	Tbsp. butter, cut into pieces

1. Preheat oven to 350°. Drain pineapple; reserving juice. Combine pineapple and next 5 ingredients in a lightly greased 11" x 7" baking dish.

2. Whisk together reserved pineapple juice, lemon juice, and next 4 ingredients until smooth. Pour juice mixture over fruit; dot with butter.

3. Bake, uncovered, at 350° for 55 minutes or until bubbly and juices are slightly thickened.

superfast APPETIZERS

These delicious recipes will help you get your holiday gathering started in 30 minutes or less.

quick & easy

Minty Green Pea and Butter Bean Hummus

This festive green hummus made from lima beans, also known as butter beans, has a lighter flavor and texture than traditional hummus, which uses chickpeas. You can also serve it with fresh vegetables.

MAKES 3 CUPS
PREP: 7 MIN.

  2 cups frozen petite peas, thawed
  2 cups frozen baby lima beans, thawed
  3 Tbsp. extra virgin olive oil
  1 Tbsp. fresh lemon juice
  2 large garlic cloves
  ½ cup fresh mint leaves
  ½ cup crumbled feta cheese
  ½ tsp. salt
  ¼ tsp. freshly ground black pepper
     Pita chips

1. Place all ingredients, except pita chips, in a food processor or blender; pulse until smooth. Cover and store in refrigerator. Serve with pita chips.

BLT Dip

The bacon, lettuce, and tomato sandwich, a diner favorite, was the inspiration for this highly rated dip. Here, the "lettuce" is Belgian endive. We liked it with bagel crisps and scoop-shaped tortilla chips, too.

MAKES ABOUT 2 CUPS
PREP: 12 MIN.   OTHER: 1 HR.

- 10 cooked bacon slices, crumbled
- 2 large plum tomatoes, seeded and chopped
- ½ cup mayonnaise
- ½ cup sour cream
- 2 Tbsp. chopped fresh flat-leaf parsley
- ⅛ tsp. garlic salt
- ⅛ tsp. freshly ground pepper
- Belgian endive leaves

1. Reserve 3 Tbsp. each bacon and tomato. Stir together remaining bacon, tomato, and next 5 ingredients in a medium bowl. Cover and chill 1 hour.

2. Sprinkle dip with reserved bacon and tomato before serving. Serve with endive leaves.

editor's favorite · quick & easy

Shrimp Martini Cocktail Appetizer

MAKES 4 SERVINGS
PREP: 12 MIN.   COOK: 1 MIN.

½   lb. medium shrimp, peeled
1   to 2 Tbsp. dry vermouth (optional)
1   Tbsp. chopped fresh cilantro
1   Tbsp. fresh lemon juice
¼   tsp. salt
2   plum tomatoes, seeded and chopped
8   pimiento-stuffed Spanish olives, coarsely chopped
1   small jalapeño pepper, seeded and minced
1   large garlic clove, minced
Garnishes: lemon zest curls, skewered olives

1. Cook shrimp in boiling water 1 minute or just until shrimp turn pink. Drain and plunge into ice water until chilled; drain.
2. Stir together vermouth, if desired, and next 7 ingredients in a medium bowl. Add shrimp, tossing gently. Spoon ½ cup shrimp mixture into each of 4 martini glasses. Garnish, if desired.

Use your favorite beverage glasses to serve this shrimp cocktail with seasonal style.

editor's favorite · quick & easy

Quick Pot Stickers with Chinese Dipping Sauce

Much of the preparation of the filling in these authentically flavored pot stickers is eliminated by the use of prepared meatballs.

MAKES 20 POT STICKERS
PREP: 14 MIN.   COOK: 9 MIN.

Chinese Dipping Sauce

¼ cup soy sauce
¼ cup rice wine vinegar
1 Tbsp. minced peeled fresh ginger
2 Tbsp. honey
1 tsp. brown sugar
½ tsp. dried crushed red pepper
1 large garlic clove, pressed

Pot Stickers

1 Tbsp. dark sesame oil, divided
1 tsp. soy sauce
4 green onions
½ medium-size red bell pepper, quartered
20 won ton wrappers
20 frozen fully cooked cocktail-size meatballs, thawed (we tested with Farm Rich)
1 Tbsp. canola oil, divided
1 cup beef broth, divided

1. Prepare Chinese Dipping Sauce: Stir together all ingredients in a small bowl.
2. Prepare Pot Stickers: Pulse 1 tsp. sesame oil and next 3 ingredients in a food processor until finely chopped. Spoon about ½ Tbsp. green onion mixture in center of each won ton wrapper; top with a meatball. Moisten edges of wrappers. Bring corners of wrappers over filling to center, pressing to seal edges.
3. Heat 1 tsp. sesame oil and 1½ tsp. canola oil in a large nonstick skillet over medium-high heat. Add half of pot stickers; cook 2 minutes or until golden. Remove pot stickers from pan. Repeat procedure with remaining oils and remaining half of pot stickers.
4. Add ½ cup broth and half of pot stickers to skillet; cover, reduce heat, and simmer 2 minutes or until tender. Transfer to a serving dish. Repeat procedure with remaining broth and remaining pot stickers. Serve pot stickers with Chinese Dipping Sauce.

Note: To quickly thaw the meatballs, place in a microwave-safe dish. Cover with a paper towel, and cook at HIGH 1 to 2 minutes.

editor's favorite · quick & easy

BBQ Pork Sliders with Blue Cheese Slaw

(pictured on page 21)

Stop by your favorite barbecue restaurant to pick up the meat for these mini sandwiches. Feel free to use your favorite barbecue sauce, too.

MAKES 12 SERVINGS
PREP: 18 MIN.

3 cups shredded coleslaw mix
½ cup refrigerated Ranch dressing (we tested with Naturally Fresh)
¼ cup crumbled blue cheese
⅛ tsp. pepper
2 slices bacon, cooked and crumbled
3 cups pulled pork barbecue, warmed
1 (15-oz.) package mini sandwich buns (we tested with Pepperidge Farm Sliders)
½ cup spicy barbecue sauce, warmed
Garnish: dill pickle slices

1. Combine first 5 ingredients in a medium bowl, stirring to coat slaw mixture.
2. Place ¼ cup pork on bottom half of each bun; top with ¼ cup slaw. Drizzle slaw with 1 to 2 tsp. barbecue sauce, and top with bun tops. Garnish, if desired.

fix it faster

Use precooked bacon bits instead of cooking and crumbling bacon.

editor's favorite · quick & easy

Asian-Style Mini Crab Cakes with Wasabi Aioli

If you can find crabmeat only in a 1-lb. container, use the extra for a crab salad. You can double the recipe for larger parties, too.

MAKES 1 DOZEN
PREP: 8 MIN.   COOK: 10 MIN.

- ½ lb. fresh crabmeat
- 2 tsp. dark sesame oil
- 1 tsp. Chinese sweet-hot mustard
- 2 small green onions, chopped
- 1 large egg, lightly beaten
- 1½ cups Japanese breadcrumbs (panko), divided
- ⅓ cup vegetable oil
- ⅓ cup mayonnaise
- 1½ tsp. wasabi paste
- Garnish: fresh cilantro sprigs

1. Pick crabmeat, removing any bits of shell. Combine crabmeat and next 4 ingredients in a bowl. Stir in ½ cup breadcrumbs. Shape crabmeat mixture into 12 balls; flatten slightly into patties.
2. Heat oil in a large nonstick skillet over medium-high heat.
3. Meanwhile, place remaining 1 cup breadcrumbs in a shallow dish. Dredge patties in breadcrumbs, pressing lightly. Fry patties in hot oil 2 to 3 minutes on each side or until golden. Drain on paper towels.
4. Stir together mayonnaise and wasabi paste until blended. Serve wasabi aioli with crab cakes. Garnish, if desired.

quick & easy

Double Cheese Tartlets

MAKES 30 TARTS
PREP: 12 MIN.   COOK: 18 MIN.

- 2 (1.9-oz.) packages frozen mini-phyllo pastry shells
- Parchment paper
- ¼ cup crumbled blue cheese
- ¼ cup whipping cream
- 2 tsp. brandy (optional)
- 2 large eggs
- ½ cup (2 oz.) finely shredded Gouda cheese

1. Preheat oven to 425°. Place pastry shells on a large baking sheet lined with parchment paper.
2. Mash blue cheese and cream with a fork in a bowl until almost smooth. Stir in brandy, if desired, until smooth; stir in eggs until well blended. Stir in cheese.
3. Spoon cheese mixture into tart shells. Bake at 425° for 18 minutes or until filling is set.

editor's favorite · quick & easy

Fried Ravioli with Marinara Sauce

These crispy, crunchy little pillows make easy pickups for guests as they mingle.

MAKES 40 RAVIOLI
PREP: 23 MIN.   COOK: 5 MIN.

- Vegetable oil
- 1 cup Italian-seasoned Japanese breadcrumbs (panko)
- ½ cup (2 oz.) shredded Parmesan cheese
- 1 tsp. garlic powder
- ¼ tsp. salt
- 1 (25-oz.) package frozen cheese ravioli, thawed
- 2 large eggs, lightly beaten
- 1½ cups bottled marinara sauce (we tested with Gia Russa)

1. Pour oil into a large Dutch oven to a depth of 1". Heat over medium-high heat to 360°.
2. Combine breadcrumbs and next 3 ingredients in a shallow dish. Dip ravioli in beaten egg; dredge in crumb mixture, shaking off excess. Fry ravioli, 10 at a time, in hot oil 20 to 30 seconds or until golden. Drain on paper towels. Serve with marinara sauce.

BBQ Pork Sliders with
Blue Cheese Slaw,
page 19

Asian-Style Mini Crab Cakes
with Wasabi Aioli

Double Cheese Tartlets

Fried Ravioli with
Marinara Sauce

Chicken and Broccoli
Cobbler

half-hour HOLIDAY FOOD

Easy meal ideas for busy people come together in this collection of casseroles and skillet dinners. Most of the recipes are one-dish wonders, and each bakes in about 30 minutes.

Chicken and Broccoli Cobbler

Leftover turkey or a rotisserie chicken works equally well in this easy casserole dotted with Christmas red and green. Crisp sourdough croutons are its crowning glory. Use bagged broccoli florets from the grocery produce section. There's no need to precook the broccoli—it will be crisp-tender when the casserole is bubbly.

MAKES 4 SERVINGS
PREP: 16 MIN.   COOK: 30 MIN.

    ¼   cup butter, melted
    5   oz. cubed sourdough bread (3 cups)
    ½   cup refrigerated grated Parmesan cheese
    3   cups small broccoli florets
    3   cups chopped cooked chicken
    ½   cup drained chopped roasted red bell pepper
    1   (10-oz.) container refrigerated Alfredo sauce
    ½   cup sour cream
    2   Tbsp. dry sherry

1. Drizzle butter over bread cubes in a large bowl; sprinkle with cheese, and toss well.
2. Preheat oven to 400°. Combine broccoli and next 5 ingredients in a large bowl. Spoon filling into a lightly greased 2-qt. rectangular or oval baking dish or individual baking dishes; top with bread cubes.
3. Bake, uncovered, at 400° for 30 minutes (20 to 25 minutes for individual cobblers) or until bubbly and top is toasted.

Chicken and Rice Casserole

To speed things up, use a rotisserie chicken for this family-friendly casserole.

MAKES 8 SERVINGS
PREP: 20 MIN.   COOK: 25 MIN.

    2   Tbsp. butter or margarine
    1   medium onion, finely chopped
    3   cups chopped cooked chicken
   1½   cups frozen petite peas
   1½   cups (6 oz.) shredded sharp Cheddar cheese
    1   cup mayonnaise
    1   (10¾-oz.) can cream of chicken soup
    1   (8.8-oz.) package microwaveable rice of choice
        (we tested with Uncle Ben's)
    1   (8-oz.) can sliced water chestnuts, drained
    1   (4-oz.) jar pimientos, drained
    3   cups coarsely crushed ridged potato chips (we tested
        with Ruffles)

1. Preheat oven to 350°. Melt butter in a skillet over medium heat. Add onion, and sauté until tender, about 5 minutes. Combine onion, chicken, and next 7 ingredients in a large bowl; toss gently. Spoon mixture into a lightly greased 13" x 9" baking dish. Top with coarsely crushed chips. Bake, uncovered, at 350° for 20 to 25 minutes or until bubbly.

Spanish Chicken, Lemon, and Potatoes

Flavors of the Mediterranean make this juicy chicken a pleasant departure from expected holiday fare.

MAKES 6 SERVINGS
PREP: 5 MIN.   COOK: 28 MIN.

    3 Tbsp. extra virgin olive oil
    6 skinned and boned chicken thighs
    ¼ tsp. salt
    ¼ tsp. freshly ground pepper
    1 (20-oz.) package refrigerated red potato wedges
    4 large garlic cloves, sliced
    2 oz. cured chorizo sausage, diced
    ½ cup pitted Spanish olives
    1 cup chicken broth
    1 Tbsp. Hungarian sweet paprika
    1 lemon, thinly sliced and seeded

1. Heat olive oil in a large skillet over medium-high heat. Sprinkle chicken thighs evenly with salt and pepper; add to skillet. Cook 5 minutes or until browned on all sides.
2. Meanwhile, combine potatoes and next 5 ingredients in a large bowl; toss to coat. Add potato mixture with broth to skillet; top with lemon slices. Cover and cook 20 minutes or until potatoes are tender.

Poppy Seed Turkey Casserole

Turkey puts a new spin on this classic cracker-topped casserole. Add some broccoli florets to introduce color and a veggie.

MAKES 6 SERVINGS
PREP: 12 MIN.   COOK: 25 MIN.   OTHER: 10 MIN.

    3 to 4 cups chopped cooked turkey
    1 (10¾-oz.) can cream of chicken and mushroom soup
    1 (16-oz.) container sour cream or light sour cream
 1½ cups (6 oz.) shredded sharp Cheddar cheese
    3 Tbsp. poppy seeds
    1 sleeve of whole wheat round buttery crackers (we tested with Ritz), crushed*
    ¼ cup butter or margarine, melted

1. Preheat oven to 350°. Combine first 5 ingredients in a large bowl; stir well. Spoon into a lightly greased 11" x 7" baking dish. Top with crushed crackers. Drizzle with melted butter. Bake, uncovered, at 350° for 25 to 30 minutes or until bubbly. Let stand 10 minutes before serving.

*You can crush the crackers while they're still in the sleeve; then open at one end, and sprinkle over casserole.

Holiday Shepherd's Pie

Fix this clever casserole whenever you're in the mood for the flavors of Christmas dinner. Substitute your leftover cornbread dressing for the cornbread to pump up the flavor.

MAKES 6 SERVINGS
PREP: 9 MIN.   COOK: 26 MIN.

    3 Tbsp. butter, divided
    3 cups prechopped fresh onion, bell pepper, and celery blend
    2 cups coarsely crumbled day-old (savory not sweet) cornbread
    3 cups chopped cooked turkey
    1 cup turkey gravy (we tested with Heinz)
    ½ tsp. salt
    ½ tsp. freshly ground black pepper
    1 (1.5-lb.) package refrigerated mashed potatoes (we tested with Simply Potatoes)
    1 cup whole-berry cranberry sauce

1. Preheat oven to 375°. Melt 2 Tbsp. butter in a large skillet over medium-high heat; add onion, bell pepper, and celery blend, and sauté 8 minutes or until tender. Combine sautéed vegetables, cornbread, turkey, and next 3 ingredients in a large bowl. Toss gently. Spoon mixture into a lightly greased 11" x 7" baking dish. Cover to keep warm.
2. Meanwhile, heat potatoes in microwave according to package directions. Stir in remaining 1 Tbsp. butter. Spread 1 cup cranberry sauce over turkey mixture. Top with potatoes. Bake, uncovered, at 375° for 15 minutes or until thoroughly heated.

Ranch Turkey Ravioli Casserole

This fun twist on lasagna uses ravioli.

MAKES 6 SERVINGS
PREP: 18 MIN.   COOK: 28 MIN.   OTHER: 15 MIN.

  1 (15-oz.) can black beans, rinsed and drained
  1 (14.5-oz.) can petite diced tomatoes, drained
  ½ cup chopped fresh cilantro
  1 tsp. ground cumin
  2 cups green enchilada sauce (we tested with
     La Preferida)
  2 (9-oz.) packages refrigerated cheese ravioli
  2 cups chopped cooked turkey
  ½ cup sliced green onions
  1 cup (4 oz.) shredded Mexican four-cheese blend

1. Preheat oven to 400°. Combine first 4 ingredients in a bowl.
2. Spread ½ cup enchilada sauce in a lightly greased 11" x 7" baking dish. Arrange half of ravioli over sauce. Top with half of black bean mixture, 1 cup turkey, ¼ cup green onions, and ½ cup enchilada sauce. Repeat layers. Pour remaining sauce over top; sprinkle with cheese.
3. Bake, uncovered, at 400° for 28 minutes or until thoroughly heated and lightly browned. Let stand 15 minutes before serving.

quick & easy

Quick Skillet Rigatoni

MAKES 4 SERVINGS
PREP: 4 MIN.   COOK: 15 MIN.

  8 oz. uncooked rigatoni
  1 Tbsp. olive oil
  1 medium onion, finely chopped
  ½ lb. ground round
  1 (8-oz.) package sliced fresh mushrooms
  2 tsp. chopped fresh rosemary
  ½ cup dry white wine or chicken or beef broth
  1 (15-oz.) can seasoned tomato sauce for lasagna
     (we tested with Hunt's)
    Grated Parmesan cheese
    Freshly ground pepper

1. Cook rigatoni according to package directions; drain and keep warm.
2. While pasta cooks, heat oil in a large skillet over medium-high heat. Add onion, ground round, mushrooms, and rosemary. Cook 8 minutes or until meat crumbles and is no longer pink. Add wine; bring to a boil. Cook 2 minutes or until almost all liquid evaporates. Stir in cooked pasta and tomato sauce; cover and simmer 3 minutes or until thoroughly heated. Sprinkle each serving with grated Parmesan cheese and pepper.

make ahead

Chili Mini Lasagna

Baking this lasagna in two loaf pans makes for easy transport to holiday get-togethers, covered-dish parties, or to a friend in need. We discovered these oven-ready noodles fit perfectly in loaf pans. Use disposable aluminum pans for no-fuss cleanup.

MAKES 2 LASAGNAS/ 8 SERVINGS
PREP: 16 MIN.   COOK: 34 MIN.   OTHER: 8 HR., 10 MIN.

  1 lb. ground round
  1 Tbsp. chili powder
  1 (15-oz.) can white kidney beans, rinsed and drained
  1 large egg, lightly beaten
  1 (15-oz.) container ricotta cheese
3¼ cups roasted tomato salsa (we tested with Ariba)
  6 oven-ready lasagna noodles
  3 cups (12 oz.) shredded Cheddar-Jack cheese
    Sour cream (optional)

1. Cook ground beef in a large skillet over medium heat, stirring until meat crumbles and is no longer pink; drain and return to pan. Stir in chili powder and kidney beans.
2. Combine egg and ricotta in a small bowl; set aside.
3. Spread 2 Tbsp. salsa in each of 2 lightly greased 9" x 5" loaf pans. Arrange 1 noodle over salsa in each pan. Spoon one-fourth ricotta mixture and one-fourth chili mixture over noodle in each pan; sprinkle each with ½ cup cheese. Spread ½ cup salsa over cheese in each pan. Repeat layers. Top each pan with another noodle, 1 cup salsa, covering noodle layer completely in each pan. Sprinkle each lasagna with remaining cheese. Cover tightly with aluminum foil, and refrigerate overnight. Bring to room temperature before baking.
4. Preheat oven to 400°. Bake, covered, at 400° for 25 minutes; uncover and bake 5 more minutes or until lightly browned and bubbly. Let stand 10 minutes before serving. Serve with sour cream, if desired.

Pasta and Greens Torte

Pasta and Greens Torte

A well-seasoned cast-iron skillet is in order for this impressive deep-dish entrée.

MAKES 6 TO 8 SERVINGS
PREP: 12 MIN. COOK: 28 MIN. OTHER: 10 MIN.

- 1 lb. fresh Swiss chard*
- 8 large eggs
- 1 cup milk
- 1 cup ricotta cheese
- 1½ tsp. dried thyme
- 1½ tsp. salt
- ½ tsp. pepper
- 1 (9-oz.) package refrigerated linguine, cut in half
- 3 Tbsp. olive oil
- 2 cups (8 oz.) shredded Italian blend cheese

1. Bring 4 qt. water to a boil in a 6-qt. Dutch oven.
2. While water comes to a boil, remove and discard stems and ribs from chard. Coarsely chop leaves. Wash chard thoroughly in cold water; drain well. Process eggs and next 5 ingredients in a blender until smooth.
3. Preheat oven to 400°. Add chard leaves and pasta to boiling water. Return water to a boil; boil 1 minute. Drain well, pressing out excess moisture from chard with the back of a spoon. Return pasta and greens to pan; toss until blended.
4. Brush a 10" cast-iron skillet with olive oil. Arrange pasta and greens in skillet; sprinkle with cheese. Pour egg mixture over cheese, pressing to submerge pasta and greens in liquid.
5. Place skillet over medium heat for 2 minutes. Immediately transfer to hot oven. Bake at 400° for 25 minutes or until golden and set. Let stand 10 minutes before inverting onto a serving platter, if desired, and cutting into wedges.

*It's easier to prepare greens if you chop or tear them first before cleaning in several washings of cold water. Drain well between washings, and finish with a whirl in a salad spinner to remove sandy grit.

editor's favorite

Southwestern Egg Casserole

This dish is great for brunch or Sunday night supper. It's spicy—for a milder flavor, choose plain Monterey Jack cheese.

MAKES 8 SERVINGS
PREP: 27 MIN. COOK: 49 MIN.

- 1 lb. mild ground pork sausage
- 1 small onion, chopped
- ½ green bell pepper, chopped
- 2 (10-oz.) cans diced tomatoes and green chiles, undrained
- 8 (10") flour tortillas, torn into bite-size pieces
- 3 cups (12 oz.) shredded Monterey Jack cheese with peppers or Monterey Jack cheese
- 6 large eggs
- 2 cups milk
- 1 tsp. salt
- ½ tsp. pepper
- ¼ cup chopped fresh cilantro

1. Cook sausage in a large skillet over medium-high heat, stirring until it crumbles and is no longer pink. Drain and return to skillet. Add chopped onion and bell pepper to sausage; sauté over medium heat 5 minutes or until vegetables are tender. Stir in tomatoes and green chiles; reduce heat. Cover and simmer 10 minutes.
2. Preheat oven to 350°. Layer half each of tortilla pieces, sausage mixture, and cheese in a lightly greased 13" x 9" baking dish. Repeat layers.
3. Whisk together eggs and next 3 ingredients; pour over layers in dish.
4. Bake, uncovered, at 350° for 25 to 30 minutes or until lightly browned and set in center. Sprinkle with cilantro before serving.

Honey-Roasted Grape
Tomato Crostini

simple CHRISTMAS

Keep things simple this holiday season. Start with these innovative and practically effortless recipes to stir you toward your goal.

editor's favorite · quick & easy

Honey-Roasted Grape Tomato Crostini

MAKES 31 CROSTINI
PREP: 2 MIN.   COOK: 20 MIN.

 1   pt. grape tomatoes
 1   Tbsp. honey
1½   tsp. olive oil
 ¼   tsp. kosher salt
 1   (4-oz.) log goat cheese
 1   (6- to 8-oz.) container crostini
Garnish: fresh rosemary

1. Preheat oven to 450°. Toss together first 3 ingredients on a lightly greased rimmed baking sheet. Bake at 450° for 20 minutes or until tomato skins burst and begin to wrinkle (do not stir). Transfer roasted tomatoes to a bowl, scraping accumulated juices into bowl. Stir salt into tomato mixture.
2. Microwave goat cheese at HIGH 8 to 10 seconds to soften. Smear goat cheese evenly over crostini; top with roasted tomatoes. Serve on a platter; garnish, if desired.

quick & easy

Parmesan-Peppercorn Snowflakes

These delicate, cheesy gems are perfect for an appetizer buffet served alongside mixed nuts and olives.

MAKES 20 SNOWFLAKES
PREP: 7 MIN.   COOK: 6 MIN.   OTHER: 3 MIN.

 2   cups freshly shredded Parmigiano-Reggiano cheese
Parchment paper
 ½   tsp. crushed tricolor peppercorn blend

1. Preheat oven to 425°. Drop cheese by slightly heaping tablespoonfuls onto parchment paper-lined baking sheets, and spread into 3½" rounds. Sprinkle each portion of cheese lightly with crushed peppercorns. Bake at 425° for 5 to 6 minutes or until bubbly and browned. Cool for 2 to 3 minutes on baking sheets. Remove with a metal spatula to wire racks to cool completely (cheese crisps up as it cools).

gift idea

Rosemary-Lemon Olives

The infused oil resulting from this recipe is great for dipping crusty baguette slices. For gift giving, replace the baked rosemary and lemon peel with fresh sprigs of rosemary and fresh lemon peel.

MAKES 2 CUPS
PREP: 4 MIN.   COOK: 40 MIN.

 6   (5") strips lemon peel
 2   (8") fresh rosemary sprigs
 ⅛   tsp. crushed red pepper flakes
 1   cup kalamata olives
 1   cup Sicilian olives
 1   cup extra virgin olive oil
Garnish: fresh rosemary

1. Preheat oven to 300°. Place lemon peel, rosemary, and red pepper flakes in an 11" x 7" baking dish. Add olives, and drizzle with olive oil. Bake, uncovered, at 300° for 40 minutes. Cool to room temperature. Garnish, if desired, and serve immediately, or store in refrigerator up to 5 days. Bring refrigerated olives to room temperature before serving.

editor's favorite • gift idea

Creole Fried Bow-Ties

This crispy snack is simply pasta that's cooked and then tossed in a spicy cornmeal coating and quickly fried. Serve these nibbles hot or at room temperature.

MAKES 6 CUPS
PREP: 7 MIN.   COOK: 4 MIN. PER BATCH

  8 oz. bow-tie pasta
  ⅓ cup yellow cornmeal
  3 Tbsp. spicy Creole seasoning (we tested with Tony Chachere's More Spice Creole Seasoning)
     Vegetable oil

1. Cook pasta according to package directions; drain well, and blot pasta dry with paper towels.
2. Combine cornmeal and Creole seasoning in a large bowl. Toss pasta, a handful at a time, in cornmeal mixture to coat; shake off excess.
3. Pour vegetable oil to a depth of 2" in a Dutch oven; heat over medium-high heat to 375°. Fry pasta, in batches, 3 to 4 minutes or until golden brown. Drain on paper towels. Store pasta snacks up to a week in an airtight container.

Creole Fried Bow-Ties

quick & easy

Balsamic-Splashed Bacon and Arugula Canapés

Ricotta salata is a dry salted ricotta cheese that can be found in specialty grocery stores.

MAKES 1 DOZEN
PREP: 9 MIN.   COOK: 5 MIN.

  6 fully cooked bacon slices
  2 tsp. honey
  ⅛ tsp. ground red pepper
 12 (½"-thick) French baguette slices, lightly toasted
 24 arugula leaves
 12 thinly shaved pieces ricotta salata or Parmesan cheese
  2 Tbsp. balsamic glaze (we tested with Gia Russa)*

1. Preheat oven to 375°. Place bacon on a baking sheet lined with aluminum foil. Combine honey and pepper; brush onto bacon. Bake at 375° for 5 minutes or until hot. Cut bacon in half crosswise.
2. Place baguette slices on a serving platter; top with arugula leaves. Arrange bacon and cheese on arugula. Drizzle each canapé with ½ tsp. balsamic glaze. Serve immediately.

*Make your own balsamic glaze by reducing balsamic vinegar. Cook ½ cup balsamic vinegar in a small saucepan over medium heat 9 minutes or until syrupy and reduced to 3 Tbsp. Cool completely.

quick & easy

Tuna Niçoise Canapés

MAKES ABOUT 3 DOZEN
PREP: 15 MIN.

  2 (5.5-oz.) cans solid light tuna in olive oil, well drained and flaked (we tested with StarKist)
  ¼ cup finely minced red onion
  3 Tbsp. chopped kalamata or niçoise olives
  2 Tbsp. capers, drained
  2 tsp. extra virgin olive oil
  2 tsp. Dijon mustard
  2 tsp. balsamic vinegar
  ¼ to ½ tsp. freshly ground pepper
  ⅛ tsp. kosher salt
     Endive leaves or cucumber slices
     Garnishes: sliced kalamata olives, fresh flat-leaf parsley

1. Combine first 9 ingredients in a medium bowl. To serve, spoon tuna mixture onto endive leaves or cucumber slices. Garnish, if desired.

Pecan, Olive, and Parmesan Rugelach

Rugelach, traditionally a Jewish pastry, is often filled with nuts and raisins or preserves. This easy savory takeoff is best served warm from the oven.

MAKES 16 PASTRIES
PREP: 12 MIN.   COOK: 15 MIN.

⅓ cup finely chopped pecans, toasted
⅓ cup finely chopped imported green olives (we tested with Picholine)
¼ cup freshly grated Parmesan cheese
2 tsp. minced fresh thyme
1 (8-oz.) can refrigerated crescent rolls
Paprika

1. Preheat oven to 375°. Combine first 4 ingredients in a medium bowl.
2. Unroll crescent rolls onto a lightly floured cutting board. Sprinkle pecan mixture evenly over dough, pressing firmly into dough. Using a sharp knife, cut dough along perforations. Cut each triangle lengthwise into 2 equal triangles.
3. Roll up each triangle, starting at wide end. Place rugelach, point sides down, on an ungreased baking sheet, curving them into a crescent shape. Sprinkle with paprika. Bake at 375° for 15 minutes or until browned. Serve hot.

making rugelach

1. Sprinkle pecan mixture over dough.

2. Press ingredients firmly into dough.

3. Cut each triangle lengthwise into 2 equal triangles. Roll up each triangle, starting at wide end.

Jalapeño-Cheese Sausage Cups

Serve these spicy sausage cups as pick-up food for a ball game get-together.

MAKES 30 APPETIZERS
PREP: 9 MIN.   COOK: 14 MIN.

1 lb. hot ground pork sausage
½ cup Ranch dressing
2 (2.1-oz.) packages frozen mini-phyllo pastry shells, thawed
½ cup pickled jalapeño slices, drained
½ cup shredded sharp Cheddar cheese

1. Preheat oven to 350°. Brown sausage in a large skillet over medium-high heat, stirring to crumble; drain. Return sausage to skillet; stir in Ranch dressing. Spoon sausage mixture evenly into phyllo shells. Place shells on a baking sheet. Top sausage cups evenly with pepper slices; sprinkle with cheese. Bake at 350° for 8 to 10 minutes or until pastry shells are browned.

Ranch Popcorn

This flavored popcorn is addictive.

MAKES 9½ CUPS
PREP: 1 MIN.   COOK: 2 MIN.

1 (3-oz.) bag butter-flavored 94% fat-free popped microwave popcorn (we tested with Pop Secret)
Butter-flavored cooking spray
1½ Tbsp. Ranch dressing mix

1. Pour popped corn into a large bowl; coat heavily with cooking spray. Sprinkle Ranch dressing mix over popcorn; toss well.

quick & easy

Bloody Mary Shrimp Cocktail

Pile these spicy marinated shrimp in martini glasses for a fun way to present a classic appetizer.

MAKES 4 TO 6 APPETIZER SERVINGS
PREP: 12 MIN.   COOK: 5 MIN.   OTHER: 8 HR.

 1 lb. unpeeled, large raw shrimp (about 30)
 1 cup hot and spicy Bloody Mary cocktail mix
 ¼ cup chopped Spanish olives
 1 to 2 Tbsp. capers, drained
 Garnishes: pimiento-stuffed Spanish olives, celery leaves

1. Bring 3 qt. water to a boil; add shrimp, and cook 3 to 5 minutes or just until shrimp turn pink. Drain and rinse with cold water. Peel shrimp.
2. Combine shrimp and cocktail mix in a large zip-top plastic freezer bag. Seal bag, and chill 8 hours.
3. Remove shrimp from marinade; discard marinade. For a fun presentation, divide shrimp among martini glasses. Sprinkle each serving with chopped olives and capers. Garnish, if desired.

editor's favorite · quick & easy

Pesto Chicken Quesadillas

These skillet quesadillas are quick and delicious. Try a flavored rotisserie chicken or add some toasted pine nuts to kick up the flavor. Marinara or sour cream makes a nice dollop on the plate.

MAKES 2 TO 4 SERVINGS
PREP: 13 MIN.   COOK: 4 MIN. PER BATCH

 1 (3.5-oz.) jar pesto (we tested with Alessi)
 4 (8") flour tortillas
 1½ cups shredded rotisserie chicken
 1 (8-oz.) package shredded Italian cheese blend
 Softened butter or yogurt-based spread (we tested with Brummel & Brown)

1. Spread about 1½ Tbsp. pesto on each tortilla. Sprinkle a slightly heaping ⅓ cup chicken onto half of each tortilla; sprinkle cheese over chicken on each tortilla.
2. Fold each tortilla in half. Butter both sides of each folded tortilla.
3. Heat a large nonstick skillet over medium-high heat. Cook quesadillas, in 2 batches, 2 minutes on each side or until browned and crusty. Remove to a cutting board, and cut each quesadilla into 3 wedges.

Chicken Yakitori

Yakitori is a Japanese grilled chicken skewer that makes a great party appetizer-on-a-stick and goes well with Japanese beer.

MAKES 8 APPETIZER SERVINGS
PREP: 11 MIN.   COOK: 8 MIN.   OTHER: 30 MIN.

 6 green onions
 ½ cup teriyaki marinade and sauce (we tested with Kikkoman)
 1½ Tbsp. grated fresh ginger
 2 large garlic cloves, pressed
 1 Tbsp. sugar
 2 Tbsp. dark sesame oil
 1 lb. boneless, skinless chicken breast, cut into 1" pieces

1. Cut white and pale green parts of green onions into 1½" pieces. Thinly slice dark green onion tops. Set aside.
2. Combine marinade, ginger, garlic, sugar, and sesame oil in a zip-top plastic freezer bag; add chicken and 1½" green onion pieces, turning to coat. Seal and chill for at least 30 minutes or up to 2 hours.
3. Meanwhile, soak 8 (6") wooden skewers in water to cover for 30 minutes. Drain.
4. Preheat grill. Thread marinated chicken and green onion pieces onto skewers, discarding marinade. Grill over medium-high heat (350° to 400°) for 3 to 4 minutes on each side or until chicken is done.
5. Transfer skewers to an appetizer platter, and sprinkle with thinly sliced green onions.

editor's favorite

Pimiento Cheese Fondue

MAKES 4 CUPS
PREP: 9 MIN.   COOK: 2 HR.

 4 cups (16 oz.) shredded extra-sharp Cheddar cheese
 1 (8-oz.) package cream cheese, softened
 1 cup heavy whipping cream
 1 (7-oz.) jar diced pimiento, well drained
 ¼ cup thinly sliced green onions
 ¼ tsp. ground red pepper

1. Combine first 3 ingredients in a 3- or 4-qt. slow cooker. Cover and cook on LOW 1 hour. Stir to combine. Cover and cook on LOW 30 more minutes. Add pimiento, green onions, and red pepper. Stir to blend. Cover and cook on LOW 30 more minutes or until thoroughly heated. Serve fondue with raw vegetables, tortilla chips, or French bread chunks.

Blue Chip Nachos

Your favorite blue cheese is essential for decadence here.

MAKES 8 TO 10 SERVINGS
PREP: 12 MIN.   COOK: 5 MIN.

- 1 (4-oz.) wedge Maytag or other blue cheese
- 3 Tbsp. tub-style cream cheese, softened
- ⅓ cup whipping cream
- 1 (5-oz.) bag lightly salted crinkle-cut potato chips (we tested with Kettle brand)
- Parchment paper
- 1 cup chopped walnuts, toasted
- 2 tsp. chopped fresh thyme
- 2 tsp. chopped fresh rosemary
- 2 to 3 Tbsp. bottled balsamic glaze (we tested with Gia Russa)

1. Preheat oven to 400°. Combine cheeses and whipping cream in a small bowl, stirring well. Spread whole potato chips in a double layer on a parchment paper-lined baking sheet. Dollop cheese onto potato chips. Sprinkle with walnuts. Bake at 400° for 5 minutes or until heated. Remove from oven, and carefully slide chips and parchment paper onto a wooden board. Sprinkle with herbs; drizzle with desired amount of balsamic glaze. Serve immediately.

Chocolate-Caramel-Pecan Potato Chips

These chips are best served the day they're made. Use the thickest ridged potato chips you can find.

MAKES ABOUT 9 DOZEN
PREP: 34 MIN.   COOK: 12 MIN.

- 1 (13-oz.) bag thick ruffled potato chips (we tested with Wavy Lays)
- Parchment paper
- 1 (14-oz.) bag caramels (we tested with Kraft)
- ⅓ cup whipping cream
- 1 (11.5-oz.) bag milk chocolate morsels
- 2 Tbsp. shortening
- 1 cup finely chopped pecans, toasted

1. Spread whole potato chips in single layers on parchment paper-lined wire racks. Combine caramels and cream in a heavy saucepan over low heat, stirring constantly, until smooth; remove from heat. Drizzle caramel over chips.
2. Melt milk chocolate morsels and shortening in a small bowl in microwave at HIGH, 1½ to 2 minutes, stirring after 1 minute; cool slightly. Drizzle chocolate over caramel on potato chips; sprinkle with pecans. Cool until chocolate and caramel harden.

Blue Chip Nachos

Chocolate-Caramel-Pecan Potato Chips

Grilled Shrimp Caesar

Smoked paprika is a delicious seasoning to have on hand. It's wonderful in marinades and as a seasoning for sauces and soups. It's made by smoke-drying red pepper pods before grinding and can range from sweet to spicy hot.

MAKES 4 SERVINGS
PREP: 7 MIN.   COOK: 6 MIN.

    2   (8-oz.) packages complete Caesar salad mix (we tested with Fresh Express)
   24   unpeeled, large raw shrimp
    2   Tbsp. olive oil
    2   Tbsp. fresh lemon juice
    2   large garlic cloves, minced, or 2 tsp. jarred minced garlic
    1   tsp. smoked paprika
    ½   tsp. salt
    ¼   tsp. freshly ground pepper

1. Empty lettuce and croutons from salad mix into a bowl; chill. Set salad dressing and Parmesan cheese packets aside.
2. Preheat grill. Peel and, if desired, devein shrimp. Combine shrimp and next 6 ingredients in a bowl; toss to coat. Thread shrimp onto 4 (10") metal skewers. Grill over medium-high heat (350° to 400°) for 3 minutes on each side or just until shrimp turn pink. Remove shrimp from skewers, if desired.
3. Lightly toss salad with desired amount of reserved dressing. Divide salad among individual serving plates. Top each salad with 6 shrimp, and sprinkle with reserved cheese.

Baked Three-Cheese Ziti

MAKES 6 TO 8 SERVINGS
PREP: 11 MIN.   COOK: 40 MIN.

   12   oz. uncooked ziti pasta
    3   cups marinara sauce, divided
    1   (8-oz.) package shredded mozzarella cheese, divided
    ½   cup freshly grated Parmesan cheese, divided
    1   cup ricotta cheese
    3   Tbsp. jarred pesto sauce
    ¼   tsp. dried crushed red pepper
        Freshly grated Parmesan cheese

1. Cook pasta according to package directions; drain and transfer to a large bowl. Add 2 cups marinara sauce, half of mozzarella cheese, half of Parmesan cheese, ricotta cheese, pesto, and red pepper, stirring gently to blend.

2. Preheat oven to 400°. Spoon pasta mixture into a lightly greased 13" x 9" baking dish. Spoon remaining marinara sauce over pasta; sprinkle with remaining mozzarella and Parmesan cheese.
3. Bake, uncovered, at 400° for 30 minutes or until cheese is melted and bubbly. Serve extra Parmesan at the table.

Chicken Fajitas

MAKES 4 SERVINGS
PREP: 12 MIN.   COOK: 10 MIN.

    2   Tbsp. olive oil
    1   red bell pepper, cut lengthwise into ½" strips
    1   medium onion, sliced
    ½   tsp. ground cumin
    ½   tsp. salt
    3   cups shredded cooked rotisserie chicken
    3   Tbsp. minced fresh cilantro
   1½   Tbsp. minced pickled jalapeño peppers
    8   (8") flour tortillas
        Toppings: salsa, guacamole, sour cream

1. Heat 2 Tbsp. olive oil in a large skillet over medium heat. Add bell pepper and next 3 ingredients. Cook 8 minutes or until pepper and onion are tender, stirring often. Add chicken, cilantro, and jalapeño peppers; cook 2 minutes or until thoroughly heated. Remove from heat, and keep warm.
2. Warm tortillas according to package directions.
3. Transfer chicken mixture to a serving platter. Serve with tortillas and desired toppings.

Chicken Pot Pie

This is easy comfort food with a puff pastry crust.

MAKES 6 SERVINGS
PREP: 9 MIN.   COOK: 46 MIN.

    2   Tbsp. butter
    1   small onion, minced
    1   (8-oz.) pkg. sliced fresh mushrooms
    ½   tsp. salt
    1   (10-oz.) package frozen mixed vegetables, thawed and drained
    3   cups chopped rotisserie chicken
    1   (10¾-oz.) can reduced-sodium cream of chicken soup
    ⅔   cup milk
    1   to 2 Tbsp. dry sherry (optional)
    1   Tbsp. fresh lemon juice
    1   sheet frozen puff pastry, thawed

Apricot-Glazed Pork
Tenderloin with Couscous

1. Melt butter in a large skillet over medium heat. Add onion and cook, stirring occasionally, 3 minutes or until tender. Add mushrooms and salt; sauté 8 minutes or until liquid evaporates and mushrooms are browned. Add vegetables and next 5 ingredients, stirring to blend.

2. Preheat oven to 375°. Pour chicken mixture into a lightly greased 10" deep-dish pie plate, and cover with pastry; trim excess pastry. Bake at 375° for 30 to 35 minutes or until filling is bubbly and pastry is golden.

Apricot-Glazed Pork Tenderloin with Couscous

A two-ingredient glaze paints this pork with rich color and tangy-sweet flavor.

MAKES 4 SERVINGS
PREP: 10 MIN.   COOK: 18 MIN.   OTHER: 5 MIN.

 1 (1¼-lb.) pork tenderloin
 1 Tbsp. olive oil
 ¼ tsp. salt
 ¼ tsp. pepper
 ⅓ cup apricot preserves
 2 Tbsp. honey mustard
 1 (10-oz.) box couscous (we tested with Far East)
 ½ cup diced dried apricots
 ⅓ cup toasted sliced almonds

1. Brush pork with olive oil; season with salt and pepper. Place on an aluminum foil-lined broiler pan.

2. Broil 5½" from heat 8 minutes or until browned, turning once.

3. Combine apricot preserves and honey mustard; spread over pork. Continue to broil 10 more minutes, turning once, or until meat thermometer inserted in center of meat registers 155°. Cover pork with aluminum foil, and let stand 5 minutes.

4. Meanwhile, prepare couscous according to package directions. Fluff couscous; stir in apricots and almonds. Slice pork, and serve with couscous.

Chocolate Cream Martini

Brownie Buttons

quick & easy

Chocolate Cream Martini

This luxurious drink is both cocktail and dessert.

MAKES 2 SERVINGS
PREP: 4 MIN.

- 1   (1-oz.) square semisweet chocolate, melted
- 3   Tbsp. vanilla-flavored vodka (we tested with Absolut Vanilla)
- 3   Tbsp. Irish cream liqueur
- 2   Tbsp. half-and-half
- ⅓   cup coffee-flavored liqueur (we tested with Tia Maria)
- ⅓   cup chocolate-flavored liqueur (we tested with Godiva)

1. Dip rims of 2 martini glasses in melted chocolate on a plate to form a thin layer. Place glasses in refrigerator until chocolate is firm.
2. Combine vodka and next 4 ingredients in a martini shaker filled with ice. Cover with lid; shake until thoroughly chilled. Remove lid; strain into chocolate-rimmed martini glasses. Serve immediately.

gift idea

Brownie Buttons

Nestle miniature chocolate candies into freshly baked brownie bites for impressive little chocolate treats.

MAKES 20 BROWNIES
PREP: 15 MIN.   COOK: 20 MIN.   OTHER: 14 MIN.

- 1   (16.5-oz.) refrigerated roll triple chocolate chunk brownie batter (we tested with Pillsbury)
- 1   bag of assorted miniature peanut butter cup candies and chocolate-coated caramels (we tested with Rolos)

1. Preheat oven to 350°. Spray miniature (1¾") muffin pans with cooking spray, or line pans with paper liners and spray liners with cooking spray. Spoon brownie batter evenly into each cup, filling almost full. Bake at 350° for 19 to 20 minutes. Cool in pans 3 to 4 minutes, and then gently press a miniature candy into each baked brownie until the top of candy is level with top of brownie. Cool 10 minutes in pans. Gently twist each brownie to remove from pan. Cool on a wire rack.

Hazelnut Mousse Crunch

Fudgy Toffee-Crunch Brownies

quick & easy

Hazelnut Mousse Crunch

For a special effect, use a decorative tip to pipe the mousse into each glass. All you need is a large star tip and piping bag.

MAKES 6 SERVINGS
PREP: 5 MIN. COOK: 1 MIN.

  1 (13-oz.) jar hazelnut spread (we tested with Nutella)
  1 (8-oz.) container frozen whipped topping, thawed
  1 (6.88-oz.) package bittersweet chocolate-dipped biscotti or other favorite biscotti (we tested with Nonni's)

1. Microwave hazelnut spread, uncovered, at HIGH for 25 seconds (be sure to completely remove foil wrap). Fold hazelnut spread and whipped topping together in a large bowl, leaving some chocolate streaks. Spoon mousse into a zip-top plastic freezer bag (do not seal). Snip 1 corner of bag to make a hole. Pipe mousse into parfait glasses. Serve with biscotti; or crush biscotti, and lightly sprinkle over each serving to provide the crunch.

gift idea · make ahead

Fudgy Toffee-Crunch Brownies

No one will know that these brownies start with a mix.

MAKES 2 DOZEN
PREP: 16 MIN. COOK: 52 MIN.

  2 (17.6-oz.) packages dark fudge brownie mix with chocolate chunks (we tested with Duncan Hines Chocolate Lover's)
  2 large eggs
  ½ cup vegetable oil or canola oil
  ¼ cup water
  1 Tbsp. instant espresso granules
  1 (12-oz.) package miniature chocolate-covered toffee bars, coarsely crushed (we tested with Heath Miniatures)

1. Preheat oven to 325°. Beat first 4 ingredients at medium speed with an electric mixer for 3 minutes or until blended; stir in coffee granules and candy bars. Spoon batter into a lightly greased 13" x 9" pan, spreading evenly (batter will be very thick).
2. Bake at 325° for 50 to 52 minutes or until center is set. Cool in pan on a wire rack. Cut into bars.

Roast Pork with Sage
and Pecan Pesto

elegant ENTRÉES

A fabulous main dish is the star of the menu. Here we offer selections perfectly suited for the holidays.

Roast Pork with Sage and Pecan Pesto

Be careful not to overprocess the flavorful pesto for this dish. The finished sauce should have some texture remaining.

MAKES 8 SERVINGS
PREP: 15 MIN.   COOK: 1 HR., 31 MIN.   OTHER: 12 HR., 10 MIN.

1   (64-oz.) bottle apple cider
¼   cup kosher salt
½   cup plus 3 Tbsp. chopped fresh sage, divided
1   (4-lb.) boneless pork loin roast
1   tsp. freshly ground pepper
2   Tbsp. olive oil
Garnishes: fresh sage, unshelled pecans
Sage and Pecan Pesto

1. Combine cider, salt, and ½ cup chopped sage, stirring until salt dissolves. Place pork in an extra-large zip-top plastic freezer bag; add cider mixture. Seal bag; chill 12 to 24 hours.
2. Preheat oven to 350°. Remove pork from brine, and pat dry with paper towels. Sprinkle pork with pepper. Heat oil in a large skillet over medium-high heat; add pork. Cook 6 minutes or until browned on all sides, turning pork occasionally. Place pork on a rack in a lightly greased roasting pan. Sprinkle remaining 3 Tbsp. sage over pork.
3. Bake, uncovered, at 350° for 1 hour to 1 hour and 25 minutes or until a meat thermometer inserted into thickest part of roast registers 150°. Remove from oven; cover and let rest 10 minutes or until thermometer reaches 160° before slicing. Garnish platter, if desired. Serve with Sage and Pecan Pesto.

Sage and Pecan Pesto

MAKES: ¾ CUP
PREP: 7 MIN.

½   cup chopped pecans, toasted
½   cup firmly packed fresh flat-leaf parsley
¼   cup firmly packed fresh sage leaves
¼   cup freshly grated Parmesan cheese
¼   cup extra virgin olive oil
1   tsp. fresh lemon juice
1   garlic clove, chopped
¼   tsp. salt

1. Combine all ingredients in a food processor; process until ingredients are finely chopped.

Coffee-Glazed Ham with Red Eye Gravy

MAKES 10 TO 12 SERVINGS
PREP: 10 MIN.   COOK: 2 HR., 30 MIN.   OTHER: 10 MIN.

1   (8- to 10-lb.) bone-in, fully cooked smoked ham half
2   cups firmly packed light brown sugar
2   cups freshly brewed coffee
¼   cup heavy whipping cream
Garnishes: fresh herbs, kumquats

1. Preheat oven to 350°. Remove skin from ham, if present, and trim fat to ¼" thickness. Place ham in a lightly greased broiler pan. Combine sugar and hot coffee in a medium bowl, stirring until sugar dissolves; pour over ham.
2. Bake at 350° for 2½ hours or until a meat thermometer inserted into thickest portion registers 140°, basting every 20 minutes. Transfer ham from pan to a serving platter. Cover and keep warm. Pour drippings into a 4-cup glass measuring cup; let stand 10 minutes. Pour off and discard fat; stir cream into remaining drippings. Serve gravy with ham. Garnish platter, if desired.

Rack of Lamb with Garlic-Herb Crust

You'll hardly believe that this elegant and flavorful dish is so easy to prepare. The initial step of searing the racks in a skillet is key to locking in flavor.

MAKES 8 SERVINGS
PREP: 10 MIN.   COOK: 33 MIN.   OTHER: 10 MIN.

  2 (8-rib) lamb rib roasts (1½ lb. each), frenched
  1 tsp. salt
  ½ tsp. pepper
  2 Tbsp. vegetable oil
  ½ cup fresh breadcrumbs
  ¼ cup minced fresh flat-leaf parsley
  1 Tbsp. minced fresh rosemary
  ½ tsp. salt
  ½ tsp. pepper
  4 large garlic cloves, minced
  2 Tbsp. mayonnaise
  2 Tbsp. Dijon mustard
  Garnish: fresh rosemary sprigs

1. Preheat oven to 350°. Pat lamb dry with paper towels; season with 1 tsp. salt and ½ tsp. pepper. Heat oil in a large skillet over high heat. Cook lamb in hot oil 3 to 4 minutes on each side or until browned. Place lamb on a rack in a broiler pan.

2. Combine breadcrumbs and next 5 ingredients in a small bowl. Combine mayonnaise and mustard in a small bowl. Brush mustard mixture over meaty top side of lamb racks; pat herb mixture evenly over mustard to adhere.

3. Bake at 350° for 20 to 25 minutes or until a thermometer inserted into thickest portion registers 145° (medium rare). Let stand 10 minutes. Garnish platter, if desired. Cut each rack into double chops.

Note: You'll want to ask your local butcher to french the racks of lamb for you, trimming them down to clean bones and small succulent eyes of meat that will be easy to cut apart after roasting.

Rosemary Beef Tenderloin with Balsamic Peppers

MAKES 8 TO 10 SERVINGS
PREP: 13 MIN.   COOK: 48 MIN.   OTHER: 10 MIN.

  1 (5- to 5½-lb.) beef tenderloin
  2 tsp. kosher salt
1½ tsp. freshly ground pepper
  2 Tbsp. olive oil
  3 Tbsp. minced garlic
  2 Tbsp. minced fresh rosemary
  Balsamic Peppers
  Garnish: fresh rosemary sprigs

1. Preheat oven to 400°. Trim fat from tenderloin. Sprinkle tenderloin all over with salt and pepper. Heat oil in a roasting pan over medium-high heat; add tenderloin. Cook 6 to 8 minutes, turning often to brown all sides. Remove tenderloin to a cutting board. Rub tenderloin with garlic and 2 Tbsp. rosemary, pressing to adhere. Return to pan. Bake, uncovered, at 400° for 40 minutes or until a meat thermometer inserted into thickest part of tenderloin registers 140° (rare) to 160° (medium). Remove tenderloin to a serving platter; let stand 10 minutes before slicing. Arrange Balsamic Peppers around tenderloin, and garnish, if desired.

Balsamic Peppers

MAKES 2¾ CUPS
PREP: 15 MIN.   COOK: 25 MIN.   OTHER: 15 MIN.

  2 large red bell peppers
  2 large yellow bell peppers
  1 red onion, cut into 8 wedges
  2 Tbsp. balsamic vinegar
  2 Tbsp. extra virgin olive oil
  2 tsp. molasses
  ½ tsp. salt
  ⅛ tsp. freshly ground black pepper
  1 Tbsp. minced fresh rosemary

1. Cut peppers in half lengthwise; discard seeds and membranes. Place pepper halves, skin side up, on a large aluminum foil-lined baking sheet; flatten peppers with palm of hand. Add onion to baking sheet. Broil 5½" from heat 20 to 25 minutes or until peppers are blackened. Place peppers in a zip-top plastic bag; seal, and let stand 15 minutes. Peel skin from peppers; cut peppers into strips.

2. Whisk together vinegar and next 4 ingredients in a medium bowl; stir in rosemary. Add pepper strips and onion to bowl; toss well.

make ahead

Sautéed Chicken with Figs in Port Wine Sauce

Adding a touch of balsamic or sherry vinegar to the sauce just before serving accents the flavor of figs and acts as a nice contrast to their sweetness. Ask your butcher to debone chicken breasts with skin if you can't find boneless portions. You can make this dish ahead, but store the chicken and sauce separately in the refrigerator. Just reheat when ready to serve.

MAKES 4 SERVINGS
PREP: 10 MIN.   COOK: 37 MIN.

- 4   boneless chicken breasts (skin on)
- 3   Tbsp. olive oil
- 2   tsp. minced fresh thyme
- ½   tsp. salt
- ¼   tsp. freshly ground black pepper
- ½   cup all-purpose flour
- 2   Tbsp. unsalted butter
- 1   cup dried Calimyrna figs, stemmed and quartered
- ⅓   cup minced shallots
- ½   cup tawny port
- 1   cup beef broth
- 1   tsp. balsamic or sherry vinegar (optional)
- Garnish: fresh thyme

1. Pat chicken dry with paper towels. Heat oil in a large non-stick skillet over medium-high heat until hot. Season chicken with thyme, salt, and pepper. Dredge in flour. Add chicken to skillet, skin side down; reduce heat to medium, and cook 16 minutes or until skin is browned. Turn and cook 5 minutes or until browned. Remove chicken from pan; keep warm. Discard pan drippings.

2. Melt butter in skillet over medium heat. Add figs and shallots; sauté 3 minutes or until shallots are tender. Add port; bring to a boil. Boil 1 minute; add beef broth, reduce heat, and simmer 3 minutes. Remove half of figs from skillet using a slotted spoon; keep warm with chicken. Process remaining figs and sauce in a food processor until smooth, stopping to scrape down sides as needed. Pour mixture through a wire-mesh strainer back into the skillet, discarding pulp and seeds. Return chicken and figs to sauce, and heat over medium-high heat 9 minutes or until chicken is done. Drizzle with vinegar, if desired. Cut chicken diagonally across the grain into thin strips. Serve sauce over chicken and figs. Garnish, if desired.

Rack of Lamb with Garlic-Herb Crust

Rosemary Beef Tenderloin with Balsamic Peppers

Roasted Lemon Chicken

Try your own combination of herbs in this simple entrée. Regular basting gives the finished bird crispy brown skin.

MAKES 4 SERVINGS
PREP: 25 MIN.   COOK: 1 HR., 16 MIN.   OTHER: 15 MIN.

1½ lemons
 2 large garlic cloves, minced
 2 Tbsp. unsalted butter, softened and divided
 2 Tbsp. minced fresh oregano, divided
 2 Tbsp. minced fresh thyme, divided
 1 tsp. salt, divided
 ½ tsp. pepper, divided
 1 (4-lb.) whole chicken
 2 Tbsp. minced fresh flat-leaf parsley

1. Preheat oven to 400°. Grate zest from 1 lemon to equal 2 tsp. Pierce zested lemon several times with a paring knife. Squeeze juice from remaining lemon half into a measuring cup to equal 1 Tbsp. Set lemon juice aside.
2. Combine zest; garlic; 1 Tbsp. each of butter, oregano, and thyme; ½ tsp. salt, and ¼ tsp. pepper in a small bowl, stirring until blended. Loosen and lift skin from chicken with fingers, without totally detaching skin; spread half of butter mixture underneath. Carefully replace skin. Sprinkle remaining 1 Tbsp. herbs, remaining ½ tsp. salt, and remaining ¼ tsp. pepper inside cavity; rub into cavity. Spread remaining half of butter mixture on skin; rub into skin. Place zested lemon in cavity. Tie ends of legs together with string; tuck wingtips under. Place chicken on a lightly greased wire rack in a lightly greased roasting pan.
3. Bake at 400° for 1 hour and 15 minutes or until a meat thermometer inserted in thickest portion of thigh registers 170°, basting with drippings every 20 minutes. Transfer chicken to a plate; transfer drippings to a small saucepan. Cover chicken with aluminum foil, and let stand 15 minutes before carving.
4. Bring drippings to a boil. Add remaining 1 Tbsp. butter to pan, stirring until melted. Remove from heat, and stir in accumulated juices from chicken, reserved lemon juice, and parsley. Carve chicken, and place on a serving platter; drizzle sauce over chicken.

editor's favorite

Crispy Chicken Salad with Dried Cranberries, Walnuts, and Blue Cheese

Panko breadcrumbs are the key to the crispy chicken strips featured in this colorful salad.

MAKES 4 SERVINGS
PREP: 23 MIN.   COOK: 17 MIN.

 ¼ cup red wine vinegar
 1 Tbsp. Dijon mustard
 ½ tsp. salt
 ¼ tsp. pepper
 ½ cup extra virgin olive oil
 8 cups gourmet mixed salad greens
 1 cup diced cucumber
 6 green onions, sliced
 ⅔ cup dried cranberries
 ½ cup crumbled blue cheese
 5 chicken cutlets (about 1 lb.)
 ½ tsp. salt
 ½ tsp. pepper
 1 large egg, lightly beaten
 1 cup Japanese breadcrumbs (panko)
 1 cup vegetable oil
 1 cup walnut halves, coarsely chopped and toasted

1. Whisk together first 4 ingredients in a small bowl. Add olive oil in a slow, steady stream, whisking constantly until smooth.
2. Combine salad greens and next 4 ingredients in a large bowl. Cover and chill while preparing chicken.
3. Sprinkle chicken with ½ tsp. each salt and pepper. Dip chicken in egg; dredge in breadcrumbs.
4. Fry chicken cutlets, in 2 batches, in hot vegetable oil in a large skillet over medium-high heat 2 to 3 minutes on each side or until golden and crisp. Drain on paper towels. Cut each cutlet crosswise into ½" slices.
5. Toss salad with ⅓ cup dressing; add walnuts, and toss gently. Divide salad among 4 serving plates; top each serving with sliced chicken, and drizzle with desired amount of dressing.

Crispy Chicken Salad with Dried Cranberries, Walnuts, and Blue Cheese

Mediterranean Chicken Kebabs

Donned with bell pepper, red onion wedges, and herbs, these tasty skewers are sure to please all year long.

MAKES 6 SERVINGS
PREP: 18 MIN. COOK: 10 MIN. OTHER: 30 MIN.

- 3 large garlic cloves, crushed
- 2 Tbsp. minced fresh rosemary
- 1 Tbsp. minced fresh oregano
- 1 tsp. salt, divided
- ½ tsp. pepper, divided
- ¼ cup fresh lemon juice, divided
- 6 Tbsp. olive oil, divided
- 1½ lb. boned and skinned chicken breasts, cut into 1" pieces
- 1 large red bell pepper, cut into 1" pieces
- 1 large red onion, cut into 1" wedges
- 6 (10" to 12") metal skewers

1. Combine first 3 ingredients, ½ tsp. salt, ¼ tsp. pepper, 3 Tbsp. lemon juice, and 5 Tbsp. oil in a large shallow dish or zip-top plastic freezer bag; add chicken, turning to coat. Cover or seal, and chill 30 minutes. Combine remaining ½ tsp. salt, ¼ tsp. pepper, 1 Tbsp. lemon juice, and 1 Tbsp. oil in a small bowl; set aside.

2. Preheat grill. Thread marinated chicken, bell pepper, and onion alternately onto skewers, discarding marinade. Grill over medium-high heat (350° to 400°) for 8 to 10 minutes or until done, turning occasionally and basting with reserved olive oil mixture.

editor's favorite · make ahead

Chicken Cobbler with Cream Cheese Crust

This old-fashioned comfort dish includes succulent chunks of chicken and saucy garden vegetables, all topped with a flaky cream cheese pastry.

MAKES 6 SERVINGS
PREP: 46 MIN.   COOK: 2 HR., 27 MIN.   OTHER: 45 MIN.

1   (3½-lb.) whole chicken
1½ tsp. salt, divided
    Cream Cheese Crust
    Parchment paper
8   oz. fresh green beans, trimmed and cut into
      1" pieces (about 1½ cups)
6   Tbsp. butter, divided
1⅓ cups sliced fresh mushrooms
2   carrots, cut in half lengthwise and sliced
1   medium onion, chopped
1   celery rib, sliced
2   garlic cloves, minced
½   cup all-purpose flour
½   cup heavy whipping cream
2   tsp. chopped fresh sage
¼   tsp. pepper
1   large egg, lightly beaten

1. Rinse chicken, and pat dry; remove excess fat. Place chicken, giblets, ¾ tsp. salt, and 3½ cups water in a Dutch oven. Bring to a boil over medium-high heat; reduce heat to low. Cover and simmer 1 hour and 15 minutes or until chicken is done. Remove from heat. Remove chicken from broth; let cool 30 minutes. Strain broth to measure 3 cups, reserving giblets for another use.

2. While chicken cools, prepare dough for Cream Cheese Crust; shape dough into a 1"-thick disk. Place disk on a large piece of parchment paper.

3. Lightly grease a 2-qt. oval baking dish. Roll out dough on parchment until it is ½" larger than diameter of baking dish. Transfer dough and paper to a large baking sheet. Chill 30 minutes to 24 hours.

4. Skin and bone chicken; chop meat into bite-size pieces to measure 4 cups. Cook green beans in boiling water to cover in a saucepan 8 minutes or until tender. Drain and set aside.

5. Melt 2 Tbsp. butter in a large skillet over medium-high heat; add mushrooms, next 4 ingredients, and ¼ tsp. salt. Cook, stirring often, 8 minutes or until vegetables are tender. Remove pan from heat.

6. Preheat oven to 400°. Melt remaining ¼ cup butter in a heavy saucepan over low heat; whisk in flour until smooth. Cook, whisking constantly, 1 minute. Gradually whisk in reserved broth; cook over medium heat, whisking constantly,

5 minutes or until thickened and bubbly. Stir in remaining ½ tsp. salt, cream, sage, and pepper. Pour sauce over vegetables in skillet. Add chicken and green beans, stirring until coated with sauce. Pour filling into prepared dish.

7. Remove pastry from refrigerator. Remove parchment from top of pastry. Cut leaves or decorative shapes in pastry using a cookie cutter. Let pastry stand 3 to 5 minutes or until pliable.

8. Cover filling with pastry, pressing edges of dough to sides of dish; brush pastry with beaten egg.

9. Bake at 400° for 35 minutes or until crust is golden and filling is bubbly. Let stand 10 minutes before serving.

Note: For ease in transferring pastry, carefully roll dough onto a rolling pin, and then unroll onto filling.

Cream Cheese Crust

MAKES ENOUGH PASTRY FOR 1 COBBLER
PREP: 5 MIN.   OTHER: 30 MIN.

1¼ cups all-purpose flour
4   oz. cold cream cheese
¼   cup cold butter, cut into 4 pieces
¼   tsp. salt

1. Process all ingredients in a food processor 1 minute or until dough forms a ball and leaves sides of bowl. Roll out dough as recipe directs.

mix 'n' match meals

For some fabulous dinners, our Test Kitchens staff recommends matching the entrées in this chapter with these particular sides. (Mixed salad greens and crusty bread will complement each plate nicely.)

· Roast Pork with Sage and Pecan Pesto — Fruit and Nut Rice Pilaf, Blue Cheese and Black Pepper Potatoes, Sweet Potato Galette, Carrot-Apricot Mash, Christmas Creamed Corn, or Butternut Squash Casserole with Pecan Streusel.
· Coffee-Glazed Ham with Red Eye Gravy — Sweet Potato Galette, Butternut Squash Casserole with Pecan Streusel, Crumb-Topped Spinach Casserole, Christmas Creamed Corn, or Green Beans with Toasted Almonds and Lemon.
· Sautéed Chicken with Figs in Port Wine Sauce — Apple-Raisin Dressing, Green Beans with Toasted Almonds and Lemon, or Broccoli with Caramelized Garlic and Pine Nuts.
· Rack of Lamb with Garlic-Herb Crust — Blue Cheese and Black Pepper Potatoes or Broccoli with Caramelized Garlic and Pine Nuts.
· Rosemary Beef Tenderloin with Balsamic Peppers — Blue Cheese and Black Pepper Potatoes, Broccoli with Caramelized Garlic and Pine Nuts, or Crumb-Topped Spinach Casserole.

Party Paella Casserole

editor's favorite

Party Paella Casserole

Here's a great use for rotisserie chicken, shrimp, and yellow rice.

MAKES 8 SERVINGS
PREP: 26 MIN.   COOK: 43 MIN.   OTHER: 30 MIN.

2   (8-oz.) packages yellow rice (we tested with Vigo)
1   lb. medium peeled shrimp
1   Tbsp. fresh lemon juice (about ½ large lemon)
½   tsp. salt
¼   tsp. pepper
2   large garlic cloves, minced
1½ Tbsp. olive oil
1   (2½-lb.) lemon-and-garlic deli-roasted whole chicken, coarsely shredded
5   large green onions, chopped (about 1 cup)
1   (8-oz.) container sour cream
1   cup frozen English peas, thawed
1   cup pimiento-stuffed Spanish olives, coarsely chopped
1½ cups (6 oz.) shredded Monterey Jack cheese
½   tsp. smoked Spanish paprika

1. Prepare rice according to package directions. Remove from heat, and let cool 30 minutes; fluff with a fork.
2. Meanwhile, toss shrimp with lemon juice, salt, and pepper in a bowl. Sauté seasoned shrimp and garlic in hot oil in a large nonstick skillet 2 minutes or just until done. Remove from heat.
3. Preheat oven to 400°. Combine shredded chicken, rice, green onions, sour cream, and peas in a large bowl; toss well. Add shrimp and olives, tossing gently. Spoon rice mixture into a greased 13" x 9" baking dish.
4. Combine cheese and paprika, tossing well; sprinkle over casserole.
5. Bake, uncovered, at 400° for 15 minutes or just until cheese is melted and casserole is thoroughly heated.

Chicken Divan

Using a whole chicken is more economical than chicken breasts alone, and the dark meat adds lots of flavor.

MAKES 8 SERVINGS
PREP: 20 MIN.   COOK: 1 HR., 55 MIN.   OTHER: 25 MIN.

1   (4-lb.) whole chicken
2   celery ribs with leaves, halved crosswise
1   tsp. salt
½   tsp. pepper
2   broccoli crowns, cut into spears
3   Tbsp. butter
3   Tbsp. all-purpose flour
3   cups milk
1½ cups (6 oz.) shredded white Cheddar cheese
1½ tsp. fresh lemon juice
¾   tsp. salt
¾   tsp. curry powder
¼   tsp. ground red pepper
2½ cups cooked rice
1   cup (4 oz.) shredded Parmesan cheese
    Paprika

1. Combine first 4 ingredients and water to cover (we used 12 cups) in a large Dutch oven. Bring to a boil over medium-high heat; reduce heat, and simmer 1 hour or until tender. Remove chicken, and cool 25 minutes or until cool enough to handle.
2. Pour broth through a wire-mesh strainer into a large bowl, discarding solids. Return broth to pan; bring to a boil. Add broccoli, and cook until crisp-tender. Drain, reserving broth for another use.
3. Skin, bone, and coarsely chop chicken; cover and keep warm.
4. Preheat oven to 350°. Melt butter in a medium saucepan over medium-low heat; add flour, stirring until smooth. Cook 1 minute, stirring constantly. Gradually add milk; cook over medium heat, stirring constantly, until thickened and bubbly. Add Cheddar cheese and next 4 ingredients, stirring until smooth.
5. Spread rice on bottom of a lightly greased 13" x 9" baking dish. Layer broccoli and chicken over rice. Pour cheese sauce over chicken mixture. Sprinkle with Parmesan cheese and paprika. Bake, uncovered, at 350° for 45 minutes or until bubbly and lightly browned.

fix it faster

Substitute 4 cups chopped cooked chicken from a rotisserie chicken. Cook broccoli in boiling salted water to cover instead of the broth.

turkey carving 101

To slice turkey easily, allow it to rest at room temperature after it's cooked, covered with aluminum foil, 15 minutes or more before carving. After the meal, remove leftover meat and stuffing from the carcass before storing in the refrigerator.

1. Carve the bird, breast side up, on a carving board in the kitchen or on a serving platter at the table.
2. Cut away string first. Remove stuffing to a serving bowl.
3. Grasp the end of a drumstick, and pull it away from the body. Cut through the skin and meat between the thigh and body; bend the leg away from the bird to expose the leg joint. Slice through the joint, and remove the leg. Cut through the joint that separates the thigh and drumstick. Slice the dark meat from the bones of the leg and thigh rather than placing them whole on the serving platter.
4. Cut the wings off at their second joint, leaving the upper part of the wing intact to steady the bird.
5. To carve the breast meat, steady the bird with a carving fork and make a deep horizontal cut into the breast just above the wing. (Use this cut to mark the end of each slice of breast meat.) Beginning at the outer top edge of breast, cut thin slices from the top down to the horizontal cut. Carve from one side of the turkey at a time, carving only as much meat as needed for serving.

Sweet-and-Spicy Glazed Turkey

editor's favorite

Sweet-and-Spicy Glazed Turkey

Crushed red pepper kicks up the brown sugar-orange glaze that paints this turkey and gives it an Asian edge.

MAKES 9 TO 10 SERVINGS
PREP: 12 MIN.   COOK: 2 HR., 48 MIN.   OTHER: 30 MIN.

 1   cup orange juice
 ¼   cup firmly packed brown sugar
 2   Tbsp. butter
 1   tsp. crushed red pepper
 1   tsp. orange zest
 ¼   tsp. salt
 ¼   tsp. freshly ground black pepper
 1   (9- to 10-lb.) fresh or frozen turkey, thawed
 1   orange, cut into 4 wedges
 1   medium onion, cut into 4 wedges
 2   Tbsp. butter, softened
 1   tsp. salt
 ½   tsp. black pepper
     Garnish: roasted Brussels sprouts

1. Combine first 7 ingredients in a medium saucepan; bring to a boil over medium-high heat. Reduce heat and simmer 15 minutes or until mixture is syrupy and reduced to about ⅔ cup. Set aside.

2. Preheat oven to 325°. Remove giblets and neck from turkey; discard or refrigerate for another use. Rinse turkey with cold water; pat dry with paper towels. Place turkey, breast side up, on a lightly greased rack in an aluminum foil-lined broiler pan. Lift wingtips up and over back, and tuck under bird.

3. Place orange and onion wedges inside turkey cavity. Rub softened butter all over outside of turkey, including legs. Tie ends of legs together with heavy string. Sprinkle turkey all over with 1 tsp. salt and ½ tsp. black pepper.

4. Bake, uncovered, at 325° for 1 hour. Brush turkey with half of the glaze; bake 1½ more hours or until a meat thermometer inserted into meaty part of thigh registers 170°, brushing with glaze every 30 minutes. Shield turkey with aluminum foil during cooking, if necessary, to prevent excessive browning.

5. Transfer turkey to a serving platter; cover turkey with foil, and let stand up to 30 minutes before carving. Garnish, if desired.

Note: Roast Brussels sprouts with a drizzle of olive oil on a rimmed baking sheet at 450° for 25 minutes or until browned.

Bay-Scented Roast Turkey

Cutting up a turkey is just like cutting up a chicken for frying; it's just a bigger bird.

MAKES 10 SERVINGS
PREP: 30 MIN.   COOK: 1 HR., 26 MIN.   OTHER: 15 MIN.

 11   garlic cloves, divided
  2   carrots, cut into 1" pieces
  3   celery ribs, cut into 2" pieces
  2   onions, cut into 2" pieces
  4   fresh thyme sprigs
  1   (32-oz.) container chicken broth
  ¼   cup butter, cut into 4 pieces
  ½   tsp. salt
 1¼   tsp. freshly ground pepper, divided
  1   (14-lb.) turkey, cut up
 12   fresh bay leaves
  ⅓   cup all-purpose flour
  ¼   cup dry white wine

1. Preheat oven to 375°. Place 3 garlic cloves and next 4 ingredients in a large roasting pan. Pour broth over vegetables.

2. With processor running, drop remaining 8 garlic cloves through food chute; process until minced. Add butter, salt, and 1 tsp. pepper through food chute; process until combined. Reserve back, wings, neck, and giblets from turkey for another use. Loosen and lift skin from turkey breast and leg quarters with fingers, without totally detaching skin; spread half of butter mixture under skin. Place 2 to 3 bay leaves under skin of each piece of turkey; carefully replace skin. Rub skin with remaining half of butter mixture. Place turkey leg quarters on top of vegetables.

3. Bake at 375° for 10 minutes; add breasts, and bake 25 more minutes. Increase oven temperature to 425°; bake 40 minutes or until a meat thermometer inserted into thickest part of breast registers 170°.

4. Transfer turkey to a platter; cover loosely with aluminum foil, and let stand 15 minutes. Strain broth through a wire-mesh strainer, discarding vegetables.

5. Pour 4 cups broth into a medium saucepan, reserving remaining broth for another use. Bring broth to a boil over medium-high heat. Stir together flour, wine, and remaining ¼ tsp. pepper; add to broth, and cook over medium-high heat, stirring constantly, 8 minutes or until thickened. Serve gravy with turkey.

Turkey Breast Roulades with Collards and Bacon

Collards and bacon—two Southern greats—are show-cased in this rolled entrée. Find packaged, chopped collard greens in the produce department of grocery stores.

MAKES 6 TO 8 SERVINGS
PREP: 16 MIN.   COOK: 1 HR., 14 MIN.   OTHER: 10 MIN.

  6 bacon slices
  1 small onion, chopped
  2 garlic cloves, minced
2¼ cups chicken broth, divided
  4 cups firmly packed chopped collard greens
  ¼ cup fine, dry breadcrumbs
  ½ tsp. salt, divided
  ½ tsp. hot sauce, divided
  1 (3-lb.) boneless turkey breast
  ½ tsp. freshly ground pepper
  1 Tbsp. all-purpose flour
  1 Tbsp. whipping cream

1. Cook bacon in a large skillet over medium heat 4 minutes just until fat is rendered. Remove 4 partially cooked bacon slices, and set aside. Cook remaining 2 bacon slices 5 minutes or until crisp. Remove bacon from skillet, and drain on paper towels, reserving drippings in pan. Crumble bacon, and set aside.

2. Sauté onion in hot drippings 3 minutes. Add garlic, and sauté 1 more minute. Add 1½ cups broth and collard greens to pan; cover and bring to a boil. Cook 18 minutes or until tender. Uncover and cook, stirring often, 3 to 4 minutes or until most of broth evaporates. Remove from heat, and stir in breadcrumbs, ¼ tsp. salt, and ¼ tsp. hot sauce.

3. Preheat oven to 400°. Butterfly turkey by making a lengthwise cut in 1 side, cutting to but not through the opposite side; unfold. Place between 2 sheets of heavy-duty plastic wrap, and flatten to ½" thickness, using a rolling pin or the flat side of a meat mallet. Sprinkle both sides of turkey with remaining ¼ tsp. salt and ½ tsp. pepper. Spoon greens mixture over turkey, leaving a 2" border. Roll up, starting at 1 long side. Arrange 4 reserved bacon slices in a crisscross pattern over turkey; tie with kitchen string, securing at 2" intervals. Place, seam side down, in a lightly greased jelly-roll pan.

4. Bake at 400° for 40 to 42 minutes or until a meat thermometer inserted into thickest portion registers 170°. Remove from oven; let stand 10 minutes before slicing.

5. For sauce, transfer drippings into a glass measuring cup, scraping pan to remove browned bits. Add enough remaining broth, about ¾ cup, to equal 1 cup. Pour into a medium saucepan; add flour, and whisk until smooth. Bring to a boil over medium-high heat, whisking constantly. Cook 3 minutes or until thickened. Whisk in cream and remaining ¼ tsp. hot sauce. Stir in reserved crumbled bacon.

editor's favorite

Chile-Rubbed Turkey Breast with Fresh Cranberry-Candied Pecan Salsa

The holiday bird goes south of the border in this spicy recipe. We especially liked the candied pecans in the salsa.

MAKES 8 TO 10 SERVINGS
PREP: 30 MIN.   COOK: 2 HR., 23 MIN.   OTHER: 15 MIN.

  2 ancho chile peppers, seeded and torn into pieces
  4 garlic cloves
  2 Tbsp. olive oil, divided
  1 tsp. sugar
  1 tsp. ground cumin
  1 tsp. fresh lime juice
  1 tsp. salt
  1 (6- to 7-lb.) bone-in turkey breast
Fresh Cranberry-Candied Pecan Salsa
Garnish: fresh cilantro sprig

1. Combine ¾ cup water, chiles, and garlic in a small saucepan. Bring to a boil; reduce heat, and simmer, uncovered, 10 to 12 minutes or until most of liquid evaporates.

2. Process chile mixture, 1 Tbsp. oil, and next 4 ingredients in a food processor 1½ to 2 minutes or until smooth.

3. Preheat oven to 400°. Loosen and lift skin from turkey with fingers, without totally detaching skin; spread chile mixture under skin. Carefully replace skin. Rub skin with remaining 1 Tbsp. oil. Place breast on a lightly greased wire rack in a roasting pan.

4. Bake at 400° for 2 hours or until a meat thermometer inserted into thickest part of breast registers 170°. (Loosely cover with aluminum foil during baking, if needed, to prevent excessive browning.) Cover breast with aluminum foil, and let stand 15 minutes before carving. Serve with Fresh Cranberry-Candied Pecan Salsa. Garnish, if desired.

editor's favorite • make ahead • quick & easy

Fresh Cranberry-Candied Pecan Salsa

MAKES 3 CUPS
PREP: 15 MIN.   COOK: 12 MIN.

Parchment paper
¼ cup sugar
½ cup chopped pecans, toasted
1 (12-oz.) package fresh or frozen cranberries,
   partially thawed
⅓ cup honey
¼ cup thinly sliced green onions
1 tsp. lime zest
2 Tbsp. fresh lime juice
1 jalapeño pepper, seeded and minced (1½ Tbsp.)
¼ cup chopped fresh cilantro

1. Place a piece of parchment paper on work surface.
2. Cook sugar in a medium skillet over medium heat 3 minutes or until melted. Stir in pecans until coated. Pour candied pecans onto parchment paper, and cool completely; chop into small pieces.
3. Pulse cranberries and next 5 ingredients in a food processor 10 to 12 times or until chopped. Transfer to a bowl. Cover and chill until ready to serve. Stir in pecans and cilantro just before serving.

**Chile-Rubbed Turkey Breast
with Fresh Cranberry-Candied
Pecan Salsa**

Turkey Panini

Try a trendy sandwich using leftover turkey after the big holiday feast. Pile on the turkey and use your homemade cranberry sauce, if desired. Shaved deli turkey is a fine substitute.

MAKES 2 SANDWICHES
PREP: 10 MIN.   COOK: 3 MIN.

¼ cup whole-berry cranberry sauce
2 to 3 tsp. prepared horseradish
2 Tbsp. mayonnaise
4 large slices ciabatta bread (½" thick)
4 (⅜"-thick) slices cooked turkey breast or deli turkey
Salt and pepper to taste
4 (¾-oz.) provolone cheese slices
4 bacon slices, cooked
1½ Tbsp. olive oil
Garnish: gourmet mixed salad greens

1. Preheat panini press according to manufacturer's instructions. Combine cranberry sauce and horseradish, stirring well.
2. Spread mayonnaise on 1 side of each slice of bread. Spread cranberry-horseradish sauce on 2 slices of bread; top each sandwich with 2 turkey slices, and sprinkle with salt and pepper.
3. Arrange 2 cheese slices on each sandwich; top with 2 bacon slices. Cover with tops of bread, mayonnaise side down.
4. Brush tops of sandwiches with olive oil. Turn and brush bottoms of sandwiches with olive oil.
5. Place sandwiches in panini press; cook 3 minutes or until cheese begins to melt and bread is toasted. Serve hot. Garnish, if desired.

Turkey Panini

Herb-Roasted Turkey Breast with Harvest Vegetables

Succulent turkey breast is surrounded by vibrant roasted fall vegetables, savory bacon, and toasted pecans.

MAKES 10 TO 12 SERVINGS
PREP: 31 MIN.   COOK: 2 HR., 18 MIN.   OTHER: 20 MIN.

1 Tbsp. chopped fresh rosemary
1 Tbsp. chopped fresh thyme
4 garlic cloves, minced
1 tsp. salt
½ tsp. pepper, divided
1 (6- to 7-lb.) bone-in turkey breast
1 Tbsp. olive oil
1 (3-lb.) butternut squash, cut into 1½" pieces
1½ lb. turnips, peeled and cut into 1½" pieces
4 medium carrots, cut into 1½" pieces
1 large onion, cut into 1½" pieces
2 Tbsp. olive oil
½ tsp. salt
⅛ tsp. pepper
4 thick bacon slices
½ cup coarsely chopped pecans
2 tsp. chopped fresh rosemary
½ tsp. salt
2½ to 2¾ cups chicken broth
3 Tbsp. all-purpose flour
Garnish: fresh rosemary sprigs

1. Preheat oven to 400°. Stir together first 4 ingredients and ¼ tsp. pepper in a small bowl. Starting at neck cavity, loosen and lift skin from turkey breast with fingers, without totally detaching skin. Rub herb mixture under skin; carefully replace skin. Rub 1 Tbsp. oil over outside of turkey. Place turkey, breast side up, on a lightly greased rack in a lightly greased large roasting pan. Bake at 400° for 1 hour and 15 minutes.
2. Meanwhile, combine squash and next 6 ingredients in a large bowl. Arrange one-third of vegetables around turkey in pan. Place remaining vegetables in another lightly greased roasting pan. Continue cooking turkey and vegetables 45 more minutes or until vegetables are tender and a meat thermometer inserted into thickest part of turkey breast registers 170°. Transfer vegetables to a bowl using a slotted spoon, reserving drippings in pan. Cover turkey with foil, and let stand 15 minutes before slicing.
3. While turkey stands, cook bacon in a skillet until crisp; remove bacon, reserving drippings in skillet. Crumble bacon; set aside. Sauté pecans in hot drippings in skillet 2 to 3 minutes or until pecans are toasted. Remove pecans from skillet using a slotted spoon. Add pecans, reserved bacon, 2 tsp.

**Herb-Roasted Turkey Breast
with Harvest Vegetables**

rosemary, and ½ tsp. salt to vegetables; toss to combine.

4. To make gravy, pour pan drippings into a 4-cup glass measuring cup, and let stand 5 minutes. Spoon 2 Tbsp. fat out of drippings in cup and return to roasting pan; discard remaining fat. Add enough chicken broth to measuring cup to yield 3 cups. Set aside.

5. Place roasting pan over 2 burners on the stovetop over medium heat. Gradually whisk in flour, and cook, whisking constantly, 2 minutes or until flour is lightly browned. Add reserved broth to pan; stir until browned bits are loosened from bottom of pan. Bring to a boil; reduce heat, and simmer 8 minutes or until gravy is reduced to 2½ cups. Stir in remaining ¼ tsp. pepper. Serve gravy with turkey and roasted vegetables. Garnish, if desired.

**Succotash with Smoked
Ham and Herbs**

choosing SIDES

Side dishes take center stage with these recipes that highlight winter's best ingredients and easy cooking methods.

editor's favorite

Succotash with Smoked Ham and Herbs

Fresh tarragon adds a subtle and intriguing flavor note to this rich, colorful side that's suitable with ham or pork roast.

MAKES 6 TO 8 SERVINGS
PREP: 12 MIN.   COOK: 36 MIN.

1 (1-lb.) package frozen baby lima beans, thawed
2 Tbsp. unsalted butter
6 oz. smoked ham, coarsely chopped (about 1½ cups)
½ cup chopped red bell pepper
⅓ cup minced shallots
1 (1-lb.) package frozen baby gold and white corn, thawed (we tested with Birds Eye)
2 tsp. sugar
½ tsp. salt
½ tsp. freshly ground black pepper
1 cup heavy whipping cream
1 Tbsp. minced fresh chives
1 Tbsp. minced fresh parsley
1 Tbsp. minced fresh tarragon

1. Cook lima beans according to microwave package directions. Drain.
2. Melt butter in a large skillet over medium-high heat. Add ham; sauté 3 minutes or until lightly browned. Add red bell pepper and shallots; sauté 3 minutes or just until tender. Add lima beans, corn, and next 3 ingredients; cook, stirring often, 6 minutes. Add cream; cook, stirring often, 10 minutes or until vegetables are tender and cream is slightly thickened. Stir in herbs.

quick & easy

Christmas Creamed Corn

Bet you never thought frozen corn could end up on your holiday table tasting this good.

MAKES 6 TO 8 SERVINGS
PREP: 10 MIN.   COOK: 15 MIN.

¼ cup butter
1 medium onion, diced
1 red bell pepper, diced
2 garlic cloves, minced
3 (10-oz.) packages frozen whole kernel corn, thawed
¾ cup heavy whipping cream
1 tsp. sugar
¾ tsp. salt
¼ tsp. pepper

1. Melt butter in a large nonstick skillet over medium heat. Add onion, bell pepper, and garlic; sauté 8 minutes or until tender.
2. Process 1 package of corn and ½ cup cream in a blender or food processor until smooth. Add puree, remaining ¼ cup cream, and remaining corn to skillet. Stir in sugar, salt, and pepper. Cook, stirring often, 5 minutes, or until heated and most of liquid evaporates.

Broccoli-Cauliflower Salad with Dried Cranberries and Pistachios

Dried cranberries and pistachios replace raisins and pecans in this traditional salad.

MAKES 6 TO 8 SERVINGS
PREP: 13 MIN.   COOK: 7 MIN.

6   bacon slices
1   cup mayonnaise
¼   cup sugar
2   Tbsp. red wine vinegar
½   tsp. salt
¼   tsp. pepper

3   cups coarsely chopped broccoli florets
2   cups coarsely chopped cauliflower (about ½ head)
1   cup sweetened dried cranberries (we tested with Craisins)
½   cup chopped pistachios
3   Tbsp. chopped red onion

1. Cook bacon in a large skillet over medium-high heat 6 to 7 minutes or until crisp; remove bacon, and drain on paper towels. Crumble bacon.

2. Meanwhile, combine mayonnaise and next 4 ingredients in a large bowl, stirring until blended. Add bacon, broccoli, and remaining ingredients. Toss until vegetables are coated.

Note: Chop the broccoli and cauliflower just enough to create uniform pieces, keeping smaller florets intact.

quick & easy

Broccoli with Caramelized Garlic and Pine Nuts

Buy bagged broccoli florets for convenience.

MAKES 6 SERVINGS
PREP: 5 MIN. COOK: 16 MIN.

⅓ cup pine nuts
¼ cup butter
1 Tbsp. olive oil
6 garlic cloves, thinly sliced
1 lb. broccoli florets
½ tsp. salt
⅛ tsp. dried crushed red pepper

1. Toast pine nuts in a large skillet over medium heat 6 minutes or until lightly browned. Remove from skillet, and set aside.

2. Heat butter and oil in same skillet over medium heat until butter melts. Add garlic, and sauté 1 to 2 minutes or until lightly browned. Add broccoli, salt, and crushed red pepper. Sauté 8 minutes or until broccoli is tender. Stir in pine nuts before serving.

Broccoli with Caramelized Garlic and Pine Nuts

editor's favorite

Tangy Cauliflower with Tomatoes, Olives, and Feta

With a great blend of Mediterranean flavors, the highlight of this big-yield side dish is pockets of warm feta.

MAKES 8 SERVINGS
PREP: 6 MIN. COOK: 31 MIN.

1 large head cauliflower (about 2 lb.), cut into florets
2 Tbsp. extra virgin olive oil
1 small red onion, thinly sliced
⅛ tsp. salt
¼ tsp. freshly ground pepper
1 (8-oz.) package feta cheese, cut into ½" cubes
2 Tbsp. white wine vinegar
2 tsp. sugar
2 plum tomatoes, chopped
1 cup pitted kalamata olives, coarsely chopped
Garnish: chopped fresh oregano

1. Bring 4 qt. salted water to a boil in a large Dutch oven over high heat. Add cauliflower; cook, stirring often, just until crisp-tender. Drain; rinse under cold water. Let cool in colander.

2. Heat oil in a large skillet or sauté pan over medium-high heat; add onion, salt, and pepper, and sauté 8 minutes or until onion is browned. Add cauliflower, cheese, and next 3 ingredients. Cook, stirring often, 3 minutes or until thoroughly heated. Sprinkle with olives. Garnish, if desired.

Crumb-Topped Spinach Casserole

This quick, cheesy side, with its crunchy herbed topping, can be ready to bake in just over the time it takes to preheat the oven.

MAKES 8 TO 10 SERVINGS
PREP: 13 MIN.   COOK: 43 MIN.

- 2 Tbsp. butter
- 1 medium onion, diced
- 2 garlic cloves, minced
- 4 (10-oz.) packages frozen chopped spinach, thawed
- ½ (8-oz.) package cream cheese, softened
- 2 Tbsp. all-purpose flour
- 2 large eggs
- ½ tsp. salt
- ¼ tsp. pepper
- 1 cup milk
- 1 (8-oz.) package shredded Cheddar cheese
- 1 cup Italian-seasoned Japanese breadcrumbs (panko) or homemade breadcrumbs
- 3 Tbsp. butter, melted

1. Preheat oven to 350°. Melt 2 Tbsp. butter in a large nonstick skillet over medium heat. Add onion and garlic, and sauté 8 minutes or until tender.

2. Meanwhile, drain spinach well, pressing between paper towels to remove excess moisture.

3. Blend cream cheese and flour in a large bowl until smooth. Whisk in eggs, salt, and pepper. Gradually whisk in milk until blended. Add sautéed onions, spinach, and Cheddar cheese, stirring to blend. Spoon into a lightly greased 11" x 7" baking dish.

4. Combine breadcrumbs and 3 Tbsp. melted butter in a small bowl; toss well, and sprinkle over casserole.

5. Bake, uncovered, at 350° for 30 to 35 minutes or until thoroughly heated and breadcrumbs are browned.

Asparagus with Gremolata

Gremolata is a parsley-lemon garnish typically sprinkled over Osso Bucco. Here it makes a nice adornment to fresh asparagus. We also recommend gremolata on baked potatoes and grilled chicken.

MAKES 4 SERVINGS
PREP: 4 MIN.   COOK: 13 MIN.

- 1 lemon
- ¼ cup chopped fresh flat-leaf parsley
- 2 garlic cloves, chopped
- 1 lb. fresh asparagus
- 2 Tbsp. unsalted butter, melted
- ½ tsp. salt
- ¼ tsp. pepper

1. Grate enough zest from lemon to yield about 2 tsp. Process parsley and garlic in a food processor until finely minced; add lemon zest, and set gremolata aside.

2. Snap off and discard tough ends of asparagus. Cook asparagus in boiling salted water to cover 5 to 6 minutes or until crisp-tender; drain. Arrange asparagus on a platter. Drizzle with butter; sprinkle with salt and pepper. Sprinkle with gremolata.

Asparagus with Gremolata

Chipotle Green Beans with Bacon

Look for canned chipotle peppers in adobo sauce in the Mexican-foods section of your grocery store.

MAKES 6 SERVINGS
PREP: 15 MIN.   COOK: 28 MIN.

- 8   bacon slices, chopped
- ½   medium onion, chopped (about 1¼ cups)
- ½   cup chicken broth
- 1   tsp. chopped canned chipotle peppers in adobo sauce
- 2   tsp. adobo sauce from can
- ¼   tsp. salt
- ¼   tsp. freshly ground black pepper
- 2   lb. fresh green beans, trimmed

1. Heat a large skillet over medium heat; add bacon, and cook 8 to 9 minutes or until browned and crisp. Drain bacon on paper towels, reserving 2 Tbsp. drippings in skillet. Sauté onion in hot drippings 4 to 5 minutes or until browned. Stir in broth and next 4 ingredients. Add green beans; toss to coat. Cover and cook 14 minutes or until tender, stirring often. Transfer beans to a serving dish; top with bacon.

make ahead • quick & easy

Green Beans with Toasted Almonds and Lemon

If your grocer doesn't carry bags of pretrimmed green beans, start with 1¾ lb. of untrimmed beans to get an equivalent amount of beans called for here.

MAKES 6 TO 8 SERVINGS
PREP: 10 MIN.   COOK: 15 MIN.

- 2   (12-oz.) packages trimmed fresh green beans
- 2   Tbsp. olive oil
- 2   large garlic cloves, minced
- 2   tsp. grated lemon rind
- ½   tsp. salt
- ¼   tsp. pepper
- 3   Tbsp. fresh lemon juice
- ⅓   cup sliced almonds, toasted

1. Cook green beans in boiling salted water to cover 5 to 7 minutes or until crisp-tender; drain. Plunge beans into a bowl of ice water to stop the cooking process; drain.
2. Heat oil in a large skillet over medium heat; add garlic, and sauté 1 minute or until golden. Stir in green beans, lemon rind, salt, and pepper; sauté 4 minutes or until beans are thoroughly heated. Add lemon juice and almonds; toss well.

Chipotle Green Beans with Bacon

editor's favorite

Braised Fennel and Leeks

Thinly sliced fennel and leeks simmer in a white wine broth and get an herbed crumb topping. Match this side with a pork roast, chicken, or fish.

MAKES 10 SERVINGS
PREP: 20 MIN.   COOK: 1 HR., 30 MIN.   OTHER: 10 MIN.

    3   medium fennel bulbs
    5   medium leeks, white and light green parts only, halved
        lengthwise and thinly sliced
    1   (14-oz.) can chicken broth
    ⅓   cup dry white wine
    2   Tbsp. chopped fresh parsley
    1   tsp. chopped fresh thyme
    ¾   tsp. salt
    ¾   tsp. pepper
    ¼   cup butter, cut into pieces
        Heavy-duty aluminum foil
    2   cups fresh breadcrumbs
    ¼   cup olive oil
    2   Tbsp. chopped fresh thyme

1. Preheat oven to 400°. Rinse fennel thoroughly. Trim and discard root ends of fennel bulbs. Trim stalks from bulbs, reserving fronds for another use. Cut bulbs into thin slices. Arrange fennel and leeks in a lightly greased 13" x 9" baking dish.
2. Combine chicken broth and next 5 ingredients, and pour over vegetables. Dot with butter, and cover tightly with heavy-duty aluminum foil. Bake at 400° for 1 hour.
3. Meanwhile, combine breadcrumbs, olive oil, and 2 Tbsp. thyme. Sprinkle breadcrumb mixture over vegetables. Bake, uncovered, 30 more minutes or until breadcrumbs are browned and liquid almost evaporates. Let stand 10 minutes before serving.

Carrot-Apricot Mash

This vivid apricot-kissed side dish is chock-full of vitamins.

MAKES 6 TO 8 SERVINGS
PREP: 15 MIN.   COOK: 20 MIN.

    2   lb. carrots, peeled and sliced
    ½   cup apricot nectar
    1   cup chicken broth
    2   garlic cloves, sliced
    3   Tbsp. grated orange rind
    ¼   cup butter
    3   Tbsp. whipping cream
    ½   tsp. salt

1. Combine first 5 ingredients in a large saucepan; bring to a boil. Cover, reduce heat, and simmer 15 to 20 minutes or until carrots are very tender.
2. Process carrot mixture, in batches, in a food processor until smooth, stopping to scrape down sides as needed. Return mixture to saucepan; add butter, whipping cream, and salt. Cook over medium heat, stirring constantly, until warm.

Mustardy Carrots with Lemon and Green Onions

Serve these glazed carrots with lemon wedges to squeeze over the top for a citrus splash.

MAKES 6 TO 8 SERVINGS
PREP: 12 MIN.   COOK: 25 MIN.

    2   lb. carrots, peeled and coarsely chopped
    2   Tbsp. olive oil
    1   Tbsp. lemon juice
    1   Tbsp. Dijon mustard
    1   Tbsp. honey
    ¾   cup thinly sliced green onions
        Salt and pepper to taste

1. Cook carrots in boiling salted water to cover 13 to 15 minutes or until tender; drain.
2. Heat a large, deep skillet over medium-high heat. Add oil and next 3 ingredients, stirring well with a whisk. Cook, whisking constantly, 1 to 2 minutes or until mixture is thickened. Stir in carrots, green onions, and desired amount of salt and pepper. Cook 1 to 2 minutes or until thoroughly heated.

Braised Fennel and Leeks

editor's favorite · quick & easy

Sautéed Mushrooms with Sage and Pistachios

Using a combination of mushrooms adds layers of flavor. Cooking them without stirring browns them nicely.

MAKES 4 TO 6 SERVINGS
PREP: 3 MIN. COOK: 17 MIN.

  2 Tbsp. olive oil
1½ lb. assorted mushrooms, quartered or sliced (we tested with shiitake, baby bella, and fresh button mushrooms)
  3 Tbsp. butter
  1 small onion, chopped
  1 Tbsp. sherry vinegar or red wine vinegar
  ½ tsp. salt
  ⅛ tsp. pepper
  ⅓ cup heavy whipping cream
1½ Tbsp. chopped fresh sage
  ¼ cup roasted and salted pistachio nuts, coarsely chopped

1. Heat oil in a large skillet over medium-high heat. Add mushrooms; cook 10 minutes (do not stir). Add butter; stir until butter melts. Add onion and next 3 ingredients; cook, stirring occasionally, 4 minutes or until onion is tender. Reduce heat to medium; add cream and sage, stirring well. Cook, stirring constantly, 1 minute or until cream thickens.
2. Transfer mushrooms to a serving bowl; sprinkle with pistachios.

editor's favorite

Roasted Beets and Oranges with Herb Butter

These beets get a citrus infusion from roasting in a foil pack along with orange slices.

MAKES 4 SERVINGS
PREP: 15 MIN. COOK: 1 HR., 29 MIN.

  4 medium beets, trimmed, peeled, and cut into 1" pieces (about 1 lb.)
  1 small orange, halved lengthwise and thinly sliced
  2 Tbsp. olive oil
  ¼ tsp. salt
  ¼ tsp. freshly ground pepper
  3 Tbsp. butter, softened
  1 Tbsp. chopped fresh flat-leaf parsley
  1 Tbsp. chopped fresh rosemary
  2 Tbsp. orange juice

1. Preheat oven to 400°. Combine first 5 ingredients in a large bowl; toss to coat. Wrap beets and oranges in lightly greased aluminum foil. Fold foil to seal. Transfer foil pack to a baking sheet.
2. Roast at 400° for 45 minutes. Carefully unfold foil with tongs, and continue roasting 40 more minutes or until beets are tender and browned. Remove beets and oranges from foil.
3. Melt butter in a large skillet over medium-high heat; whisk in herbs and orange juice, and cook 1 to 2 minutes or until slightly thickened. Add beets and oranges; sauté 1 to 2 minutes or until thoroughly heated. Transfer to a serving bowl.

editor's favorite

Caramelized Turnips

If you don't like turnips, this recipe may just change your mind. If you can only get baby turnips, cook them whole, and add 2 to 3 minutes to the cook time.

MAKES 4 TO 6 SERVINGS
PREP: 8 MIN. COOK: 40 MIN.

  2 lb. turnips, peeled and cut into 1" pieces (about 5 cups)
  2 Tbsp. unsalted butter
1½ Tbsp. sugar
  ½ tsp. salt
  ¼ tsp. freshly ground pepper

1. Place turnips in a single layer in a large skillet. Add enough water to cover two-thirds of turnips (to a depth of about ½"). Add butter and remaining ingredients. Bring to a boil; cover, reduce heat, and simmer 5 minutes. Uncover; cook over medium-high heat 30 to 32 minutes or until water evaporates and turnips are browned. Add 2 Tbsp. water; cook 1 minute to deglaze skillet, stirring to loosen particles from bottom of skillet and glaze turnips. Serve hot.

make ahead

Butternut Squash Casserole with Pecan Streusel

As an option, you can use canned pumpkin puree or yams instead of the squash in this recipe.

MAKES 8 TO 10 SERVINGS
PREP: 15 MIN.   COOK: 40 MIN.   OTHER: 5 MIN.

  3 (12-oz.) packages frozen cooked butternut squash, thawed (we tested with McKenzie)
  1 cup firmly packed light brown sugar
  ½ cup half-and-half
  ¼ cup butter, melted
  2 large eggs, lightly beaten
  ½ tsp. salt
  ½ tsp. ground cinnamon
  ¼ tsp. ground allspice
  ¼ tsp. ground cloves
  1 tsp. vanilla extract
  ¼ cup all-purpose flour
  ¼ cup firmly packed light brown sugar
  3 Tbsp. cold butter, cut into pieces
  ½ cup chopped pecans

1. Combine first 10 ingredients in a large bowl; stir well. Place in a lightly greased 11" x 7" baking dish.
2. Preheat oven to 375°. Combine flour and ¼ cup brown sugar. Cut in 3 Tbsp. butter with a pastry blender until crumbly. Stir in nuts. Sprinkle over squash. Bake, uncovered, at 375° for 40 minutes or until edges are lightly browned. Let casserole stand 5 minutes before serving.

Whole Acorn Squash Cream Soup

This unique recipe celebrates the beauty of squash by using it as a serving vessel. Choose squash that stand upright for ease in baking and serving.

MAKES 4 SERVINGS
PREP: 16 MIN.   COOK: 1 HR., 45 MIN.

  4 medium acorn squash
  ¼ cup cream cheese
  1 cup heavy whipping cream
  1 cup chicken broth
  ½ tsp. salt
  1 tsp. ground cinnamon

Whole Acorn Squash Cream Soup

1. Preheat oven to 350°. Cut off about 1" of stem ends of squash to reveal seeds. Scoop out and discard seeds and membranes. Arrange squash in a 13" x 9" baking dish.
2. Place 1 Tbsp. cream cheese in each squash cavity. Pour ¼ cup each heavy cream and chicken broth over cream cheese in each squash, and sprinkle each cavity with ⅛ tsp. salt and ¼ tsp. cinnamon. Add water to baking dish to a depth of ½".
3. Bake squash, uncovered, at 350° for 1 hour and 45 minutes or until squash are very tender.
4. To serve, carefully set each squash in a shallow soup bowl.

Squash and Cornbread Dressing

MAKES 12 SERVINGS
PREP: 45 MIN.   COOK: 1 HR., 45 MIN.

 5 Tbsp. canola oil, divided
 2 cups self-rising white cornmeal mix (we tested
    with White Lily)
 1 large egg
1⅓ cups milk
 2 (16-oz.) packages frozen sliced yellow squash
 2 cups chopped celery
 ½ cup butter
 3 large onions, chopped (about 6 cups)
1½ sleeves saltine crackers, coarsely crushed
1½ cups (6 oz.) shredded sharp Cheddar cheese
 2 large eggs
1½ tsp. poultry seasoning
1½ tsp. pepper
 ¼ tsp. salt
 1 cup chicken broth

1. Preheat oven to 450°. Place 1 Tbsp. oil in a 9" cast-iron skillet; place skillet in oven while it preheats. Place cornmeal mix in a large bowl; make a well in center. Whisk together 1 egg, milk, and remaining ¼ cup oil; add to cornmeal mix, stirring just until moistened. Pour batter into preheated skillet.
2. Bake at 450° for 20 to 25 minutes or until golden brown. Place cornbread in a large bowl. Set aside. Reduce oven temperature to 350°.
3. Meanwhile, place squash, celery, and ¼ cup water in a large microwave-safe bowl. Cover, vent, and microwave at HIGH 25 minutes or until vegetables are tender, stirring every 10 minutes. (Do not drain.)
4. Meanwhile, melt butter in a large skillet over medium-high heat; add onion, and cook, stirring often, 10 minutes or until tender. Stir in crackers. Reserve 3 cups of cracker mixture. Crumble cornbread in bowl; add remaining cracker mixture and 1½ cups cheese, tossing well. Stir squash mixture into cornbread mixture.
5. Whisk together 2 eggs and next 3 ingredients in a medium bowl; stir in broth. Stir egg mixture into cornbread mixture. Spoon into 2 greased 11" x 7" baking dishes. Top each casserole with 1½ cups reserved cracker mixture.
6. Bake, uncovered, at 350° for 45 to 50 minutes or until golden.

Roasted Tomatoes Provençal

An herb-and-garlic crumb topping dresses up fresh tomatoes for an easy accompaniment to meat, poultry, or fish.

MAKES 4 SERVINGS
PREP: 17 MIN.   COOK: 30 MIN.

 4 medium-size firm ripe tomatoes (about 2 lb.),
    cut in half crosswise
 ¼ cup extra virgin olive oil, divided
 3 large garlic cloves, thinly sliced
 1 Tbsp. minced fresh thyme
 ¾ tsp. salt
 ¼ tsp. pepper
 ⅔ cup fresh breadcrumbs
 3 Tbsp. minced fresh flat-leaf parsley

1. Preheat oven to 425°. Place tomato halves in a shallow baking dish. Drizzle 2 Tbsp. oil over tomatoes; sprinkle with garlic slices, thyme, salt, and pepper.
2. Bake at 425° for 20 minutes or until tomato juices are bubbly and tomatoes are just tender.
3. Combine breadcrumbs, parsley, and remaining 2 Tbsp. oil in a small bowl. Sprinkle crumb mixture over tomatoes. Bake 10 more minutes or until crumbs are browned.

Note: Make fresh breadcrumbs from your favorite crusty bread. Tear off or cut 1 or 2 thick slices, and pulse in a mini chopper or food processor until coarse crumbs form.

editor's favorite • quick & easy

Blue Cheese and Black Pepper Potatoes

You'll love these spuds made luscious with blue cheese.

MAKES 8 TO 10 SERVINGS
PREP: 2 MIN.   COOK: 8 MIN.

- 2 (24-oz.) packages refrigerated mashed potatoes (we tested with Bob Evans)*
- 4 oz. blue cheese, crumbled
- ¼ cup butter, cut into pieces
- ¼ tsp. salt
- ¼ tsp. freshly ground black pepper

1. Heat potatoes in a large saucepan over medium heat, stirring often, 6 to 8 minutes. Add blue cheese, butter, salt, and pepper, stirring just until butter is melted.

*Look for this brand of mashed potatoes in the meat department of your grocery store.

Sweet Potato Galette

MAKES 6 SERVINGS
PREP: 15 MIN.   COOK: 33 MIN.

- 2 lb. sweet potatoes, peeled and sliced into ⅛"-thick rounds
- ¼ cup unsalted butter, melted and divided
- 2 Tbsp. all-purpose flour
- 1 tsp. salt
- ½ tsp. pepper
- ¼ tsp. freshly grated nutmeg

1. Preheat oven to 375°. Combine sweet potatoes and 2 Tbsp. butter in a large bowl, tossing to coat. Combine flour and next 3 ingredients; sprinkle over potatoes. Toss potatoes to coat.
2. Place remaining 2 Tbsp. butter in a 10" cast-iron skillet or other large ovenproof skillet. Arrange 1 layer of sweet potatoes in slightly overlapping concentric circles in skillet. Top with remaining sweet potatoes.
3. Cut a circle of nonstick aluminum foil; place over potatoes. Place a 9" cast-iron skillet on top of foil to weight the galette. Cook galette over medium heat 5 minutes without disturbing. Transfer weighted skillet to oven; bake at 375° for 10 minutes. Remove top skillet and foil, and bake galette 15 more minutes or until potatoes are tender. Loosen edges of galette with a spatula to prevent sticking. Invert onto serving plate; serve warm.

Sweet Potato Galette

Fruit and Nut Rice Pilaf

Apple-Raisin Dressing

If you're a fan of moist dressing, use the larger amount of broth.

MAKES 10 TO 12 SERVINGS
PREP: 16 MIN.   COOK: 1 HR., 14 MIN.

¼ cup butter
1 large onion, diced
2 celery ribs, diced (about 1 cup)
2 Granny Smith apples, diced (about 3 cups)
2 tsp. rubbed sage
½ tsp. salt
¼ tsp. freshly ground black pepper
1 (16-oz.) package herb-seasoned stuffing mix
   (we tested with Pepperidge Farm)
1 cup golden raisins
1 cup chopped pecans, toasted
2½ to 3 cups chicken broth
2 large eggs, lightly beaten

1. Preheat oven to 325°. Melt butter in a large skillet over medium-high heat. Add onion and celery, and sauté 10 minutes or until tender. Add apple; sauté 3 minutes or until tender. Stir in sage, salt, and pepper.
2. Combine sautéed mixture, stuffing, raisins, and pecans in a large bowl. Add chicken broth and eggs; stir well. Spoon dressing into a lightly greased 13" x 9" baking dish. Bake, uncovered, at 325° for 50 to 60 minutes or until well browned.

editor's favorite · quick & easy
Fruit and Nut Rice Pilaf

MAKES 6 TO 8 SERVINGS
PREP: 5 MIN.   COOK: 16 MIN.

2 Tbsp. butter
1 medium onion, diced
2 celery ribs, diced
½ cup chicken broth
1 (7-oz.) package dried fruit bits
2 (8.8-oz.) packages microwave-ready long grain and
   wild rice (we tested with Uncle Ben's)
1 cup chopped walnuts or pecans, toasted
¼ cup chopped flat-leaf parsley
¼ tsp. pepper

1. Melt butter in a large skillet over medium heat. Add onion and celery, and sauté 5 minutes or until tender. Add broth and fruit; bring to a boil. Cover; reduce heat, and cook 5 minutes or until fruit is softened. Stir in rice; cook, stirring often, 4 minutes or until rice is heated. Stir in walnuts, parsley, and pepper.

Vanilla Crumb Cakes

heavenly CHOCOLATE & VANILLA

Chocolate and vanilla are classic dessert themes. Discover these ingredients anew with fresh and deliciously unexpected flavor pairings. Your palate will be happily surprised.

Vanilla Crumb Cakes

MAKES 4 CRUMB CAKES
PREP: 14 MIN.   COOK: 30 MIN.   OTHER: 10 MIN.

 ¼ cup plus 2 Tbsp. granulated sugar
 ¼ cup plus 2 Tbsp. firmly packed light brown sugar
 1½ cups plus 2 Tbsp. all-purpose flour
 ¼ tsp. freshly grated nutmeg
 ½ cup unsalted butter, cut into pieces
 ½ cup buttermilk
 1 tsp. vanilla bean paste or vanilla extract
 ½ tsp. baking powder
 ¼ tsp. baking soda
 ¼ tsp. salt
 1 large egg
 Vanilla Glaze

1. Preheat oven to 350°. Stir together sugars in a large bowl. Add flour and nutmeg, whisking until blended. Cut butter into flour mixture with a pastry blender or fork until crumbly. Remove and reserve ½ cup crumb mixture.
2. Combine buttermilk, vanilla, baking powder, baking soda, and salt; whisk in egg. Pour over crumb mixture in large bowl; stir with a fork until dry ingredients are moistened.
3. Spoon batter evenly into a greased jumbo muffin pan, filling 4 muffin cups with batter. Fill 2 empty cups halfway with water. Sprinkle reserved crumb mixture evenly over batter, pressing lightly into batter. Bake at 350° for 28 to 30 minutes or until a wooden pick inserted in center comes out clean. Cool in pan on a wire rack 10 minutes; remove cakes from pan, and let cool completely on wire rack. Drizzle with Vanilla Glaze.

Vanilla Glaze

MAKES ¼ CUP

 ⅔ cup powdered sugar
 1 Tbsp. milk
 ½ tsp. vanilla bean paste or vanilla extract

1. Whisk all ingredients until smooth.

Chocolate-Chipotle Fondue

This updated fondue gets a kick from spicy chipotle pepper. Enjoy leftovers over ice cream.

MAKES 3¼ CUPS
PREP: 5 MIN.   COOK: 11 MIN.

 4 (4-oz.) sweet dark chocolate baking bars, chopped (we tested with Ghirardelli)
 1½ cups whipping cream
 ½ cup canned dulce de leche (we tested with La Lechera)
 1 tsp. ground chipotle chile powder
 ⅓ cup coffee liqueur (we tested with Kahlúa)
 Dippers: Candied fruit (we tested with mango slices, papaya strips, and pineapple chunks); banana slices; pound cake cubes; marshmallows

1. Combine first 3 ingredients in a medium saucepan; cook, stirring constantly, over medium-low heat until chocolate melts and mixture is smooth. Stir in chile powder and coffee liqueur. Pour mixture into a fondue pot; place over fondue burner. Serve with candied fruit, banana slices, cake cubes, and marshmallows as dippers.

vanilla math

Vanilla beans and vanilla bean paste (which is thick like syrup with an abundance of seeds) have more intense vanilla flavor than vanilla extract. Recipes in this chapter that call for vanilla bean or paste work just as well if vanilla extract is what you have on hand (Vanilla Sugar, page 72, and Vanilla Bean Oil, page 72, are exceptions). Here are the conversions:

• 1 tsp. vanilla bean paste = 1 tsp. vanilla extract
• Seeds from 1 whole vanilla bean = 1 Tbsp. vanilla extract
• Seeds from 1 (2") piece vanilla bean = 1 tsp. vanilla extract

gift idea · make ahead

Deep Dark Fudge with Candied Ginger

A dab of wasabi paste gives this fudge an intriguing Asian influence.

MAKES 1½ LB.
PREP: 5 MIN.   COOK: 8 MIN.   OTHER: 2 HR.

1¼ cups sugar
 1   (5-oz.) can evaporated milk
 2   Tbsp. butter
 ⅛   tsp. salt
 2   cups miniature marshmallows
 2   tsp. wasabi paste (optional)
1⅔ cups 60% cacao bittersweet chocolate morsels
      (we tested with Ghirardelli)
 1   tsp. vanilla extract
 3   Tbsp. minced crystallized ginger

1. Line a lightly greased 8" square pan with nonstick aluminum foil; set aside.

2. Combine first 4 ingredients in a medium-size heavy saucepan. Cook over medium heat, stirring constantly, until mixture comes to a boil; boil 4 minutes, stirring constantly. Remove from heat. Add marshmallows, wasabi paste, if desired, plus chocolate morsels, and vanilla. Beat by hand with a wooden spoon until melted and smooth. Spread fudge into prepared pan. Sprinkle top with crystallized ginger, and press lightly into fudge. Refrigerate 2 hours or until firm. Cut into squares.

make ahead

Vanilla-Banana-Caramel Flans

Toasted walnut halves are the perfect finish for these smooth, dense custards.

MAKES 6 SERVINGS
PREP: 10 MIN.   COOK: 46 MIN.   OTHER: 8 HR.

1½ cups sugar, divided
 2   small very ripe bananas
 1   Tbsp. vanilla bean paste
1½ cups half-and-half
 5   large eggs
 6   walnut halves, toasted

1. Place 1 cup sugar in an 11" skillet over medium heat. Shake skillet to evenly distribute sugar over bottom of skillet. When sugar begins to melt (clear liquid will form around edges), shake pan as needed to keep sugar evenly covering the bottom of the skillet. When sugar in center of pan begins to turn golden (this will take about 6 minutes), stir with a wooden spoon just often enough to maintain an even color, shaking pan and allowing sugar to continue to melt between stirrings. When sugar is completely melted and amber in color, quickly spoon about 1 Tbsp. syrup into each of 6 (6-oz.) custard cups, tilting to coat bottoms evenly. Set cups in a 13" x 9" pan.

2. Preheat oven to 325°. Mash bananas slightly with a fork to measure ¾ cup. Place banana in blender; add remaining ½ cup sugar, vanilla bean paste, and half-and-half. Process 5 seconds or just until smooth. Add eggs; process 5 seconds or just until thoroughly blended, but not foamy. Be sure not to overprocess the eggs. Pour custard evenly into prepared cups. Add hot water to pan to depth of 1".

3. Bake, uncovered, at 325° for 40 minutes or until custards are set and a knife inserted near center comes out clean.

4. Remove cups from water bath, and cool completely on a wire rack. Cover and chill at least 8 hours. Run a paring knife around edge of each cup to loosen custards, and invert onto a serving platter, letting melted caramel drizzle down sides of custards. Top each dessert with a walnut half.

Tip: It's easiest if you place the pan containing filled custard cups on oven rack before adding hot water. Wear rubber gloves to easily remove cups from water after baking.

Chile Caribe Brownies

Although these slick brownies harbor spicy red pepper, chocolate and a hint of cinnamon tame the fire.

MAKES 20 BROWNIES
PREP: 5 MIN.   COOK: 31 MIN.

- 1 to 1½ tsp. chile caribe pepper flakes or crushed red pepper flakes (we tested with Penzeys)*
- 1 (19.5-oz.) package fudge brownie mix (we tested with Pillsbury)
- 1½ tsp. ground cinnamon
- 2 large eggs
- ½ cup canola oil
- ¼ cup water
- 2 cups dark chocolate morsels, divided (we tested with Nestlé Chocolatier)
- 3 Tbsp. unsalted butter, cut into small pieces
- 2 Tbsp. heavy whipping cream
- Chile caribe pepper flakes (optional)

1. Preheat oven to 350°. Grind 1 to 1½ tsp. pepper flakes with a mortar and pestle or spice grinder until pieces are small. Combine brownie mix, ground pepper flakes, and cinnamon in a medium bowl; whisk until well blended. Stir in eggs, oil, and water until blended. Add ¾ cup chocolate morsels to batter; spoon batter into a lightly greased 13" x 9" pan. Bake at 350° for 28 to 31 minutes. Cool completely in pan on a wire rack.

2. Place 1 cup chocolate morsels and butter in a large glass bowl. Microwave at HIGH 1 minute or until melted; stir in whipping cream. Pour mixture over cooled brownies, spreading to form a thin even layer. Place remaining ¼ cup chocolate morsels in a 1-cup glass measuring cup, and microwave at HIGH 30 seconds or until melted. Pour melted chocolate in a zip-top plastic freezer bag; snip a tiny hole in 1 corner of bag. Pipe a zigzag drizzle over iced brownies; sprinkle lightly with chile caribe flakes, if desired. Refrigerate brownies for easy cutting.

*Caribe red pepper flakes are typically medium heat, but not overwhelming. Find them on the spice aisle or order a jar from www.penzeys.com or www.thespicehouse.com.

Chile Caribe Brownies

Vanilla-Banana-Caramel Flan

Double Chocolate Surprise Cupcakes

Dark Chocolate Truffles with Fleur de Sel

Double Chocolate Surprise Cupcakes

MAKES 20 CUPCAKES
PREP: 14 MIN.   COOK: 18 MIN.   OTHER: 5 MIN.

1   cup butter, softened
1   cup granulated sugar
½   cup firmly packed brown sugar
4   large eggs
6   (1-oz.) unsweetened chocolate squares, melted
    and cooled
1   tsp. vanilla extract
2   cups all-purpose flour
1   tsp. baking soda
¼   tsp. salt
1   cup buttermilk
1   (7-oz.) jar marshmallow crème
1   (15.5-oz.) can triple chocolate fudge chip frosting
    (we tested with Betty Crocker)
Assorted Christmas sprinkles and candies

1. Preheat oven to 350°. Beat butter at medium speed with an electric mixer until fluffy; gradually add sugars, beating well. Add eggs, 1 at a time, beating after each addition. Add melted chocolate and vanilla, mixing well.

2. Combine flour, baking soda, and salt; add to batter alternately with buttermilk, beginning and ending with flour mixture. Mix at low speed after each addition until blended.

3. Spoon batter into paper-lined standard muffin pans, filling each cup full. Bake at 350° for 15 to 18 minutes or until a wooden pick inserted in center comes out clean. Cool 5 minutes in pans. Remove from pans, and cool completely on a wire rack.

4. Take a plug out of center top of each cupcake, going pretty deep but not quite to the bottom of each cake. (Reserve these little cupcake pieces.)

5. Spoon marshmallow crème into a zip-top freezer bag; seal bag, and cut a hole (about ½") in 1 corner. Squirt crème into hole of each cupcake. Replace just the top portion of each cupcake piece to regain a smooth top. Gently frost cupcakes; decorate as desired.

editor's favorite · gift idea

Dark Chocolate Truffles with Fleur de Sel

These sinfully rich truffles earned our Test Kitchens' highest rating. For information on fleur de sel, see page 99.

MAKES ABOUT 2 DOZEN
PREP: 30 MIN. COOK: 12 MIN. OTHER: 3 HR.

  8 oz. bittersweet chocolate, chopped
  ¼ cup sugar
  1 Tbsp. water
  ⅔ cup heavy whipping cream
  ¼ tsp. fleur de sel or coarse sea salt
  ½ cup Dutch process cocoa, sifted
 12 oz. bittersweet chocolate, broken
     Parchment paper
     Fleur de sel or coarse sea salt to taste

1. Microwave 8 oz. chocolate in a glass bowl at HIGH 1 minute or until melted.

2. Combine sugar and water in a small heavy saucepan; cook over medium heat until sugar dissolves, stirring gently. Continue to simmer, without stirring, about 7 minutes or until syrup is golden, brushing down sides of pan with a pastry brush dipped in water; remove pan from heat. Carefully add cream (mixture will bubble). Return pan to low heat, and simmer, stirring until smooth. Stir in ¼ tsp. fleur de sel. Remove from heat. Add cream mixture to melted chocolate; stir until smooth, and let cool. Cover and chill 3 hours or until firm.

3. Place cocoa in a bowl. Shape chocolate mixture into 1" balls (we used a 1" ice cream scoop); roll in cocoa. Place truffle balls on a baking sheet; chill until firm.

4. Place 12 oz. chocolate in top of a double boiler over simmering water until a thermometer inserted into chocolate registers 115°.* Remove top insert; working quickly, dip truffles in melted chocolate, coating completely. Lift out truffles with a small fork, letting excess chocolate drip off. Tilt double boiler insert, if needed, to make dipping and coating easier. Return top insert to heat every few minutes to keep chocolate at 115°. Transfer truffles to parchment paper. Sprinkle truffles lightly with additional fleur de sel. Let stand until chocolate coating is set.

*It's important to keep the saucepan of melted chocolate at 115° for coating the truffles. As your guide, use a candy or digital thermometer, easily found at your local cook store. Once this chocolate coating hardens on the candy, it will lend a nice crunch when you bite into it.

editor's favorite · make ahead

Vanilla Spice Pistachio Cheesecake

Vanilla, cardamom, and white chocolate unite in this creamy holiday dessert.

MAKES 12 SERVINGS
PREP: 21 MIN. COOK: 1 HR., 31 MIN. OTHER: 8 HR., 10 MIN.

  ½ (10-oz.) package shortbread cookies (we tested with Lorna Doone)
  ½ cup unsalted pistachio nuts
  ¼ cup sugar
  ¼ cup butter, melted
  3 (8-oz.) packages cream cheese, softened
 1¼ cups sugar
  1 tsp. ground cardamom
 2¾ cups sour cream, divided
  1 Tbsp. all-purpose flour
  1 Tbsp. vanilla bean paste or vanilla extract
  4 large eggs
  5 oz. white chocolate, chopped
     Garnish: additional unsalted pistachio nuts

1. Preheat oven to 350°. Place first 3 ingredients in a food processor; process until finely ground. Stir in butter. Press cookie crumb mixture into bottom of an ungreased 9" springform pan. Bake at 350° for 15 minutes.

2. Meanwhile, beat cream cheese, 1¼ cups sugar, and cardamom at medium speed with an electric mixer until smooth. Add 1½ cups sour cream, flour, and vanilla bean paste; beat until blended. Add eggs, 1 at a time, beating just until yellow disappears. Pour batter into baked crust. Reduce oven temperature to 300°.

3. Bake at 300° for 1 hour and 15 minutes or until almost set. Immediately run a knife around edge of pan, releasing sides. Let cool on a wire rack 10 minutes.

4. Meanwhile, place white chocolate in a microwave-safe bowl; microwave at HIGH for 1 minute or until chocolate is soft. Stir until smooth. Whisk in remaining 1¼ cups sour cream. Spread white chocolate mixture over warm cheesecake. Let cool completely in pan on wire rack. Cover and chill 8 hours. Remove sides of pan. Garnish cheesecake, if desired.

make ahead · quick & easy

Vanilla Sugar

This recipe provides a great way to enjoy the essence of a vanilla bean. Substitute this vanilla-flecked sugar for regular granulated sugar to add richness to just about anything you bake.

MAKES 3 CUPS
PREP: 5 MIN.

2   vanilla bean pods (seeds already scraped and used in another recipe)
3   cups sugar

1. Cut each vanilla bean pod into 4 pieces, splaying open each piece to expose any remaining vanilla seeds and essence. Place in a canister or a plastic container with sugar, and stir gently. Cover canister, and store in a cool, dry place. Discard pod pieces after 1 month.

gift idea · make ahead

Vanilla Bean Oil

Vanilla bean oil is very delicate in flavor and quite versatile—use it to flavor salads, seafood, or poultry; or drizzle it over sweet potatoes before roasting.

MAKES 2 CUPS
PREP: 3 MIN.   COOK: 3 MIN.   OTHER: 24 HR.

2   cups canola oil
2   vanilla beans, split lengthwise

1. Pour oil into a saucepan. Using the tip of a small sharp knife, scrape vanilla bean seeds into oil; add vanilla bean pods to pan. Bring oil just to a simmer over medium-low heat. Remove from heat; let cool completely.
2. Pour oil into a clean jar with a tight fitting lid; cover and chill 24 hours. Discard vanilla bean pods. Store oil in refrigerator up to 1 month. Before each use, let oil stand at room temperature at least 30 minutes.

Note: Here's our favorite recommendation for Vanilla Bean Oil. Lightly drizzle mixed baby greens with the oil; squeeze a lemon half over greens, sprinkle with salt, and gently toss. Add a handful of fresh or dried blueberries and toasted almonds, if desired.

Candy Cane Soufflés

These soufflés are impressive when served straight from the oven. The crème anglaise can be prepared a day ahead and then chilled.

MAKES 6 SERVINGS
PREP: 7 MIN.   COOK: 30 MIN.

1   cup hard peppermint candies (about 35 candies)
Butter
2   Tbsp. sugar
4   egg yolks
2   Tbsp. sugar
4   Tbsp. butter
6   oz. dark chocolate, chopped (we tested with Ghirardelli)
6   Tbsp. all-purpose flour
1   cup milk
1   cup heavy whipping cream
2   tsp. vanilla extract
1   tsp. peppermint extract
7   egg whites
⅛   tsp. cream of tartar
Very Vanilla Crème Anglaise
Garnish: small candy canes

1. Place 1 cup candies in a food processor; process until candies are ground. Set aside.
2. Preheat oven to 375°. Lightly butter bottoms and sides of 6 (8-oz.) individual soufflé ramekins. Sprinkle 2 Tbsp. sugar evenly into ramekins, tilting ramekins to coat sides. Place ramekins on a baking sheet; set aside.
3. Whisk together 4 egg yolks and 2 Tbsp. sugar in a large bowl. Melt 4 Tbsp. butter and chocolate in a small heavy saucepan over medium-low heat. Whisk in flour; cook 1 minute. Gradually whisk in milk and cream; cook, stirring constantly, 3 minutes or until thickened. Remove from heat; add a small amount of chocolate mixture to egg yolk mixture, whisking constantly. Continue adding chocolate mixture in small amounts, whisking constantly until thoroughly blended. Stir in reserved candies, vanilla, and peppermint extract.
4. Beat egg whites and cream of tartar at high speed with an electric mixer until stiff peaks form. Fold into peppermint mixture. Pour into prepared soufflé dishes. Bake at 375° for 24 minutes or until puffed and slightly browned on top. Serve immediately with Very Vanilla Crème Anglaise. Garnish, if desired.

Very Vanilla Crème Anglaise

MAKES 1 CUP
PREP: 2 MIN.   COOK: 10 MIN.

3 egg yolks
2 Tbsp. sugar
½ vanilla bean or 1½ tsp. vanilla extract
1 cup heavy whipping cream

1. Whisk egg yolks and sugar in a bowl until blended.
2. Split vanilla bean piece lengthwise; scrape seeds into cream using knife blade. Bring cream and vanilla bean seeds just to a boil in a medium-size heavy saucepan; reduce heat, and simmer 4 minutes. Stir one-fourth of hot milk mixture gradually into yolks; add yolk mixture to remaining milk mixture, stirring constantly. Cook over medium-low heat, stirring constantly, 6 minutes or until custard reaches 160° and coats the back of a spoon. Remove from heat, and set aside to cool. Store in refrigerator.

Cacao and Milk Chocolate Scones

This recipe is like a sweet version of drop biscuits. Find cacao nibs packaged at gourmet food stores.

MAKES 14 SCONES
PREP: 12 MIN.   COOK: 18 MIN.

3 cups all-purpose flour
⅔ cup sugar
1 Tbsp. baking powder
½ tsp. salt
¾ cup cold unsalted butter, cut into pieces
1 cup milk chocolate morsels or chopped milk
   chocolate bar (we tested with Hershey's)
½ cup cacao nibs or chopped toasted pecans
1 large egg
1 cup whipping cream
2 tsp. vanilla extract
Whipping cream (optional)
Coarse or granulated sugar (optional)

1. Preheat oven to 425°. Stir together first 4 ingredients in a large bowl; cut in butter with a pastry blender until crumbly. Stir in chocolate morsels and cacao nibs.
2. Whisk together egg, 1 cup whipping cream, and vanilla; add to flour mixture, stirring with a fork just until dry ingredients are moistened and mixture forms a shaggy dough. Using a ⅓-cup measuring cup, scoop dough into mounds onto parchment paper-lined baking sheets. Brush scones with additional cream, and sprinkle with sugar, if desired.
3. Bake at 425° for 18 minutes or until golden. Serve warm.

Cacao and Milk Chocolate Scones

1. Cacao nibs are unsweetened, roasted, and crushed cacao beans. They give these scones a toasty, bittersweet flavor.
2. Brush scones with cream; sprinkle with sugar for a crunchy finish.

Candied Orange Truffle Tart

editor's favorite

Candied Orange Truffle Tart

Buy a fresh jar of curry powder and premium chocolate for this fudgy dessert. You'll be pleasantly surprised that curry permeates the trufflelike filling, candied orange topping, and yummy syrup. A sharp knife will cut easily through the decorated tart.

MAKES 10 TO 12 SERVINGS
PREP: 12 MIN.   COOK: 1 HR.   OTHER: 4 HR.

1⅔ cups all-purpose flour
2 Tbsp. sugar
¼ tsp. salt
10 Tbsp. unsalted butter, chilled and cut into ½" pieces
2 to 3 Tbsp. ice water
1 large egg yolk
1 tsp. vanilla extract
1 cup whipping cream
2 Tbsp. sugar
2½ Tbsp. frozen orange juice concentrate
2½ tsp. curry powder (optional)
12 oz. dark chocolate, finely chopped (we tested with Ghirardelli Intense Dark 72% Cacao)
1 cup water
1 cup sugar
½ tsp. curry powder (optional)
2 navel oranges, thinly sliced
Garnishes: orange wedges, rosemary sprig

1. Pulse first 3 ingredients in a food processor 3 or 4 times or until combined. Add butter, and pulse 5 or 6 times or until crumbly. With processor running, gradually add 2 Tbsp. water, egg yolk, and vanilla; process until dough forms a ball and leaves sides of bowl, adding more water if necessary. Cover and chill 1½ hours.
2. Preheat oven to 375°. Roll dough to a 12" circle on a lightly floured surface. Fit pastry in a 9" tart pan with removable bottom. Trim off excess pastry, allowing edges to overhang ½"; fold in overhang against inside edge of pan to form double-thick sides. Pierce bottom of pastry with a fork; freeze 20 minutes. Bake at 375° for 30 minutes or until lightly browned. Cool completely in pan on a wire rack.
3. Whisk together whipping cream and next 3 ingredients in a medium saucepan. Bring to a simmer over medium-low heat. Add chocolate, and whisk until smooth. Pour filling into baked crust. Refrigerate 2 hours or until firm.
4. Whisk together 1 cup water, 1 cup sugar, and, if desired, ½ tsp. curry powder in a large heavy skillet. Bring to a simmer over medium-high heat, stirring until sugar dissolves. Add orange slices to pan. Reduce heat to medium-low; simmer 25 to 30 minutes, turning slices occasionally, or until orange slices

are translucent. Remove pan from heat; allow orange slices to cool in syrup.
5. Arrange orange slices on top of tart before serving. Spoon remaining syrup over each serving. Garnish, if desired.

fix it faster

Omit the homemade crust (first 7 ingredients), and use ½ of a 15-oz. package of refrigerated piecrusts. Unroll piecrust and fit into pan. Prick with a fork. Bake at 375° for 18 minutes or until golden. Cool completely and proceed with filling.

gift idea · make ahead

Speckled Vanilla-Hazelnut Brittle

Banana chips add texture in this vanilla bean-freckled brittle. Your kitchen will smell like Bananas Foster as they're stirred into the hot candy.

MAKES 1¾ LB.
PREP: 7 MIN.   COOK: 29 MIN.

1½ cups hazelnuts with skins
1¾ cups granulated sugar
½ cup light corn syrup
¼ tsp. salt
½ cup hot water
½ cup dried banana chips
3 Tbsp. butter, melted
½ tsp. baking soda
1 Tbsp. vanilla bean paste

1. Preheat oven to 350°. Spread hazelnuts in a single layer on a 15" x 10" jelly-roll pan. Bake at 350° for 5 to 10 minutes or until skins begin to split. Transfer warm nuts to a colander; using a towel, rub briskly to remove skins. Coarsely chop nuts.
2. Cook sugar and next 3 ingredients in a large heavy saucepan over medium heat, stirring constantly, until mixture starts to boil. Boil without stirring until a candy thermometer registers 290°. Carefully stir in nuts using a clean spoon. Remove from heat, and stir in banana chips and remaining ingredients. (Baking soda will cause candy to foam.) When foaming subsides, quickly pour candy onto a buttered baking sheet. Pour as thinly as possible without spreading. After 2 to 3 minutes, use 2 buttered forks to stretch and pull brittle as fast as possible before brittle starts to break. Cool completely, and break into irregular-size pieces. Store in an airtight container.

editor's favorite · make ahead

Chocolate-Bourbon-Pecan Cake

Serve this ultra-Southern cake on the second day, moist and saturated with bourbon flavor.

MAKES 12 SERVINGS
PREP: 14 MIN.   COOK: 40 MIN.   OTHER: 10 HR., 10 MIN.

    3   cups all-purpose flour
    2¼ tsp. baking soda
    ¾   tsp. salt
    1½ cups boiling water
    1¼ cups unsweetened cocoa
    ¾   cup milk
    1   Tbsp. vanilla extract
    1½ cups unsalted butter, softened
    3   cups firmly packed light brown sugar
    6   large eggs
    ½   cup bourbon
        Two-Part Frosting
        Garnish: pecans

1. Preheat oven to 350°. Grease and flour 2 (9") round cake pans. Whisk together flour, baking soda, and salt.

2. Whisk together 1½ cups boiling water and cocoa, whisking until smooth. Whisk in milk and vanilla.

3. Beat butter at medium speed with an electric mixer until creamy. Gradually add brown sugar, beating at medium speed 3 minutes or until light and fluffy. Add eggs, 1 at a time, beating well after each addition.

4. With mixer at low speed, add dry ingredients alternately with cocoa mixture, beginning and ending with dry ingredients. Pour batter into prepared pans.

5. Bake at 350° for 35 to 40 minutes or until a wooden pick inserted in center comes out clean. Let cool in pans on wire racks 10 minutes; remove from pans, and cool completely on wire racks (about 1 hour). Wrap and freeze cake layers 1 hour. (This step enables you to split cake layers with ease.)

6. Using a serrated knife, slice cake layers in half horizontally to make 4 layers. Brush cut side of each layer with bourbon. Spread pecan frosting between layers. Spread top and sides of cake with chocolate frosting. For best flavor, cover and let stand at room temperature 8 to 24 hours before serving. Garnish, if desired.

Two-Part Frosting

Split this frosting in half; add pecans to one part that becomes the filling, and cocoa to the rest that becomes the outer frosting.

MAKES 3 CUPS PECAN FROSTING PLUS 1¾ CUPS CHOCOLATE FROSTING
PREP: 7 MIN.

    1   cup butter, softened
    2   (16-oz.) packages powdered
        sugar, divided
    ½   cup milk
    2   tsp. vanilla extract
    1¼ cups chopped pecans, toasted
    2   Tbsp. milk, divided
    ½   cup unsweetened cocoa

1. Beat butter at medium speed with an electric mixer until creamy. With mixer at low speed, gradually add 2 cups powdered sugar, beating until blended. Add ½ cup milk and vanilla, beating until blended.

2. Gradually add remaining powdered sugar, beating until smooth. Remove 3 cups frosting, and place in a separate bowl; stir in pecans and 1 Tbsp. milk. (This pecan frosting will be used as the filling.) Add cocoa and remaining 1 Tbsp. milk to frosting in mixing bowl, beating until blended.

Chocolate-Cherry Galettes

These individual freeform pastries are packed with plump cherries and chocolate chunks.

MAKES 6 GALETTES
PREP: 27 MIN.   COOK: 22 MIN.   OTHER: 40 MIN.

- 4 cups all-purpose flour
- 1¼ cups granulated sugar, divided
- 2 tsp. salt
- 1½ cups butter, cut up and divided
- 1 cup ice water
- 1½ cups pecan halves, toasted
- 1 large egg
- 1½ cups semisweet chocolate chunks, divided
- Parchment paper
- 2 (12-oz.) packages frozen dark, sweet cherries, thawed and well-drained
- ¼ tsp. almond extract
- 1 egg white
- 2 Tbsp. turbinado sugar

1. Whisk together flour, ½ cup granulated sugar, and salt; cut in 1 cup butter with a pastry blender or fork until mixture resembles small peas and is crumbly. Sprinkle 1 cup ice water, ¼ cup at a time, over surface; stir with a fork until dry ingredients are moistened. Divide dough into 2 equal portions; wrap and chill.

2. While dough chills, process pecans and remaining ¾ cup granulated sugar in a food processor 30 seconds. Add remaining ½ cup butter and 1 egg; process 1 minute or until smooth. Place 1 cup chocolate chunks in a microwave-safe bowl. Microwave at HIGH 1 minute or until melted; stir into pecan mixture. Cover and chill 30 minutes.

3. Preheat oven to 400°. Working with 1 portion at a time, roll dough to ⅛" thickness on a lightly floured surface. Cut 3 (8") circles from dough, and place each on a parchment paper-lined baking sheet. Spread ⅓ cup pecan filling over each dough circle, leaving a ½" border around edges.

4. Combine cherries and almond extract in a bowl. Spread ⅓ cup cherry mixture over each dough circle to within 2" of edges. Fold 1" borders of dough over cherries. Repeat with remaining dough, pecan filling, and cherries.

5. Whisk together egg white and 1 Tbsp. water in a small bowl. Brush outer edges of galettes with egg wash; sprinkle with turbinado sugar.

6. Bake at 400° for 20 to 22 minutes or until golden. Sprinkle galettes with remaining ½ cup chocolate chunks. Let stand 10 minutes before serving.

Chocolate Extreme Cupcakes

These triple chocolate cupcakes are a chocolate lover's dream.

MAKES 1 DOZEN
PREP: 24 MIN.   COOK: 30 MIN.   OTHER: 50 MIN.

- 1 cup unsalted butter, softened
- ½ cup granulated sugar
- 1 cup firmly packed light brown sugar
- 4 large eggs
- 3 (1-oz.) unsweetened chocolate baking squares, melted
- 3 (1-oz.) semisweet chocolate baking squares, melted
- 1 tsp. vanilla extract
- 2 cups all-purpose flour
- 1 tsp. baking soda
- ½ tsp. salt
- 1 cup buttermilk
- Jumbo paper baking cups
- Thick Chocolate Frosting

1. Preheat oven to 350°. Beat butter at medium speed with an electric mixer until creamy. Gradually add sugars, beating well. Add eggs, 1 at a time, beating after each addition. Add melted chocolates and vanilla, beating well.

2. Combine flour, baking soda, and salt; add to batter alternately with buttermilk, beginning and ending with flour mixture. Beat at low speed after each addition until blended.

3. Place baking cups in jumbo muffin pans. Spoon batter into cups, filling three-fourths full.

4. Bake at 350° for 30 minutes or until a wooden pick inserted in center comes out clean. Cool in pans on wire racks 5 minutes. Remove from pans, and cool completely on wire racks (45 minutes). Spread with Thick Chocolate Frosting.

Thick Chocolate Frosting

MAKES 3½ CUPS
PREP: 5 MIN.

- ½ cup butter, softened
- 1 (16-oz.) package powdered sugar
- 1 cup semisweet chocolate morsels, melted
- ½ cup whipping cream
- 2 tsp. vanilla extract
- Pinch of salt

1. Beat butter at medium speed with an electric mixer until creamy; gradually add powdered sugar alternately with melted chocolate and whipping cream. Beat at low speed after each addition until blended. Stir in vanilla and salt.

Chocolate Extreme Cupcakes

Chocolate Bread

1. Combine milk, ½ cup warm water, and yeast in a large bowl; whisk until smooth. Let stand 5 minutes. Stir 2 cups flour, cocoa, granulated sugar, and salt into yeast mixture; beat at medium speed with an electric mixer until smooth. Beat in egg, butter, and 2 cups flour until a soft dough forms.
2. Turn out dough onto a floured surface, and knead until smooth (about 6 minutes), adding remaining ½ cup flour, 1 Tbsp. at a time as needed, to prevent dough from sticking. Fold in chopped chocolate during last minute of kneading.
3. Place dough in a large, lightly greased bowl, turning to coat top. Cover with plastic wrap, and let rise in a warm place (85°), free from drafts, 1 hour and 40 minutes or until doubled in bulk.
4. Punch down dough. Divide dough in half; gently shape each portion into an 8" x 4" oval. Place dough in 2 lightly greased 8½" x 4½" loaf pans. Cover and let rise 1½ hours or until doubled in bulk.
5. Preheat oven to 375°. Sprinkle loaves with turbinado sugar. Bake at 375° for 25 minutes or until loaves sound hollow when tapped. Remove from pans. Let cool on a wire rack.

editor's favorite

Chocolate Bread Pudding

MAKES 12 SERVINGS
PREP: 16 MIN.   COOK: 1 HR., 6 MIN.   OTHER: 10 MIN.

  2 cups milk
  2 cups whipping cream
  1 tsp. ground cinnamon
  4 large eggs
1¼ cups sugar
  2 Tbsp. butter, melted
1½ tsp. vanilla extract
  1 loaf day-old Chocolate Bread (recipe at left), cut into 1" cubes
  4 (1.4-oz.) chocolate-coated toffee candy bars, chopped (we tested with SKOR)
  1 cup semisweet chocolate morsels, divided

1. Preheat oven to 350°. Combine first 3 ingredients in a medium saucepan; cook over medium heat just until bubbles appear (do not boil). Whisk together eggs, sugar, and butter in a large bowl. Gradually add hot milk mixture to eggs, whisking constantly. Stir in vanilla.
2. Add bread cubes, chopped candy bars, and ½ cup chocolate morsels to milk mixture, stirring until bread is moistened. Pour into a lightly greased 13" x 9" baking dish.
3. Bake, covered, at 350° for 30 minutes. Uncover and bake 30 more minutes or until set. Remove from oven, and sprinkle with remaining ½ cup chocolate morsels. Let stand 10 minutes before serving.

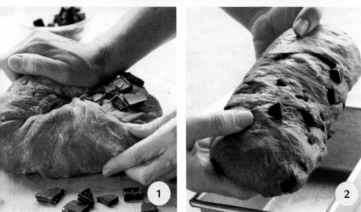

1. Fold/knead chopped chocolate into bread dough.
2. Place dough in loaf pans to rise.

Chocolate Bread

Save one of the loaves to turn into luscious Chocolate Bread Pudding (recipe at right), if you'd like.

MAKES 2 LOAVES
PREP: 21 MIN.   COOK: 25 MIN.   OTHER: 3 HR., 15 MIN.

1¼ cups warm milk (100° to 110°)
 ½ cup warm water (100° to 110°)
  1 (¼-oz.) package active dry yeast
4½ cups all-purpose flour, divided
 ½ cup unsweetened cocoa
 ¼ cup granulated sugar
  1 tsp. salt
  1 large egg
  2 Tbsp. butter, softened
  2 (4-oz.) semisweet chocolate bars, chopped (we tested with Ghirardelli)
1½ Tbsp. turbinado sugar

editor's favorite • gift idea • make ahead

Chocolate Chunk Scones

Serve these big chocolate wedges for breakfast or brunch with coffee, or for dessert with a dollop of whipped cream.

MAKES 1 DOZEN
PREP: 25 MIN.   COOK: 36 MIN.

4	cups all-purpose flour
⅔	cup sugar
½	cup unsweetened cocoa
4	tsp. baking powder
1½	tsp. baking soda
1	tsp. salt
½	tsp. freshly grated nutmeg
¾	cup cold butter, cut up
1	(11.5-oz.) package semisweet chocolate chunks
1	cup coarsely chopped walnuts or pecans (optional)
1¾	cups buttermilk
1	large egg, lightly beaten
2	tsp. vanilla extract
	Parchment paper
2	Tbsp. sugar

1. Preheat oven to 350°. Whisk together flour and next 6 ingredients in a large bowl.

2. Cut butter into flour mixture with a pastry blender or fork until mixture resembles small peas and is crumbly. Stir in chocolate chunks and, if desired, nuts.

3. Combine buttermilk, egg, and vanilla. Pour over crumb mixture; stir just until dry ingredients are moistened.

4. Turn out dough onto a lightly floured surface, and gently knead 3 or 4 times.

5. Divide dough in half; shape each half into a ball. Pat each into a 6" circle on parchment paper-lined baking sheets. Cut each circle into 6 wedges using a sharp knife (do not separate wedges). Sprinkle 2 Tbsp. sugar over dough.

6. Bake at 350° for 36 minutes or until a wooden pick inserted in center comes out clean. Separate into wedges. Serve warm, or remove to a wire rack to cool. Reheat scones in microwave at HIGH 20 to 25 seconds each.

Chocolate Bread Pudding

Chocolate Chunk Scones

Triple-Layer Peanut Butter Brownie Bars

3. Add 2 cups granulated sugar to melted chocolate mixture; beat at medium speed with an electric mixer until blended. Add eggs, 1 at a time, beating just until blended. Add vanilla. Add flour; beat at low speed just until blended. Stir in ¾ cup peanuts.

4. Spread batter into prepared pan.

5. Bake at 350° for 30 to 34 minutes. (Wooden pick will not test clean.) Remove to a wire rack, and cool completely.

6. Meanwhile, beat peanut butter and ½ cup butter in a large mixing bowl at medium speed until blended. Add powdered sugar; beat until blended. Spread over brownies.

7. Melt 8 oz. chocolate squares and remaining 1 oz. chopped chocolate in a small glass bowl according to microwave package directions; stir in corn syrup. Spoon dollops of melted chocolate over peanut butter layer; spread gently to cover peanut butter layer. Sprinkle with ⅓ cup peanuts, if desired. Cover and chill 2 hours or until set. Use foil to lift uncut brownies out of pan. Peel foil away from sides of uncut brownies, and cut into bars.

editor's favorite · gift idea · make ahead

Triple-Layer Peanut Butter Brownie Bars

MAKES 2 DOZEN
PREP: 17 MIN.   COOK: 36 MIN.   OTHER: 2 HR., 5 MIN.

1   cup butter
7   (1-oz.) semisweet chocolate baking squares, divided and chopped
2   cups granulated sugar
4   large eggs
1   tsp. vanilla extract
1   cup all-purpose flour
¾   cup dry-roasted peanuts, chopped
1   cup creamy peanut butter
½   cup butter, softened
1   cup powdered sugar
8   (1-oz.) semisweet chocolate baking squares
1   Tbsp. light corn syrup
⅓   cup dry-roasted peanuts, chopped (optional)

1. Preheat oven to 350°. Line a lightly greased 13" x 9" pan with aluminum foil, allowing foil to extend over ends of pan; set aside.

2. Melt 1 cup butter in a saucepan over medium heat. Remove from heat; add 6 oz. chopped chocolate, and let stand 5 minutes. Stir until smooth; transfer to a large mixing bowl.

editor's favorite · make ahead · quick & easy

Ultimate Chocolate Pudding

Definitive in flavor and silky texture, this pudding deserves a place in the chocolate hall of fame.

MAKES 3½ CUPS
PREP: 10 MIN.   COOK: 12 MIN.   OTHER: 10 MIN.

1¼   cups sugar
½   cup Dutch process cocoa
¼   cup cornstarch
½   tsp. salt
2½   cups milk
⅓   cup unsalted butter, cut up
2   tsp. vanilla extract
Unsweetened whipped cream
Chocolate-filled vanilla wafer sandwich cookies (we tested with Pepperidge Farm Milano cookies)

1. Whisk together first 4 ingredients in a medium saucepan. Gradually whisk in milk. Cook over medium heat, stirring constantly, until pudding boils and is thickened (about 8 to 10 minutes). Reduce heat to medium-low, and cook 2 more minutes. Remove from heat; add butter and vanilla, stirring gently until butter melts. Place heavy-duty plastic wrap directly on warm pudding (to keep a film from forming); cool 10 minutes.

2. Serve warm, or chill until ready to serve. Top with whipped cream. Serve with cookies.

Note: For rich chocolate flavor, order double-Dutch dark cocoa online at www.kingarthurflour.com

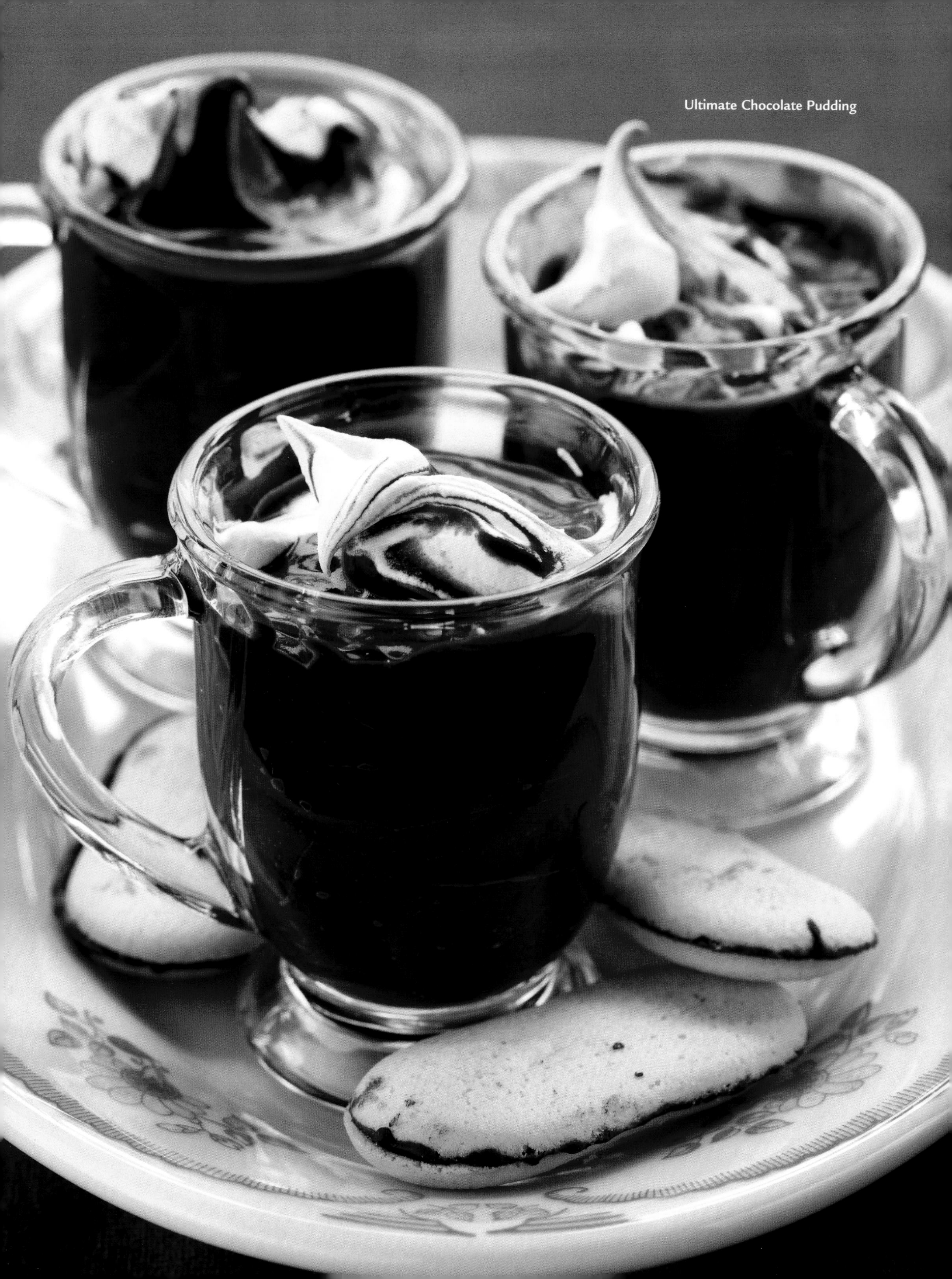
Ultimate Chocolate Pudding

holiday BAKING

For many folks baking is one of the most anticipated activities during the yuletide season. This collection of classics has something sweet for every age.

make ahead

Gingerbread Girls

These firm, crisp, delicious cookies are perfect for topping off a stocking, decorating a mantel, or forming a centerpiece.

MAKES 16 COOKIES
PREP: 1 HR., 20 MIN.   COOK: 14 MIN. PER BATCH   OTHER: 2 HR.

- ¼ cup granulated sugar
- ¼ cup firmly packed dark brown sugar
- ½ cup molasses
- 2 tsp. ground ginger
- 1 tsp. ground allspice
- 1 tsp. ground cinnamon
- 1 tsp. ground cloves
- 2 tsp. baking soda
- ½ cup unsalted butter, cut into pieces
- 1 large egg, lightly beaten
- 3 cups all-purpose flour
- ¼ tsp. salt
- Parchment paper
- ½ cup raisins (optional)
- ¼ cup red cinnamon candies (optional)
- Royal Icing (see next page)
- Candy decorations (optional)

1. Combine first 7 ingredients in a 3-qt. saucepan. Bring to a boil over medium heat, stirring occasionally. Remove pan from heat; stir in baking soda. Transfer to a mixing bowl. Add butter and egg, beating at medium speed with an electric mixer until smooth. Gradually stir in flour and salt, beating just until blended.
2. Shape dough into a ball, and divide in half. Flatten each half into a round disk; wrap each in plastic wrap, and chill at least 1 hour or until firm.
3. Line several large baking sheets with parchment paper. Roll out dough, 1 section at a time, to ¼" thickness on a floured

surface. Cut into gingerbread girl shapes (we used a 5½" cookie cutter from www.rochowcutters.com). Reroll trimmings to make additional cookies. Place cutouts ½" apart on prepared baking sheets.
4. Preheat oven to 325°. Bake cutouts plain, or press raisins and cinnamon candies in each gingerbread girl for eyes, nose, mouth, and buttons, if desired.
5. Bake at 325° for 14 minutes or until cookies are puffed and slightly darker around edges. Cool 1 minute on baking sheets; remove to wire racks to cool completely.
6. Decorate cookies with Royal Icing by first outlining desired patterns for each cookie. Then fill in with additional icing, letting icing flow into outlined area. Apply candy decorations, if desired. Let icing harden at least 1 hour.

1. Fill a zip-top plastic freezer bag with icing, snip a small hole in 1 corner of bag, and first outline desired patterns on each cookie.
2. After outlining, fill in with same icing. Allow to dry at least 1 hour before handling cookies.

Royal Icing

MAKES 3⅔ CUPS
PREP: 20 MIN.

1 (16-oz.) package powdered sugar
3 Tbsp. meringue powder
½ cup lukewarm water
Paste food coloring

1. Combine first 3 ingredients in a large bowl; beat at medium speed with an electric mixer 5 to 6 minutes or until icing is firm enough to pipe, but still of spreading consistency, adding a few drops of additional water if necessary for right consistency. Divide icing into small bowls, and tint each by dipping a wooden pick into paste coloring and stirring it into icing until desired color is reached. Icing dries quickly; keep it covered at all times.
2. Spoon icing into zip-top plastic freezer bags, and snip a small hole in 1 corner of each bag.

Christmas Panettone

We chose to bake this European holiday bread in a springform pan instead of the traditional cylinder-shaped pan.

MAKES 10 TO 12 SERVINGS
PREP: 12 MIN.   COOK: 45 MIN.   OTHER: 4 HR.

⅔ cup currants
⅔ cup diced dried apricots
⅔ cup raisins
¼ cup bourbon
1 (¼-oz.) package active dry yeast
½ cup warm milk (100° to 110°)
1 cup all-purpose flour
½ cup unsalted butter, softened
½ cup granulated sugar
½ tsp. salt
3 Tbsp. grated orange rind
2 tsp. vanilla extract
3 cups all-purpose flour
4 large eggs, lightly beaten
2 Tbsp. unsalted butter, melted
Powdered sugar (optional)
Mascarpone Cream

1. Combine currants, apricots, raisins, and bourbon in a small bowl. Let stand 1 hour or up to 4 hours.
2. Combine yeast and milk in a medium bowl; whisk until smooth. Stir in 1 cup flour until well blended; cover and let rise 30 minutes.

3. Combine ½ cup butter, granulated sugar, and salt in a bowl; beat at medium speed with an electric mixer 3 to 5 minutes or until light and fluffy. Add orange rind and vanilla; beat 2 minutes. Add 3 cups flour alternately with eggs, beginning and ending with flour. Stir in yeast mixture. Turn out dough onto a floured surface, and knead until smooth while gradually folding in fruit mixture (8 to 10 minutes). Place dough in a buttered bowl, turning to butter the top. Cover with plastic wrap, and let rise in warm place (85°), free from drafts, 1½ hours or until doubled in bulk.
4. Preheat oven to 350°. Butter a 10" springform pan. Place dough in pan, pressing to evenly fill pan. Cover with plastic wrap, and let rise 1 hour, or until dough reaches top of pan. Bake at 350° for 45 minutes or until a wooden pick inserted in center comes out clean, shielding with foil after 30 minutes to prevent excessive browning. Remove from oven, and brush with 2 Tbsp. melted butter. Cool in pan on a wire rack 5 minutes. Remove sides of pan, and allow bread to cool. Dust with powdered sugar, if desired. Serve with Mascarpone Cream.

Mascarpone Cream

MAKES ABOUT 1½ CUPS
PREP: 2 MIN.

1 (8-oz.) container mascarpone cheese
2 Tbsp. amaretto liqueur
1 Tbsp. powdered sugar

1. Combine all ingredients in a small bowl, stirring well to blend. Store in refrigerator.

Candy Bar Brown Sugar Cakes

MAKES 1 DOZEN
PREP: 22 MIN.   COOK: 25 MIN.   OTHER: 10 MIN.

¾ cup butter, softened
⅓ cup shortening
1½ cups firmly packed light brown sugar
¾ cup granulated sugar
3 large eggs
2¼ cups all-purpose flour
1 tsp. baking powder
½ tsp. salt
¾ cup milk
2 tsp. vanilla extract
¾ cup toffee bits
3 (2.7-oz.) chocolate-coated caramel-peanut nougat bars, coarsely chopped
Powdered sugar

1. Preheat oven to 325°. Beat butter and shortening at medium speed with an electric mixer 2 minutes or until creamy. Gradually add brown and granulated sugars, beating until light and fluffy. Add eggs, 1 at a time, beating just until blended.

2. Combine flour, baking powder, and salt. Add to butter mixture alternately with milk, beginning and ending with dry ingredients. Stir in vanilla and toffee bits.

3. Spoon batter into 2 greased and floured Bundtlette pans, filling each cup ⅔ full. Sprinkle with chopped nougat bars, pressing candy gently into batter.

4. Bake at 325° for 25 minutes or until a wooden pick inserted in center comes out clean. Cool in pans 10 minutes. Remove from pans to cool on wire racks. Sprinkle with powdered sugar before serving.

Note: See page 94 for more about Bundtlette pans.

editor's favorite · gift idea

Big Crunchy Sugar Cookies

Sparkling sugar cookies are holiday classics. These goodies, which earn their name from a coating of coarse sugar, received our Test Kitchens' highest rating.

MAKES 18 COOKIES
PREP: 20 MIN.   COOK: 15 MIN.   OTHER: 2 HR.

  1 cup unsalted butter, softened
  1 cup granulated sugar
  1 large egg
1½ tsp. vanilla extract
  2 cups all-purpose flour
  ½ tsp. baking powder
  ¼ tsp. salt
     Assorted coarse decorator sugars
     Parchment paper

1. Beat butter at medium speed with an electric mixer until creamy. Gradually add 1 cup sugar, beating until smooth. Add egg and vanilla, beating until blended.

2. Combine flour, baking powder, and salt; gradually add to butter mixture, beating just until blended. Shape dough into a ball; cover and chill 2 hours.

3. Preheat oven to 375°. Divide dough into 3 portions. Work with 1 portion of dough at a time, storing remaining dough in refrigerator. Shape dough into 1½" balls; roll each ball in decorator sugar. Place 2" apart on parchment paper-lined baking sheets. Gently press and flatten each ball of dough to ¾" thickness. Bake at 375° for 13 to 15 minutes or until edges of cookies are lightly browned. Cool 5 minutes on baking sheets; remove to wire racks to cool.

Big Crunchy Sugar Cookies

Part of the charm of these cookies is that the dough balls are heavily sugar coated. Coarse sugar comes in a variety of colors. Pick your favorite solids, and then mix complementary sugars.

editor's favorite · make ahead

Whipped Cream Caramel Cake

Shy away from making caramel frosting? No worries here—this is the easiest caramel frosting ever. It takes its time firming up, so there's no need to rush while frosting the layers.

MAKES 1 (4-LAYER) CAKE
PREP: 27 MIN.   COOK: 28 MIN.   OTHER: 1 HR., 10 MIN.

- 1 cup unsalted butter, softened
- 1½ cups sugar
- 4 large eggs
- 2¼ cups sifted cake flour
- 2 tsp. baking powder
- ½ tsp. salt
- ¾ cup milk
- 1 Tbsp. vanilla extract
- Whipped Cream Caramel Frosting
- 2 (1.4-oz.) chocolate-covered toffee candy bars, coarsely broken
- 1 (4.5-oz.) package dark chocolate-covered almonds, halved (we tested with Dove)

1. Preheat oven to 350°. Beat butter and sugar at medium speed with an electric mixer until fluffy. Add eggs, 1 at a time, beating until blended after each addition.

2. Combine flour, baking powder, and salt; add to butter mixture alternately with milk, beginning and ending with flour mixture. Beat at low speed after each addition. Stir in vanilla. Pour batter into 2 greased and floured 8" round cake pans.

3. Bake at 350° for 26 to 28 minutes or until a wooden pick inserted in center comes out clean. Cool in pans on wire racks 10 minutes; remove from pans, and cool completely on wire racks. Wrap and chill cake layers at least 1 hour or up to 24 hours. (This step enables you to split layers with ease.)

4. Using a serrated knife, slice cake layers in half horizontally to make 4 layers. Place 1 layer on a cake plate. Spread with ½ cup Whipped Cream Caramel Frosting. Repeat procedure with remaining 3 layers. Frost sides and top of cake with remaining frosting. Decorate cake with broken toffee bars and chocolate-covered almonds. Store in refrigerator.

Whipped Cream Caramel Frosting

MAKES 3¾ CUPS
PREP: 7 MIN.   COOK: 6 MIN.   OTHER: 1 HR.

- 1 cup unsalted butter
- 2 cups firmly packed dark brown sugar
- ¼ cup plus 2 Tbsp. whipping cream
- 2 tsp. vanilla extract
- 3¾ cups powdered sugar

1. Melt butter in a 3-qt. saucepan over medium heat. Add brown sugar; bring to a boil, stirring constantly. Stir in whipping cream and vanilla; bring to a boil. Remove from heat, and let cool 1 hour. Transfer to a mixing bowl.

2. Sift powdered sugar into icing. Beat at high speed with an electric mixer until creamy and spreading consistency.

fix it faster

This impressive cake also works well as a 2-layer cake if you don't want to split the layers. You'll have some frosting left over, but that was okay with us!

editor's favorite • make ahead

Toffee-Tiramisù Layer Cake

Just like traditional tiramisù, this towering cake is best when made ahead so the flavors can meld. Our Test Kitchens staff gave this dessert our highest rating.

MAKES 12 SERVINGS
PREP: 27 MIN.   COOK: 30 MIN.   OTHER: 16 HR.

Wax paper
1 (18.25-oz.) package French vanilla cake mix
   (we tested with Pillsbury)
1 (1.16-oz.) package Swiss mocha cappuccino mix
   (we tested with Land O'Lakes)
⅓ cup vegetable oil
3 large eggs
¾ cup Cinnamon-Espresso Syrup
Mascarpone Frosting
3 (1.4-oz) chocolate-covered toffee candy bars, chopped
   (we tested with SKOR)
Garnishes: additional chopped chocolate-covered toffee
   candy bars, semisweet chocolate and white chocolate
   shavings

1. Preheat oven to 350°. Lightly grease 2 (8") round cake pans; line with wax paper. Lightly grease wax paper. Dust pans with flour; shake out excess, and set aside.
2. Beat cake mix, next 3 ingredients, and 1 cup water in a large bowl at low speed with an electric mixer 30 seconds; then beat at medium speed 2 minutes. Pour batter into prepared pans.
3. Bake at 350° for 28 to 30 minutes or until a wooden pick inserted in center comes out clean. Let cool in pans on wire racks 10 minutes; remove from pans. Discard wax paper, and cool layers completely on wire racks (1 hour). Wrap and chill cake layers 1 to 24 hours. (This step enables you to split layers with ease.)
4. Using a serrated knife, slice layers in half horizontally to make 4 layers. Place 1 layer, cut side up, on a cake plate. Brush with one-fourth of Cinnamon-Espresso Syrup. Spread with 1½ cups Mascarpone Frosting; sprinkle with one-fourth chopped chocolate-covered toffee pieces. Repeat process with remaining 3 layers, syrup, frosting, and chopped candy bar. Frost sides of cake with remaining 2½ cups frosting. Garnish, if desired. Cover and refrigerate overnight. Store in refrigerator.

Cinnamon-Espresso Syrup

MAKES 1¼ CUPS
PREP: 2 MIN.   COOK: 4 MIN.   OTHER: 15 MIN.

⅔ cup sugar
1 (3") cinnamon stick, broken in half
1 Tbsp. instant espresso powder
¼ cup coffee liqueur

1. Bring 1 cup water, sugar, and cinnamon stick to a boil in a small saucepan; boil 1 minute. Remove from heat; let stand 15 minutes. Remove and discard cinnamon stick. Stir in espresso powder and liqueur.

Mascarpone Frosting

MAKES 8½ CUPS
PREP: 13 MIN.

2 (8-oz.) containers mascarpone cheese
1 cup powdered sugar
2 tsp. vanilla extract
½ cup Cinnamon-Espresso Syrup
2½ cups whipping cream, whipped

1. Beat first 3 ingredients at low speed with an electric mixer until creamy. Gradually add Cinnamon-Espresso Syrup, beating until smooth. Fold in whipped cream. Cover and chill until ready to use.

Using cake mix for this impressive yet easy dessert makes the holidays just a bit more relaxed.

White Christmas Coconut Sheet Cake

White Christmas Coconut Sheet Cake

Enjoy this portable, moist sheet cake slathered with lemon curd, whipped cream, and plenty of coconut.

MAKES 15 SERVINGS
PREP: 28 MIN.   COOK: 36 MIN.   OTHER: 10 HR.

1   (18.25-oz.) package white cake mix (we tested with Duncan Hines)
¾   cup cream of coconut
¼   cup unsalted butter, melted
3   large eggs
¾   cup lemon curd (we tested with Dickinson's)
4   oz. white chocolate, chopped
½   cup sour cream
1   cup whipping cream
¼   cup powdered sugar
1   (6-oz.) package frozen grated coconut, thawed
Garnishes: maraschino cherries with stems, lemon zest

1. Preheat oven to 350°. Combine first 4 ingredients and ½ cup water in a large bowl; beat at low speed with an electric mixer 1 minute. Increase speed to medium, and beat 1½ minutes. Spread batter into a greased and floured 13" x 9" pan.

2. Bake at 350° for 35 minutes or until a wooden pick inserted in center comes out clean. Remove pan to a wire rack; spread lemon curd over hot cake. Let cool completely in pan on a wire rack. (Cake will sink slightly in center.)

3. Microwave white chocolate in a small microwave-safe bowl at HIGH 1 minute or until melted, stirring after 30 seconds. Stir in sour cream. Cover and chill 30 minutes.

4. Beat whipping cream and powdered sugar in a large bowl at medium speed until stiff peaks form. Add white chocolate mixture, and beat at low speed just until combined. Spread whipped cream topping over cake; sprinkle with coconut. Cover and chill 8 hours. Garnish, if desired. Store in refrigerator.

editor's favorite · make ahead

Dark Rum Spice Cake

This moist sweet potato cake tastes even better the second day.

MAKES 12 SERVINGS
PREP: 19 MIN.   COOK: 40 MIN.   OTHER: 1 HR. 5 MIN.

¾   cup pecan halves
1   (15-oz.) can sweet potatoes in syrup, drained
3   large eggs
1   cup sour cream
¼   cup vegetable oil
1   (18.25-oz.) package spice cake mix (we tested with Duncan Hines)
¾   cup firmly packed light brown sugar
¼   cup butter
2   Tbsp. whipping cream
¼   cup dark rum
Powdered sugar

1. Preheat oven to 350°. Grease and flour a 12-cup Bundt pan (we recommend greasing pan with shortening). Arrange pecan halves in bottom of pan.

2. Beat sweet potatoes at low speed with an electric mixer until smooth. Add eggs, sour cream, and oil, beating until blended. Add cake mix; beat 1 minute or until blended. Scrape sides of bowl; beat at medium speed 2 minutes. Pour batter into prepared pan.

3. Bake at 350° for 35 minutes or until a wooden pick inserted in center comes out clean. Cool in pan on a wire rack 5 minutes.

4. Meanwhile, combine brown sugar, butter, and cream in a small saucepan. Bring to a boil; boil, stirring often, 1 minute or until sugar melts. Remove pan from heat; carefully stir in rum (mixture will start to foam). Pierce cake multiple times using a metal or wooden skewer. Pour rum syrup over cake. Cool cake completely in pan on wire rack.

5. To serve, invert cake onto a serving platter; sprinkle with powdered sugar.

Pumpkin Spice Bars

Spice cake mix serves double duty as the crust and topping.

MAKES 2 DOZEN
PREP: 12 MIN.   COOK: 45 MIN.   OTHER: 40 MIN.

  1   (18.25-oz.) package spice cake mix (we tested
       with Duncan Hines)
  ½   cup butter, melted
  ½   cup finely chopped pecans
  1   Tbsp. vanilla extract
  1   (8-oz.) package cream cheese, softened
  ⅓   cup firmly packed light brown sugar
  1   cup canned unsweetened pumpkin
  1   large egg
  1   tsp. vanilla extract
  ½   cup finely chopped white chocolate
  1   Tbsp. butter, melted
  ⅓   cup uncooked regular oats
      Powdered sugar (optional)

1. Preheat oven to 350°. Combine first 4 ingredients, mixing well with a fork. Reserve 1 cup crumbs for streusel topping. Press remaining crumbs into a lightly greased 13" x 9" pan.

2. Bake at 350° for 13 to 15 minutes or until puffy and set. Cool in pan on a wire rack 20 minutes.

3. Beat cream cheese at medium speed with an electric mixer 30 seconds or until creamy. Add brown sugar, pumpkin, egg, and 1 tsp. vanilla; beat until blended. Pour filling over baked crust.

4. Stir white chocolate, 1 Tbsp. melted butter, and oats into reserved 1 cup streusel. Sprinkle over filling.

5. Bake at 350° for 30 minutes or until edges begin to brown and center is set. Cool completely in pan on a wire rack. Sprinkle with powdered sugar, if desired. Cut into bars. Serve at room temperature or chilled.

editor's favorite · make ahead

Chocolate Chunk Candy Cane Cheesecake

Loaded with chocolate chunks and peppermint candies, slathered in a decadent chocolate ganache, and decorated with classic Christmas candies, this dessert is a "must-make" for the holidays.

MAKES 12 SERVINGS
PREP: 35 MIN.   COOK: 1 HR., 10 MIN.   OTHER: 9 HR., 10 MIN.

1½   cups chocolate wafer cookie crumbs (about
        32 cookies)
¼   cup butter, melted
2   Tbsp. sugar
4   (8-oz.) packages cream cheese, softened
1   (14-oz.) can sweetened condensed milk
⅓   cup whipping cream
¼   cup sugar
2   Tbsp. all-purpose flour
2   tsp. vanilla extract
3   large eggs
1½   cups semisweet chocolate chunks
½   cup coarsely crushed hard peppermint candies
        (about 18 candies)
¾   cup whipping cream
1½   cups semisweet chocolate morsels
     Garnishes: 65 soft peppermint sticks (5 small bags),
        broken, peppermint bark

our best basic baking tips

· You'll get optimal results when you place eggs, butter, and other dairy needed at room temperature for about 30 minutes before you begin baking. (There are exceptions, however, in which recipes may call for cold butter, ice water, etc.)
· To measure flour accurately, lightly spoon flour from the canister into a measuring cup. Fill the cup full to barely overflowing; then level the top with the edge of a knife.
· If a dough seems soft after blending and shaping, pop it in the refrigerator for 15 to 20 minutes. If dough seems soft after rolling out cookies or punching out biscuits, place baking sheet of cutouts or biscuits in refrigerator briefly before baking. This helps cookies and biscuits keep a nice shape.
· Always preheat your oven 10 minutes before baking. If your oven tends to bake hot, purchase an oven thermometer at the grocery store, and clip it in your oven. This way you can regulate the temperature so recipes bake accurately.

tools for gift giving

In testing the holiday confections in this chapter, our Test Kitchens staff gave thumbs-up on these baking items and ingredients. Stock them in your holiday pantry, or consider them for gift giving.
· Gingerbread girl cookie cutters. We tested with a handsome 5½" cutter from www.rochowcutters.com
· Nonstick Bundtlette pans. We tested with both Nordic Ware® and Wilton pans. Each pan makes six 1-cup Bundtlettes.
· Mini loaf pans. These are available at kitchen shops, or you can use the disposable aluminum pans available at the grocery store.
· Coarse decorating sugars. These are available online and in cook stores in a variety of colors and jar sizes. They make a nice gift basket addition along with sugar cookie dough.

1. Preheat oven to 325°. Combine first 3 ingredients; stir well. Press mixture firmly on bottom of a lightly greased 9" springform pan. Bake at 325° for 14 minutes; let cool.
2. Beat cream cheese at medium-high speed with an electric mixer until creamy. Gradually add sweetened condensed milk, beating just until blended. Add ⅓ cup whipping cream and next 3 ingredients, beating just until blended. Add eggs, 1 at a time, beating just until yellow disappears. Stir in chocolate chunks and crushed candies.
3. Pour batter into baked crust. Bake at 325° for 52 to 55 minutes or until edges are set and center is almost set. Turn off oven. Immediately run a knife around edge of pan, releasing sides. With oven door slightly open, let cheesecake stand in oven 1 hour. Remove from oven; cool completely on a wire rack. Cover and chill 8 hours. Remove sides and bottom of pan; place cheesecake on a serving plate.
4. Pour ¾ cup whipping cream into a microwave-safe bowl. Microwave at HIGH 1 minute or until hot. Add 1½ cups semisweet morsels; stir until chocolate melts and mixture is smooth. Pour ganache over chilled cheesecake, allowing ganache to spill over edges of cheesecake; smooth ganache with an offset spatula. Let stand 10 minutes before garnishing, if desired. Store in refrigerator.

Note: For easy cleanup, place wax paper strips under edges of cheesecake on serving plate. When you pour the ganache, it will drip onto the wax paper. Gently remove wax paper strips after the 10-minute standing time.

Chocolate-Drenched Chipotle-Roasted Nuts;
Chile-Spiced Sugared Nuts

GIFTS

Keep everyone on your gift list happy this holiday season with sweet ideas from the kitchen.

gift idea • make ahead

Chocolate-Drenched Chipotle-Roasted Nuts

Serve these spicy-sweet nuts as a fun pickup dessert, or wrap them in cellophane bags to give as gifts.

MAKES 3 CUPS
PREP: 5 MIN.   COOK: 1 HR., 4 MIN.

3 Tbsp. sugar
2 Tbsp. water
2 tsp. minced chipotle pepper in adobo sauce
½ tsp. salt
2 Tbsp. butter, melted
1 cup pecan halves
1 cup walnut halves
Parchment paper
½ cup semisweet chocolate morsels
1 Tbsp. shortening
¼ cup white chocolate morsels, melted

1. Preheat oven to 250°. Combine first 4 ingredients in a medium-size nonstick skillet. Cook over medium heat until mixture comes to a boil. Remove from heat; stir in butter. Add nuts, and gently stir to coat. Spoon coated nuts in a single layer onto a rimmed baking sheet lined with parchment paper.
2. Bake at 250° for 1 hour, stirring every 15 minutes. Spread nuts on wax paper or parchment paper to cool, breaking apart large clumps as nuts cool.
3. Melt semisweet chocolate morsels and shortening in a small saucepan over low heat, stirring until smooth. Remove from heat; cool slightly. Toss cooled nuts in semisweet chocolate until well coated. Return nuts to wax paper, and let harden. Drizzle white chocolate over nuts (do not toss). Let harden.

Tip: Speed up the chocolate hardening process by popping the jelly-roll pan into the freezer for 5 to 10 minutes.

A drizzling of white chocolate makes these chipotle-roasted nuts even more decadent.

editor's favorite • gift idea • make ahead

Chile-Spiced Sugared Nuts

MAKES ABOUT 6 CUPS
PREP: 9 MIN.   COOK: 30 MIN.

2 large egg whites
1 Tbsp. water
1⅔ cups (½ lb.) pecan halves
1⅔ cups (½ lb.) whole natural almonds
1½ cups sugar
2 Tbsp. ground cinnamon
2 tsp. salt
1½ tsp. chipotle chile powder or other chile powder

1. Beat egg whites and water in a bowl until blended. Add nuts to egg whites, stirring to coat; drain in a colander.
2. Preheat oven to 300°. Combine sugar and next 3 ingredients in another bowl. Add nuts, in batches, to spiced sugar, shaking bowl to coat nuts. Transfer nuts with a slotted spoon to a large rimmed baking sheet lined with parchment paper, spreading nuts into a single layer.
3. Bake at 300° for 30 minutes or until coating is crisp, stirring after 25 minutes. Cool completely. Break big clusters apart. Store in airtight containers.

gift idea • make ahead • quick & easy

White Chocolate Cookies 'n' Cream Fudge

Beloved chocolate sandwich cookies stud a vanilla fudge landscape.

MAKES 4 LB.
PREP: 7 MIN. COOK: 13 MIN. OTHER: 2 HR.

  1 cup sugar
  ¾ cup butter
  1 (5-oz.) can evaporated milk
  2 (12-oz.) packages white chocolate morsels
  1 (7-oz.) jar marshmallow cream
  3 cups coarsely crushed cream-filled chocolate
      sandwich cookies (about 25 cookies), divided
Pinch of salt

1. Line a greased 9" square pan with aluminum foil; set aside.
2. Combine first 3 ingredients in a medium saucepan. Cook over medium-high heat, stirring constantly, until mixture comes to a boil; cook 3 minutes, stirring constantly. Remove from heat; add white chocolate morsels, marshmallow cream, 2 cups crushed cookies, and salt. Stir until morsels melt.
3. Pour fudge into prepared pan. Sprinkle remaining 1 cup cookies over fudge, gently pressing cookies into fudge. Cover and chill until firm (about 1 to 2 hours).
4. Lift uncut fudge in aluminum foil from pan; remove foil, and cut fudge into squares.

White Chocolate
Cookies 'N Cream
Fudge

editor's favorite · gift idea · quick & easy

editor's favorite · gift idea · quick & easy

Ultimate Fudge Sauce

This sauce is rich, thick, and so delicious. It received our highest rating.

MAKES 2½ CUPS
PREP: 6 MIN.   COOK: 5 MIN.

  1   cup heavy whipping cream
  ¾   cup sugar
  8   oz. unsweetened chocolate, finely chopped
  ⅓   cup corn syrup
  ¼   cup unsalted butter
  1½ tsp. vanilla extract
  ⅛   tsp. salt

1. Combine whipping cream and sugar in a heavy saucepan. Place over medium heat, and cook, stirring constantly, until sugar dissolves. Stir in chocolate, corn syrup, and butter. Cook over medium-low heat, stirring occasionally, until chocolate melts and all ingredients are blended. Remove from heat; stir in vanilla and salt. Let cool to room temperature. Transfer sauce to jars with tight-fitting lids. Store in refrigerator. To serve, spoon sauce into a microwave-safe bowl, and microwave at HIGH for 20-second intervals until pourable.

Fleur de Sel Caramel Crunch Cups

French sea salt is the perfect finish for these candy cups. This hand-harvested fine salt looks like tiny snowflakes. Reserve it for recipes that highlight its texture and distinctive clean flavor.

MAKES 45 CANDY CUPS
PREP: 31 MIN.   COOK: 9 MIN.

  2   Tbsp. heavy whipping cream
  1   (14-oz.) package caramels
  1   cup chopped macadamia nuts, toasted
  1   cup coarsely crushed thin pretzel sticks (we tested with Rold Gold)
  ¼   tsp. vanilla extract
  1¾ cups bittersweet chocolate morsels
      Fleur de sel (French sea salt) or coarse sea salt

1. Combine heavy cream and caramels in a small microwave-safe bowl; microwave at HIGH 2 to 3 minutes or until caramels are melted, stirring after every minute. Stir in nuts, pretzels, and vanilla. Spoon mixture into 45 (1½") foil petit four cups lightly greased with cooking spray, filling each two-thirds full; cool completely.

2. Place chocolate morsels in a small microwave-safe bowl, and microwave at HIGH 1 minute or until melted; stir until smooth. Spoon chocolate evenly over caramel in cups; cool slightly. Sprinkle with fleur de sel, and let candy cups set completely. Store candy cups in an airtight container in a cool, dry place.

gift idea

Honey-Baked Chunky Granola

Enjoy this whole grain crunchy snack sprinkled over ice cream, pancakes, or yogurt.

MAKES ABOUT 10 CUPS
PREP: 13 MIN.   COOK: 1 HR., 10 MIN.

  ½   cup butter
  ½   cup honey
  ½   cup firmly packed light brown sugar
  ¼   tsp. salt
  1   Tbsp. grated orange rind
  1   Tbsp. ground cinnamon
  2   tsp. vanilla extract
  4   cups uncooked regular oats
  1   cup raw sunflower seeds
  ½   cup toasted wheat germ
  ½   cup whole natural almonds
  ½   cup coarsely chopped walnuts
  ½   cup flax seeds
      Butter-flavored cooking spray
  1   cup dried cherries
  1   cup dried cranberries or blueberries
  1   cup chopped dried apricots
  ¾   cup dried organic coconut flakes

1. Preheat oven to 275°. Combine first 4 ingredients in a small saucepan. Bring to a simmer over medium heat, and cook 5 minutes, stirring occasionally. Remove from heat; stir in orange rind, cinnamon, and vanilla.

2. While syrup cooks, toss together oats and next 5 ingredients in a large bowl until blended. Pour syrup over oat mixture, and stir until coated. Using hands coated with butter-flavored cooking spray, very firmly press oat mixture into a large lightly greased rimmed baking sheet.

3. Bake at 275° for 1 hour and 10 minutes or until toasted and browned (do not stir). Let cool completely in pan.

4. Toss together cherries and next 3 ingredients in a large bowl. When granola is cool, break apart into chunks, and gently stir into dried fruit and coconut. Store granola in airtight jars up to 5 days.

Red Velvet Petits Cakes

MAKES 6 DOZEN
PREP: 48 MIN.   COOK: 33 MIN.   OTHER: 5 MIN.

Miniature baking cups*
1 (18.25-oz.) package red velvet cake mix (we tested
   with Duncan Hines)
2 (16-oz.) containers cream cheese frosting
Finely chopped toasted pecans (optional)

1. Preheat oven to 350°. Line miniature muffin pans with
baking cups. Prepare cake mix batter according to package
directions. Spoon about 1 heaping Tbsp. batter into each baking cup, filling two-thirds full. Bake at 350° for 11 minutes
or until a wooden pick inserted in center comes out clean.
Remove from oven; let cool 5 minutes in pans on wire racks.
Remove from pans; let cool completely on wire racks.
2. Spread cream cheese frosting on tops of cakes, and sprinkle
with pecans, if desired.

Coconut Petits Cakes

MAKES 5½ DOZEN
PREP: 1 HR., 3 MIN.   COOK: 24 MIN.   OTHER: 5 MIN.

Miniature baking cups*
1 (18.25-oz.) package coconut supreme cake mix
   (we tested with Duncan Hines)
1 (7.2-oz.) package fluffy white frosting mix (we tested
   with Betty Crocker)
1 (10-oz.) jar lemon curd (we tested with Dickinson's)
1 (3.5-oz.) can sweetened flaked coconut

1. Preheat oven to 350°. Line miniature muffin pans with
baking cups. Prepare cake mix batter according to package
directions. Spoon about 1 heaping Tbsp. batter into each
baking cup, filling two-thirds full. Bake at 350° for 10 to 12
minutes or until a wooden pick inserted in center comes out
clean. Remove from oven; let cool 5 minutes in pans on wire
racks. Remove from pans; let cool completely on wire racks.
2. Meanwhile, prepare frosting mix according to package
directions. Spoon about ½ tsp. lemon curd on top of each cake.
Spread frosting on tops of cakes, and sprinkle with coconut.

Brownie Ganache Bites

MAKES 35
PREP: 23 MIN.   COOK: 13 MIN.   OTHER: 5 MIN.

Miniature baking cups*
1 (20-oz.) package double-chocolate brownie mix
   (we tested with Ghirardelli)
⅓ cup semisweet chocolate morsels
⅓ cup whipping cream

1. Preheat oven to 350°. Line miniature muffin pans with
baking cups. Prepare brownie mix batter according to package
directions. Let batter stand 5 minutes until thickened. Spoon
1 level Tbsp. batter into each baking cup. Bake at 350° for 12
minutes. Remove from pans. Cool completely on wire racks.
2. Combine chocolate morsels and cream in a 1-cup glass
measuring cup. Microwave at HIGH 1 minute; stir until
smooth. Spread ganache over tops of brownies, ending in a
decorative swirl.

*We used baking cups that were about 1½" in diameter. They
are available, both in paper and in foil, in a variety of patterns
and colors.

Variation: Brownie bites may be removed from baking cups
and turned upside down. Spoon ganache over bites, and
top with a walnut half or sprinkle with chopped hazelnuts.
Carefully set prepared bites in new slightly larger baking cups
(the tops are larger than the bottoms of the cups in which they
were baked) for presentation.

Arrange an assortment of these tiny cakes on a tiered cake stand for a show-stopping presentation at your holiday party, or package in boxes for delightful gifts.

Chocolate-Mint Brownie Pops

editor's favorite · great gift

Chocolate-Mint Brownie Pops

The Test Kitchen gave these decadent brownies-on-a-stick our highest rating.

MAKES 31 POPS
PREP: 1 HR., 19 MIN.   COOK: 34 MIN.   OTHER: 1 HR., 30 MIN.

½ cup butter
2 (1-oz.) squares unsweetened chocolate
1 (10-oz.) package crème de menthe baking morsels
   (we tested with Andes)
1 cup sugar
2 large eggs, lightly beaten
1 tsp. vanilla extract
¾ cup all-purpose flour
¼ tsp. salt
Parchment paper
2 Tbsp. shortening
5 (2-oz.) chocolate candy coating squares
31 (4") white craft sticks
4 (2-oz.) vanilla candy coating squares
Crushed peppermint candies

1. Preheat oven to 350°. Combine butter, unsweetened chocolate, and 1 cup baking chips in a medium saucepan. Cook over low heat, stirring constantly until melted. Remove from heat; add sugar, eggs, and vanilla, beating until smooth.
2. Combine flour and salt; stir into chocolate mixture until blended. Stir in remaining baking morsels.
3. Pour batter into a lightly greased 8" square pan. Bake at 350° for 32 minutes. Cool completely in pan on a wire rack.
4. Using a 2-Tbsp. scoop, scoop out balls from cooked brownie in pan. Gently reshape into smooth balls; place on a large baking sheet lined with parchment paper. Chill 30 minutes.
5. Place shortening and chocolate candy coating in a 2-cup glass measuring cup. Microwave at HIGH 1 minute or until melted. Stir until smooth. Insert a craft stick into each brownie ball. Dip each ball into melted chocolate mixture, reheating as necessary to keep mixture liquid. Place dipped balls on a large baking sheet lined with parchment paper. Let stand until firm.
6. Place vanilla candy coating in a bowl. Microwave at HIGH 40 seconds or until melted. Spoon into a large zip-top plastic freezer bag; seal bag. Snip a small hole (about ⅛" in diameter) in 1 corner of bag . Squeeze white chocolate onto dipped brownie balls to decorate as desired; sprinkle with crushed peppermint.

editor's favorite · great gift

Pistachio-Lime Wedding Cookies

MAKES ABOUT 3 DOZEN
PREP: 37 MIN.   COOK: 15 MIN.   OTHER: 1 HR., 5 MIN.

1 cup unsalted butter, softened
1½ cups powdered sugar, divided
2 Tbsp. frozen limeade concentrate, thawed
⅔ cup finely chopped pistachios
2 tsp. lime zest, divided
½ tsp. vanilla extract
2 cups all-purpose flour
⅛ tsp. salt

1. Beat butter, ½ cup powdered sugar, and limeade concentrate at medium speed with an electric mixer until creamy. Stir in nuts, 1 tsp. lime zest, and vanilla.
2. Whisk together flour and salt; gradually add to butter mixture, beating at medium speed until a soft dough forms. Cover and chill 1 hour.
3. Preheat oven to 375°. Shape dough into 1" balls, and place on ungreased baking sheets. Bake at 375° for 14 to 15 minutes or until lightly browned. Remove cookies to wire racks, and cool 5 minutes.
4. Stir together remaining 1 tsp. lime zest and remaining 1 cup powdered sugar; roll warm cookies in powdered sugar mixture, and cool completely on wire racks.

great gift

Candy Bar Sugar Cookies

MAKES 4 DOZEN
PREP: 25 MIN. COOK: 40 MIN. OTHER: 8 MIN.

- ½ cup shortening
- ¼ cup butter, softened
- ½ cup firmly packed light brown sugar
- 1 large egg
- 1½ tsp. vanilla extract
- 2 cups all-purpose flour
- 1½ tsp. baking powder
- ½ tsp. baking soda
- ½ tsp. salt
- 2 (2.1-oz.) chocolate-covered crispy peanut-buttery candy bars, coarsely chopped (we tested with Butterfinger)
- 6 Tbsp. turbinado sugar
- Parchment paper

1. Preheat oven to 375°. Beat shortening and butter at medium speed with an electric mixer until creamy. Gradually add brown sugar, beating until smooth. Add egg and vanilla, beating until blended.
2. Combine flour and next 3 ingredients; gradually add to shortening mixture, beating just until blended. Stir in candy. Shape dough into 1" balls; roll each ball in turbinado sugar. Place balls 3" apart on parchment paper-lined baking sheets.
3. Bake at 375° for 9 to 10 minutes or until lightly browned. Cool 2 minutes on baking sheets; remove to wire racks to cool completely.

editor's favorite • great gift • make ahead

Orange Pralines

For a delightful gift of this New Orleans specialty, attach a copy of the recipe to a bottle of high-quality orange extract nestled in a basketful of these sweet treats.

MAKES 2½ DOZEN
PREP: 13 MIN. COOK: 8 MIN.

- Wax paper
- 1¼ cups sugar
- 1 cup firmly packed dark brown sugar
- ½ cup heavy cream
- 6 Tbsp. unsalted butter
- ¾ cup chopped pecans, toasted
- ¾ cup pecan halves, toasted
- 1 tsp. orange extract (we tested with Massey)
- 2 tsp. orange zest

1. Lightly grease 1 (24"-long) sheet of wax paper; set aside.
2. Combine sugar and next 5 ingredients in a heavy 3-qt. saucepan. Bring to a boil over medium heat, stirring constantly. Wash down crystals from sides of pan with a pastry brush dipped in hot water; insert a candy thermometer. Cook until thermometer registers 234° to 238° (soft ball stage), about 6 minutes, stirring occasionally.
3. Remove from heat, and stir in orange extract and zest. Beat with a wooden spoon 5 minutes or just until mixture begins to thicken and lose its gloss. Working rapidly, drop by tablespoonfuls onto prepared wax paper; let stand until firm.

Candy Bar Sugar Cookies

Orange Pralines

Stained Glass Christmas Trees

Multicolored sanding sugar makes these tasty trees look as if they've been trimmed in holiday lights.

MAKES 14 COOKIES
PREP: 23 MIN. COOK: 18 MIN. OTHER: 1 HR., 30 MIN.

  1 cup unsalted butter, softened
  ½ cup powdered sugar
  1 tsp. lemon zest
  1 Tbsp. vanilla bean paste
  ¼ tsp. almond extract
2¼ cups all-purpose flour
  ½ tsp. salt
    Parchment paper
  1 egg white, lightly beaten
  1 (5-oz.) jar multicolored sanding sugar (we tested with Williams-Sonoma decorating sugar)

1. Beat butter at medium speed with an electric mixer until creamy. Gradually add powdered sugar, beating until smooth. Add lemon zest, vanilla bean paste, and almond extract, beating until blended.

2. Combine flour and salt; gradually add to butter mixture, beating just until blended. Shape dough into a ball, and divide in half. Flatten each half into a round disk; wrap each in plastic wrap, and chill at least 1 hour or until firm.

3. Preheat oven to 350°. Line 2 large baking sheets with parchment paper. Roll out dough, 1 portion at a time, to ¼" thickness on a floured surface. Cut into Christmas tree shapes using a 5½" Christmas tree cookie cutter. Place Christmas tree cutouts 1" apart on prepared baking sheets. Brush cookies with egg white, and sprinkle with multicolored sugar.

4. Bake at 350° for 18 minutes or until edges of cookies are lightly browned. Cool 5 minutes on baking sheets; remove cookies to wire racks to cool completely.

Note: Other brands of decorating sugar would also work; the sugar might be finer in texture if using grocery store brands.

Cranberry-Pecan Coffee Cakes

These tender cranberry-and-nut streusel loaves are sure to please friends and neighbors.

MAKES 4 MINI COFFEE CAKES
PREP: 29 MIN. COOK: 50 MIN. OTHER: 45 MIN.

  ½ cup butter, softened
  1 cup sugar
  2 large eggs
  2 cups all-purpose flour
  2 tsp. baking powder
  ½ tsp. baking soda
  ½ tsp. salt
  1 (8-oz.) container sour cream
  1 tsp. almond extract
  1 tsp. vanilla extract
  1 (16-oz.) can whole-berry cranberry sauce, stirred
  1 cup coarsely chopped pecans
    Almond Cream Glaze

1. Preheat oven to 350°. Beat butter at medium speed with an electric mixer until creamy. Gradually add sugar, beating well. Add eggs, 1 at a time, beating until blended after each addition.

2. Combine flour and next 3 ingredients. Add flour mixture to butter mixture alternately with sour cream, beginning and ending with flour mixture. Stir in extracts.

3. Spoon ½ cup batter into each of 4 greased and floured 5¾" x 3" mini loaf pans. Spoon 3 Tbsp. cranberry sauce over batter in each pan, and spread lightly to edges; sprinkle 2 Tbsp. pecans over cranberry sauce in each pan. Repeat layers in each pan using remaining batter, cranberry sauce, and pecans.

4. Bake at 350° for 48 to 50 minutes or until a wooden pick inserted in center comes out clean. Cool in pans on a wire rack 15 minutes; remove from pans, and let cool completely. Drizzle glaze over cooled cakes.

Almond Cream Glaze

MAKES ⅓ CUP
PREP: 6 MIN.

  ¾ cup powdered sugar
  2 Tbsp. whipping cream
  ½ tsp. almond extract

1. Stir together all ingredients.

editor's favorite · gift idea · make ahead

Chocolate Granola Brittle

The beauty of this recipe is that you can make a decadent brittle in the microwave in half the time it takes to make the traditional candy. If you want to make more than one pound, don't double the recipe— it won't give you the same result. Just make it twice.

MAKES ABOUT 1 LB.
PREP: 6 MIN.   COOK: 10 MIN.

Cranberry-Pecan Coffee Cakes

Chocolate Granola Brittle

 1 cup sugar
 ½ cup light corn syrup
 ⅛ tsp. salt
 1 cup coarsely chopped pecans
 1 Tbsp. butter
 1 tsp. vanilla extract
 1 tsp. baking soda
 Parchment paper
 ¾ cup chocolate granola (we tested with Bear Naked chocolate granola)
 3 (1-oz.) semisweet chocolate baking squares
 1½ Tbsp. shortening

1. Combine first 3 ingredients in a 2-qt. glass bowl. Microwave at HIGH 5 minutes, using an 1100-watt microwave oven (add 1 more minute if using a 700-watt microwave oven). Stir in pecans. Microwave 1 minute and 30 seconds in an 1100-watt oven (add 1 more minute in 700-watt oven). Stir in butter and vanilla. Microwave 1 minute and 45 seconds in an 1100-watt oven (add 1 more minute in 700-watt oven) or until candy is the color of peanut butter. Stir in baking soda (mixture will bubble).

2. Quickly pour candy onto a lightly greased rimless baking sheet. (Pour as thinly as possible without spreading candy.) Cover brittle quickly with parchment paper, and use a rolling pin to thin out candy; peel off parchment. Sprinkle granola over brittle. Replace parchment, and use rolling pin to adhere granola to brittle; peel off parchment. Cool brittle completely; break into desired-size pieces.

3. Melt semisweet chocolate squares and shortening in a small bowl in the microwave oven at HIGH, 1½ to 2 minutes, stirring after 1 minute. Dip each piece of brittle halfway into chocolate mixture. Place dipped brittle on parchment paper to harden. Store in an airtight container.

classic CELEBRATIONS

RING IN THE YULETIDE SEASON WITH FRIENDS AND FAMILY.
WE'VE MADE PLANNING A BREEZE WITH READY-TO-GO MENUS
AND GAME PLANS TO HELP ORGANIZE YOUR TIME.

Christmas TREE CUTTING PARTY

Let the tree trimming begin! Make a tradition of this simple menu of soul-satisfying comforts to be enjoyed while you select the pick of the forest.

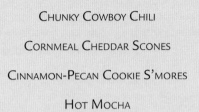

menu

CHUNKY COWBOY CHILI

CORNMEAL CHEDDAR SCONES

CINNAMON-PECAN COOKIE S'MORES

HOT MOCHA

serves 8 to 10

Chunky Cowboy Chili, page 110;
Cornmeal Cheddar Scones, page 110

game plan

1 day ahead:

- [ ] Prepare Chunky Cowboy Chili. Cover and chill in an airtight container.
- [ ] Bake cookies for Cinnamon-Pecan Cookie S'mores.
- [ ] Organize marshmallows, chocolate bars, and roasting sticks for S'mores.

2 hours ahead:

- [ ] Prepare Cornmeal Cheddar Scones; wrap tightly in plastic wrap.

1 hour ahead:

- [ ] Prepare Hot Mocha and pour into a thermos.
- [ ] Reheat chili and pour into a thermos.
- [ ] Pack in a picnic basket.

editor's favorite · make ahead

Chunky Cowboy Chili

(pictured on page 109)

The flavor of this chili, like many soups and stews, is better the next day.

MAKES ABOUT 14 CUPS
PREP: 17 MIN. COOK: 2 HR., 5 MIN.

- 2 Tbsp. canola oil, divided
- 4 lb. boneless chuck roast, cut into ½" pieces
- 1 large onion, chopped
- 1 green bell pepper, chopped
- 2 garlic cloves, minced
- 1 Tbsp. Worcestershire sauce
- 2 Tbsp. tomato paste
- 2 tsp. chili powder
- ¼ tsp. ground cumin
- 2 (14.5-oz.) cans petite diced tomatoes with jalapeños, undrained
- 2 (8-oz.) cans tomato sauce
- 1 (16-oz.) can red beans
- 1 (15-oz.) can whole kernel corn, drained
- 1 (12-oz.) bottle dark beer (we tested with Michelob AmberBock)

1. Heat 1 Tbsp. oil in a large Dutch oven over medium-high heat; add half of beef. Cook 12 minutes or until dark brown, turning after 5 minutes. Remove beef from pan, and keep warm. Repeat procedure with remaining half of beef.

2. Add remaining 1 Tbsp. oil to pan. Add onion, bell pepper, and garlic to pan. Sauté 5 minutes or until tender. Return beef and accumulated juices to pan. Stir in 1 cup water, Worcestershire sauce, and remaining ingredients. Bring to a boil; cover, reduce heat, and simmer 1 hour and 30 minutes or until beef is tender and chili is thick.

editor's favorite

Cornmeal Cheddar Scones

(also pictured on page 109)

Cornmeal provides a little crunch to these tender, cheesy brunch favorites. They pair well with soups, stews, chili, or fried chicken.

MAKES 15 SCONES
PREP: 20 MIN. COOK: 20 MIN.

- 2 cups all-purpose flour
- ¾ cup stone-ground cornmeal
- 1 Tbsp. sugar
- 1 Tbsp. baking powder
- ½ tsp. baking soda
- ½ tsp. salt
- ⅛ tsp. ground red pepper
- ¾ cup unsalted butter, cut into chunks
- 1 cup (4 oz.) shredded extra-sharp Cheddar cheese
- 1 large egg
- ¾ cup buttermilk
- Parchment paper
- Unsalted butter, melted
- Sea salt

1. Preheat oven to 425°. Place first 7 ingredients in a food processor. Add ¾ cup butter; pulse 3 or 4 times or until mixture resembles coarse meal. Place flour mixture in a large bowl; stir in cheese. Whisk together egg and buttermilk until blended. Make a well in center of dry ingredients; add egg mixture, stirring just until dry ingredients are moistened.

2. Turn dough out onto a floured surface; knead lightly 3 or 4 times. Pat dough into a 10" x 7" rectangle. Cut into 15 squares. Place squares on a parchment paper-lined baking sheet. Brush tops with melted unsalted butter, and sprinkle with sea salt. Bake at 425° for 20 minutes or until golden.

Cornmeal Cheddar Scones

editor's favorite

Cinnamon-Pecan Cookie S'mores

This variation on the campfire staple is over the top, thanks to the nutty homemade cookies that replace the graham crackers.

MAKES 8 SERVINGS
PREP: 13 MIN.   COOK: 19 MIN.   OTHER: 1 MIN.

½ cup butter, softened
½ cup firmly packed dark brown sugar
¼ cup granulated sugar
1 large egg
1½ tsp. vanilla extract
1¼ cups all-purpose flour
1 tsp. baking powder
1 tsp. ground cinnamon
¼ tsp. salt
1 cup coarsely chopped pecans, toasted
1 (4-oz.) bittersweet chocolate baking bar (we tested with Ghirardelli)
8 large marshmallows

1. Preheat oven to 350°. Beat butter at medium speed with an electric mixer until creamy; gradually add sugars, beating well. Add egg and vanilla, beating well.
2. Combine flour and next 3 ingredients; add to butter mixture. Beat at low speed until blended. Stir in pecans.
3. Divide dough into 16 equal portions; roll each portion into a ball. Place balls 1" apart on lightly greased baking sheets; flatten slightly.
4. Bake at 350° for 16 minutes or until lightly browned. Cool cookies on pans 1 minute. Transfer cookies to wire racks. Cool completely.
5. Preheat broiler. Separate chocolate bar into 8 squares. Place a chocolate square on flat side of each of 8 cookies.
6. Place marshmallows on a baking sheet. Broil 3 minutes or until toasted. Immediately transfer marshmallows to tops of chocolate squares, using a small spatula. Top marshmallows with remaining cookies, flat sides down; press down gently.

editor's favorite

Hot Mocha

Whether the Hot Mudslide version or the nonalcoholic one, this yummy drink will warm you down to your toes.

MAKES ABOUT 10 CUPS
PREP: 2 MIN.   COOK: 10 MIN.

1 cup unsweetened cocoa
1 cup sugar
¼ cup instant espresso*
2 cups half-and-half
6 cups milk
4 tsp. vanilla extract
Sweetened whipped cream
Chocolate syrup

1. Whisk together first 4 ingredients in a large saucepan. Cook, whisking constantly, over medium heat until sugar dissolves. Whisk in milk; cook over medium-high heat, whisking constantly 5 minutes or until very hot. (Do not boil.) Whisk in vanilla.
2. Pour chocolate mixture into mugs; top with whipped cream, and drizzle with chocolate syrup.

*Omit or substitute decaffeinated espresso for the youngsters.

Note: To make a Hot Mudslide, omit espresso. Stir ½ cup Kahlúa, ½ cup Baileys Irish Cream, and, if desired, ¼ cup vodka into the hot milk mixture along with the vanilla. Proceed as directed.

Keep cocoa hot in a thermos while you search for a tree. Add whipped cream and syrup before serving.

Hot Mocha

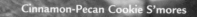

Cinnamon-Pecan Cookie S'mores

holiday OPEN HOUSE

Ring in the holidays with a hearty menu of flavor combinations your party guests will not soon forget.

menu

Açaí-Berry Mulled Cider

Blood Orange Martinis

Mediterranean Roasted Almonds

Fig, Prosciutto, and Blue Cheese Squares

Caramelized Vidalia Onion Dip

Mini Sun-dried Tomato Cheese Toasts

Mini Muffulettas

Grilled Flat-Iron Steak Crostini

Marinated Vegetables

Dark Chocolate-Toffee Brownie Shooters

serves 18 to 24

editor's favorite · make ahead

Caramelized Vidalia Onion Dip

Here's a new take on an old favorite appetizer. Look for sturdy sweet potato chips for scooping up this mega-cheesy family favorite.

MAKES 4 CUPS
PREP: 14 MIN. COOK: 1 HR., 10 MIN.

2   Tbsp. butter
3   large Vidalia or other sweet onions, thinly sliced
1   (8-oz.) package cream cheese, softened
1   (8-oz.) block Swiss cheese, shredded
1   cup freshly grated Parmesan cheese
1   cup regular or light mayonnaise
Sweet potato chips

1. Preheat oven to 375°. Melt butter in a large skillet over medium heat; add sliced onions. Cook, stirring often, 30 to 40 minutes or until onions are caramel colored.
2. Combine onions, cream cheese, and next 3 ingredients, stirring well. Spoon dip into a lightly greased 1½- to 2-qt. baking dish. Bake, uncovered, at 375° for 30 minutes or until golden and bubbly. Serve with sweet potato chips.

make ahead

Prepare dip a day ahead, but do not bake. Cover and refrigerate overnight. Bake, uncovered, at 375° for 45 minutes or until golden and bubbly.

Caramelized Vidalia Onion Dip

editor's favorite

Fig, Prosciutto, and Blue Cheese Squares

Refrigerated pizza crust dough unrolls to almost the perfect dimensions needed for this recipe. Briefly heating the oil and garlic infuses the oil with garlic flavor before it is brushed on the dough. This is a uniquely flavored appetizer pizza not to be missed.

MAKES 3 DOZEN
PREP: 14 MIN. COOK: 26 MIN. OTHER: 5 MIN.

2   Tbsp. olive oil
2   garlic cloves, pressed
3   oz. thinly sliced prosciutto, chopped
1   (11-oz.) can refrigerated thin pizza crust dough
1   Tbsp. chopped fresh rosemary
½   cup fig preserves (we tested with Braswell's)
¾   cup crumbled blue cheese
½   tsp. freshly ground pepper
Garnishes: fresh rosemary, figs

1. Preheat oven to 400°. Combine oil and garlic in a small microwave-safe bowl. Microwave at HIGH 20 seconds or just until warm. Let stand while prosciutto cooks.
2. Cook prosciutto in a large skillet over medium-high heat 11 minutes or until browned and crisp; remove prosciutto, and drain on paper towels.
3. Unroll dough, and place on a lightly greased large baking sheet. Press out dough with hands to form a 15" x 13" rectangle. Brush dough with garlic-flavored oil; sprinkle rosemary over dough. Spread fig preserves over dough; sprinkle with prosciutto, cheese, and pepper.
4. Bake at 400° for 15 minutes or until crust is browned and crisp. Let stand 5 minutes before cutting. Garnish, if desired.

make ahead

Cook prosciutto up to 2 days ahead. Store in an airtight container in refrigerator until ready to assemble recipe.

game plan

up to 1 month ahead:

☐ Make and freeze Mini Sun-dried Tomato Cheese Toasts.

2 days ahead:

☐ Make Olive Salad for Mini Muffulettas; assemble muffulettas, if desired.

☐ Make brownies for Dark Chocolate-Toffee Brownie Shooters.

☐ Make Mediterranean Roasted Almonds.

☐ Cook prosciutto for Fig, Prosciutto, and Blue Cheese Squares; cool and store in airtight container in refrigerator.

1 day ahead:

☐ Marinate Flat-Iron Steak; prepare Herbed Caper Butter. Cover and chill both recipes.

☐ Combine ingredients for Blood Orange Martinis; cover and chill.

☐ Prepare Caramelized Vidalia Onion Dip, but don't bake; cover and chill.

☐ Prepare Marinated Vegetables; cover and chill.

4 hours ahead:

☐ Assemble Dark Chocolate-Toffee Brownie Shooters; chill.

☐ Assemble muffulettas, if not already completed.

☐ Prepare Açaí-Berry Mulled Cider.

☐ Prepare Fig, Prosciutto, and Blue Cheese Squares.

1 to 2 hours ahead:

☐ Bake Caramelized Vidalia Onion Dip.

☐ Grill Flat-Iron Steak, and assemble crostini.

☐ Bake Mini Sun-dried Tomato Cheese Toasts.

☐ Arrange Marinated Vegetables on serving platter.

☐ Pour Blood Orange Martinis into pitchers or martini glasses.

---

editor's favorite

Açaí-Berry Mulled Cider

The açaí-raspberry juice blend in this soothing brew features açaí juice, a now readily available superfood packed with powerful antioxidants.

MAKES 18½ CUPS
PREP: 7 MIN.   COOK: 1 HR., 2 MIN.

2 (1.5-liter) bottles apple cider
6 cups açaí-raspberry juice blend (we tested with Tropicana)
⅓ cup firmly packed light brown sugar
3 (3") cinnamon sticks
5 whole allspice
5 whole cloves
1 (1") piece fresh ginger, peeled
3 orange slices
3 lemon slices

1. Combine first 3 ingredients in a very large Dutch oven. Cook over medium-high heat, stirring until sugar dissolves.
2. Tie cinnamon sticks and next 3 ingredients in a cheesecloth bag; add spice bag to cider. Add orange and lemon slices. Bring mixture to a boil; reduce heat to medium-low, and simmer 45 minutes. Discard spice bag.

editor's favorite · make ahead

Blood Orange Martinis

Serve this stunning sipper in miniature, sugar-rimmed martini glasses.

MAKES ABOUT 8 CUPS
PREP: 6 MIN.

4 cups blood orange juice
2 cups orange-flavored vodka
1 cup orange liqueur
Simple Syrup
Garnish: blood orange slices
Coarse sugar (optional)

1. Combine first 4 ingredients in a large pitcher. Cover and chill until ready to serve. Garnish, if desired. Serve in sugar-rimmed glasses, if desired.

Note: For sugared rims, dip rims of stemmed glasses into a thin coating of light corn syrup or water, and then spin rims in a plateful of coarse sugar.

Simple Syrup

MAKES ⅔ CUP
PREP: 1 MIN.   COOK: 6 MIN.   OTHER: 1 HR.

½ cup sugar

1. Bring sugar and ½ cup water to a boil in a saucepan. Boil, stirring often, 3 minutes or until sugar dissolves and syrup is reduced to ⅔ cup. Remove from heat; cool completely. Store in refrigerator.

gift idea • make ahead

Mediterranean Roasted Almonds

A gourmet sea salt blend is the star ingredient that transforms plain almonds into a memorable snack.

MAKES 5 CUPS
PREP: 9 MIN.   COOK: 45 MIN.

2 egg whites
2 tsp. Worcestershire sauce
2 (10-oz.) packages whole natural almonds
3 Tbsp. Mediterranean spiced sea salt (we tested with McCormick)
3 Tbsp. sugar
1 tsp. garlic powder
¼ tsp. dried crushed red pepper

1. Preheat oven to 300°. Whisk together egg whites, Worcestershire sauce, and 1 Tbsp. water in a large bowl until frothy. Add nuts, stirring to coat.
2. Combine sea salt and next 3 ingredients in another bowl. Using a slotted spoon, transfer coated nuts to spice mixture; toss well to coat nuts. Transfer nuts with a slotted spoon to a lightly greased large rimmed baking sheet, spreading nuts into a single layer.
3. Bake at 300° for 45 minutes, stirring after 25 minutes. Remove almonds from oven; cool completely on wire racks to help nuts dry out and gain some crunch. Store in airtight containers up to 1 month.

Blood Orange Martinis

editor's favorite • make ahead

Caramelized Vidalia Onion Dip

Here's a new take on an old favorite appetizer. Look for sturdy sweet potato chips for scooping up this mega-cheesy family favorite.

MAKES 4 CUPS
PREP: 14 MIN.   COOK: 1 HR., 10 MIN.

- 2   Tbsp. butter
- 3   large Vidalia or other sweet onions, thinly sliced
- 1   (8-oz.) package cream cheese, softened
- 1   (8-oz.) block Swiss cheese, shredded
- 1   cup freshly grated Parmesan cheese
- 1   cup regular or light mayonnaise
- Sweet potato chips

1. Preheat oven to 375°. Melt butter in a large skillet over medium heat; add sliced onions. Cook, stirring often, 30 to 40 minutes or until onions are caramel colored.
2. Combine onions, cream cheese, and next 3 ingredients, stirring well. Spoon dip into a lightly greased 1½- to 2-qt. baking dish. Bake, uncovered, at 375° for 30 minutes or until golden and bubbly. Serve with sweet potato chips.

make ahead

Prepare dip a day ahead, but do not bake. Cover and refrigerate overnight. Bake, uncovered, at 375° for 45 minutes or until golden and bubbly.

Caramelized Vidalia Onion Dip

editor's favorite

Fig, Prosciutto, and Blue Cheese Squares

Refrigerated pizza crust dough unrolls to almost the perfect dimensions needed for this recipe. Briefly heating the oil and garlic infuses the oil with garlic flavor before it is brushed on the dough. This is a uniquely flavored appetizer pizza not to be missed.

MAKES 3 DOZEN
PREP: 14 MIN. COOK: 26 MIN. OTHER: 5 MIN.

- 2   Tbsp. olive oil
- 2   garlic cloves, pressed
- 3   oz. thinly sliced prosciutto, chopped
- 1   (11-oz.) can refrigerated thin pizza crust dough
- 1   Tbsp. chopped fresh rosemary
- ½   cup fig preserves (we tested with Braswell's)
- ¾   cup crumbled blue cheese
- ½   tsp. freshly ground pepper
- Garnishes: fresh rosemary, figs

1. Preheat oven to 400°. Combine oil and garlic in a small microwave-safe bowl. Microwave at HIGH 20 seconds or just until warm. Let stand while prosciutto cooks.
2. Cook prosciutto in a large skillet over medium-high heat 11 minutes or until browned and crisp; remove prosciutto, and drain on paper towels.
3. Unroll dough, and place on a lightly greased large baking sheet. Press out dough with hands to form a 15" x 13" rectangle. Brush dough with garlic-flavored oil; sprinkle rosemary over dough. Spread fig preserves over dough; sprinkle with prosciutto, cheese, and pepper.
4. Bake at 400° for 15 minutes or until crust is browned and crisp. Let stand 5 minutes before cutting. Garnish, if desired.

make ahead

Cook prosciutto up to 2 days ahead. Store in an airtight container in refrigerator until ready to assemble recipe.

Fig, Prosciutto, and Blue Cheese Squares

Marinated Vegetables, page 120

make ahead

Marinated Vegetables

(pictured on page 119)

Hosts will welcome this colorful make-ahead vegetable dish for the party table. Whole green beans or asparagus spears can be substituted for broccoli.

MAKES 15 TO 18 APPETIZER SERVINGS
PREP: 17 MIN.   COOK: 3 MIN.   OTHER: 8 HR.

 1   (12-oz.) package fresh broccoli florets
 4   medium carrots, cut into thin (2") sticks
 1   yellow, orange, or red bell pepper, cut into thin strips
 1   lb. fresh button or baby portobello mushrooms
 1   (5.75-oz.) jar pimiento-stuffed Spanish olives, drained
 1   cup pitted kalamata olives, drained
 ¾   cup Italian white wine vinegar
 2   Tbsp. sugar
 1   tsp. salt
 ½   tsp. freshly ground black pepper
 ½   tsp. dried oregano
 ½   cup olive oil
 1   (12-oz.) jar roasted red bell peppers, drained and cut into ½"-thick strips

1. Combine first 6 ingredients in a large bowl.
2. Combine vinegar and next 4 ingredients in a small saucepan; bring to a boil. Reduce heat, and cook 1 minute or until sugar dissolves. Remove from heat; whisk in oil. Pour over vegetables in bowl; toss gently to coat. Add roasted red bell pepper; toss gently.
3. Transfer vegetables to a 2-gal. zip-top plastic freezer bag. Seal and chill 8 hours, turning bag occasionally.
4. Drain vegetables, reserving marinade. Arrange vegetables on a serving platter; drizzle with a small amount of reserved marinade, if desired.

editor's favorite • make ahead

Mini Muffulettas

Make these small bites of New Orleans up to 2 days ahead. The longer the flavorful Olive Salad marinade soaks into the sandwiches, the tastier they'll be.

MAKES 28 SANDWICHES
PREP: 37 MIN.

 28   (1.1-oz.) crusty bakery rolls, split (see note)
      Olive Salad
 28   thin slices Genoa salami (about ¾ lb.)
 ¾   lb. very thinly sliced deli ham
 28   (.76-oz.) slices provolone cheese
      Garnish: pimiento-stuffed olives

1. Arrange bottom halves of rolls on work surface. For each sandwich, spoon about 1 Tbsp. Olive Salad on a roll bottom. Layer salami, ham, and cheese over salad. Spoon 1 Tbsp. more Olive Salad over cheese, and cover with top of roll. Cut in half, and secure with wooden picks. Garnish, if desired. Store in an airtight container in refrigerator up to 2 days before serving.

Note: Muffulettas are traditionally made with a crusty, round French loaf. For our minis, look for small crusty rolls that are about 1 oz. each and 2" to 4" in diameter. We tested with "water rolls."

Olive Salad

MAKES 4¾ CUPS
PREP: 15 MIN.

 1   (12-oz.) jar roasted red bell peppers with garlic and oregano, undrained (we tested with B&G)
 1   (13-oz.) jar pimiento-stuffed Spanish olives, drained
 1   (6-oz.) can pitted ripe black olives, drained
 ½   cup coarsely chopped red onion
 5   pepperoncini peppers, cut in half
 3   garlic cloves, cut in half
 2   tsp. dried Italian seasoning
 ¼   cup olive oil
 ¼   tsp. freshly ground black pepper

1. Drain roasted red bell peppers; reserve 1 Tbsp. liquid.
2. Pulse all ingredients and reserved liquid in a food processor until coarsely chopped. Cover and store in refrigerator until ready to use.

Mini Muffulettas

Grilled Flat-Iron Steak Crostini

editor's favorite • make ahead

Grilled Flat-Iron Steak Crostini

Store-bought crostini are slathered with herbed caper butter and topped with steak to make these elegant bites that are impressive but easy.

MAKES 46 CROSTINI
PREP: 10 MIN.   COOK: 10 MIN.   OTHER: 8 HR., 10 MIN.

    1 Tbsp. chopped fresh rosemary
    4 garlic cloves, minced
    2 Tbsp. olive oil
    1 Tbsp. lemon juice
    2 lb. flat-iron steak
    ¾ tsp. kosher salt
    ½ tsp. freshly ground pepper
       Herbed Caper Butter
    1 (7-oz.) container crostini
       Garnish: fresh rosemary

1. Combine first 4 ingredients in a small bowl; rub over steak. Cover and chill 8 hours.
2. Preheat grill. Sprinkle steak with salt and pepper. Grill steak, covered with grill lid, over medium-high heat (350° to 400°) for 5 minutes on each side or until desired degree of doneness. Let stand 10 minutes. Cut diagonally across the grain into thin strips.
3. Spread Herbed Caper Butter over crostini; top with steak slices. Garnish, if desired.

Herbed Caper Butter

MAKES 1¼ CUPS
PREP: 6 MIN.

    1   cup butter, softened
    1   Tbsp. drained, chopped capers
    1   Tbsp. chopped fresh parsley
    1½ tsp. chopped fresh rosemary
    ½   tsp. lemon zest

1. Stir together all ingredients in a small bowl.

make ahead

Prepare Herbed Caper Butter a day ahead; cover and refrigerate overnight. Let butter soften before spreading onto crostini.

editor's favorite · gift idea · make ahead

Mini Sun-dried Tomato Cheese Toasts

Think gourmet grilled cheese with a surprise bite of sun-dried tomato hidden inside. These appetizers travel straight from the freezer to the oven. The large yield makes enough to serve for a party, to give as gifts to friends, and still have a few left to enjoy with a glass of wine on a cold January night.

MAKES 6 DOZEN
PREP: 1 HR., 13 MIN.   COOK: 18 MIN. PER BATCH   OTHER: 2 HR., 45 MIN.

- 2 (5-oz.) jars sharp process cheese spread (we tested with Old English)
- ¾ cup butter, softened
- ½ cup crumbled feta cheese
- ¾ tsp. dried basil
- ½ tsp. garlic powder
- ¼ tsp. ground red pepper
- 2 (16-oz.) loaves sandwich bread, chilled (we tested with Pepperidge Farm)
- 1 (10-oz.) jar sun-dried tomato pesto sauce (we tested with Classico)

1. Beat first 3 ingredients at medium speed with an electric mixer until creamy; stir in basil, garlic powder, and red pepper.
2. Work with 1 bread loaf at a time, leaving remainder chilled. Stack 4 slices of bread on a cutting board; remove crusts using a serrated knife. Spread 1 tsp. sun-dried tomato pesto over 1 slice bread; stack with another slice of bread. Spread cheese mixture over top and sides of sandwich; cut into 4 squares. Spread cheese mixture on bare sides of each square. Place stacks on an ungreased baking sheet; place in freezer 45 minutes or until firm. Repeat procedure with remaining bread loaf, pesto, and cheese mixture; freeze 45 minutes.
3. Transfer partially frozen squares from baking sheet to a large zip-top plastic freezer bag. Freeze 2 hours or up to 1 month.
4. Preheat oven to 350°. Place frozen squares on ungreased baking sheets. Bake at 350° for 18 minutes or until lightly browned and toasted.

Note: A small amount of cheese may ooze onto the baking sheets during baking. We call this a good thing.

editor's favorite · make ahead

Dark Chocolate-Toffee Brownie Shooters

You'll get your chocolate fix in short order with these shot glasses of decadent mousse and brownie chunks doused with Kahlúa.

MAKES 3 DOZEN
PREP: 47 MIN.   COOK: 30 MIN.   OTHER: 2 HR.

- 1 (18-oz.) package triple-chocolate brownie mix (we tested with Duncan Hines Triple Chocolate Decadence)
- 3 Tbsp. Kahlúa (optional)
- 3 (3.5-oz.) dark chocolate with toffee bits and caramelized almonds candy bars, chopped (we tested with Ghirardelli)
- 1½ cups whipping cream, divided
- 6 Tbsp. caramel topping
- 1 (7-oz.) can refrigerated instant nondairy whipped topping (we tested with Cool Whip)
- Garnish: fresh mint sprigs

1. Bake brownies according to package directions for fudgy brownies. If desired, poke holes in baked brownies using a straw, and pour Kahlúa over brownies, allowing it to seep into holes. Let cool completely in pan.
2. Microwave chocolate and ¼ cup whipping cream in a large microwave-safe bowl at HIGH 1 to 1½ minutes or until chocolate melts, stirring after 1 minute. Let stand 45 minutes or until almost cool.
3. Beat remaining 1¼ cups whipping cream at high speed with an electric mixer until soft peaks form; gently fold into chocolate mixture.
4. Crumble brownies into bite-size pieces. Layer brownies, caramel topping, and chocolate mousse into 2-oz. shot glasses. Top each dessert shot with whipped topping. Garnish, if desired.

fix it faster

Substitute 2 (8.6-oz.) packages Soft Baked Chocolate Chunk Brownie Cookies (we tested with Pepperidge Farm) for brownies. Toss crumbled cookies with Kahlúa, if desired.

make ahead

Make brownies up to 2 days before assembly. Assemble shooters up to 4 hours before party; cover and chill until ready to serve. Don't prepare mousse until ready to assemble desserts; it firms up quickly.

Dark Chocolate-Toffee
Brownie Shooters

holiday TEX-MEX PARTY

It's the perfect time of year for throwing a fiesta. Zesty chiles, tangy citrus, and hints of cinnamon come together in this casual menu. Olé!

menu

Cranberry-Lime Margaritas

Smoky Guacamole

Spicy Queso Dip

Chicken Meatballs in Mole Sauce

Mexican Lasagna

Black Beans with Saffron Rice

Mini Churros

Mexican Chocolate Bar Cookies with Bittersweet Chocolate Frosting

Pineapple Agua Fresca

serves 8

game plan

1 week ahead:

- [ ] Prepare sugar syrup for Cranberry-Lime Margaritas. Cover and chill.

2 days ahead:

- [ ] Prepare Chicken Meatballs; cool and place in a large zip-top plastic freezer bag. Seal and freeze.
- [ ] Prepare Pineapple Agua Fresca; chill.

1 day ahead:

- [ ] Combine ingredients for margaritas.
- [ ] Prepare Mole Sauce; cover and chill.
- [ ] Assemble Mexican Lasagna; cover with plastic wrap, and chill.
- [ ] Thaw meatballs overnight in refrigerator.

4 hours ahead:

- [ ] Prepare Mexican Chocolate Bar Cookies. Store in airtight container.
- [ ] Set up chips for Queso and Guacamole bar.
- [ ] Cook meatballs; keep warm in a slow cooker.

2 hours ahead:

- [ ] Prepare Black Beans with Saffron Rice; keep warm.
- [ ] Prepare Smoky Guacamole. Cover tightly with plastic wrap, and chill.
- [ ] Let lasagna come to room temperature; bake lasagna.

1 hour ahead:

- [ ] Prepare Spicy Queso Dip; keep warm in slow cooker.
- [ ] Prepare Mini Churros.

---

editor's favorite • quick & easy

Cranberry-Lime Margaritas

If you like frozen margaritas, try processing the margarita mixture with crushed ice in a blender.

MAKES 13 CUPS
PREP: 5 MIN.   COOK: 5 MIN.   OTHER: 20 MIN.

- 1 cup sugar
- 1 cup fresh lime juice
- 1½ cups tequila
- ½ cup orange liqueur
- 1 (64-oz.) bottle cranberry juice cocktail (we tested with Ocean Spray)
- Lime wedges
- Coarse salt
- Garnish: additional lime wedges

1. Stir together sugar and 1 cup water in a small saucepan. Cook over medium heat until sugar dissolves. Remove from heat. Pour into a large pitcher; cover and chill 20 minutes.
2. Add lime juice and next 3 ingredients to sugar syrup in pitcher. Chill until ready to serve. Rub glass rims with lime wedges, and dip rims in salt. Serve margaritas over crushed ice. Garnish, if desired.

Spicy Queso Dip

If you prefer, you may reduce or omit the peppers.

MAKES 4 CUPS
PREP: 8 MIN.   COOK: 10 MIN.

- 1 cup milk
- 8 oz. queso melt cheese, shredded
- 8 oz. white American cheese slices, diced
- 2 Tbsp. butter
- 1 cup finely chopped onion
- 1 garlic clove, minced
- 1 cup finely chopped seeded tomato
- 1 (4-oz.) can diced jalapeño peppers, drained
- Tortilla chips

1. Combine first 3 ingredients in a 2-qt. glass bowl. Microwave at HIGH 5 minutes or until creamy, stirring every minute.
2. Melt butter in a large skillet over medium-high heat. Add onion and garlic; sauté 3 minutes or until tender. Stir in tomato, and sauté 2 minutes or until onion is tender. Stir in jalapeño peppers.
3. Stir vegetable mixture into cheese mixture until blended. Transfer dip to a 2-qt. slow cooker. Heat on low or warm setting for up to 2 hours, stirring occasionally. Serve with tortilla chips.

Cranberry-Lime Margaritas

editor's favorite

Smoky Guacamole

MAKES 2 CUPS
PREP: 8 MIN.

3   ripe avocados
1   Tbsp. chopped fresh cilantro
3   Tbsp. fresh lime juice
1   Tbsp. chipotle chile hot sauce (we tested with
     Tabasco)
½   tsp. salt
2   garlic cloves, minced
Garnish: 1 small canned chipotle chile pepper in adobo
     sauce, drained and sliced

1. Cut avocados in half. Scoop avocado pulp into bowl; mash with a fork or potato masher until almost smooth. Stir in cilantro and next 4 ingredients. Garnish, if desired.

Spoon prepared guacamole into empty avocado shells if you want to offer individual portions.

editor's favorite · *make ahead*

Chicken Meatballs in Mole Sauce

MAKES 16 APPETIZER SERVINGS
PREP: 20 MIN.   COOK: 30 MIN.   OTHER: 20 MIN.

- 1 large egg
- 2 lb. ground chicken
- 1 cup fine, dry breadcrumbs
- ¼ cup chopped fresh cilantro
- 1 tsp. salt
- 2 large garlic cloves, minced
- Mole Sauce

1. Whisk egg in a large bowl. Stir in chicken and next 4 ingredients. Cover and chill 20 minutes.
2. Preheat oven to 375°. Coat 2 racks and 2 large rimmed baking sheets with cooking spray; place racks in prepared pans. Shape chicken mixture into 1" balls; place on racks. Bake at 375° for 20 minutes.
3. Place meatballs in large Dutch oven; stir in Mole Sauce. Cook over medium heat until thoroughly heated. Transfer to a chafing dish or slow cooker, if desired. Serve hot.

editor's favorite · *make ahead*

Mole Sauce

MAKES 5 CUPS
PREP: 22 MIN.   COOK: 11 MIN.   OTHER 30 MIN.

- 4 ancho chiles
- 1½ cups chopped onion
- 2 garlic cloves, minced
- 2 Tbsp. vegetable oil
- ⅓ cup raisins
- ¼ cup slivered almonds, toasted
- 1 Tbsp. toasted sesame seeds (we tested with McCormick)
- 1 tsp. salt
- ½ tsp. ground cinnamon
- ¼ tsp. dried oregano
- ¼ tsp. ground cumin
- ⅛ tsp. ground cloves
- ⅛ tsp. ground coriander
- ⅛ tsp. anise seeds
- 1 (14.5-oz.) can petite-cut diced tomatoes with jalapeños, undrained
- ½ cup chicken broth
- 1 (1-oz.) square bittersweet chocolate, chopped

1. Remove stems and seeds from chiles; soak in hot water to cover in a medium bowl 30 minutes or until softened.
2. Meanwhile, sauté onion and garlic 3 minutes in oil in a large Dutch oven over medium heat until crisp-tender. Stir in raisins and next 9 ingredients; cook 2 minutes, stirring often.
3. Drain chiles, reserving ⅓ cup soaking liquid. Process chiles and reserved soaking liquid in a food processor until pureed. Press chile puree through a wire-mesh strainer into a large skillet to measure about ⅓ cup, using back of a spoon to remove skins. (Mixture will be very thick.) Discard skins and any seeds.
4. Process onion mixture, tomatoes, and chicken broth in a food processor until smooth; stir into chile puree. Add chocolate. Cook over medium heat, whisking constantly, 5 minutes or until chocolate melts.

make ahead

Prepare meatballs up to 2 days ahead; cool and place in a large zip-top plastic freezer bag. Seal bag; freeze. Prepare Mole Sauce up to 1 day ahead; cover and chill. Thaw meatballs overnight in refrigerator. Combine meatballs and sauce in a 3-qt. slow cooker; cover and cook on HIGH 2 hours or until thoroughly heated.

Mexican Lasagna

This twist on traditional lasagna is on the spicy side. Use mild pork sausage if you prefer a tamer casserole.

MAKES 8 SERVINGS
PREP: 14 MIN.   COOK: 42 MIN.   OTHER: 10 MIN.

½ lb. hot ground pork sausage
½ lb. ground round
1 (15-oz.) can ranch-style pinto beans, drained
1 (10-oz.) can diced tomatoes and green chiles, drained
1 tsp. garlic powder
1 tsp. ground cumin
½ tsp. salt
½ tsp. pepper
1 (10¾-oz.) can cream of celery soup
1 (10¾-oz.) can cream of mushroom soup
1 (10-oz.) can enchilada sauce
9 (6") corn tortillas, divided
2 cups (8 oz.) shredded sharp Cheddar cheese
2 cups (8 oz.) shredded Monterey Jack or pepper Jack cheese, divided
1 medium tomato, chopped
4 green onions, chopped
1 medium avocado, chopped

1. Preheat oven to 350°. Cook sausage and ground round in a large nonstick skillet over medium-high heat, stirring often until meat crumbles and is no longer pink; drain. Return meat to pan; stir in beans and next 5 ingredients. Cook 2 minutes or until thoroughly heated.

2. Stir together soups and enchilada sauce in a medium saucepan; cook, stirring constantly, 3 minutes or until thoroughly heated.

3. Spoon one-third of sauce into a lightly greased 13" x 9" baking dish; top with 3 tortillas. Spoon half of beef mixture and one-third of sauce over tortillas; sprinkle with half of Cheddar cheese. Top with 3 tortillas; repeat layers with remaining beef, sauce, Cheddar cheese, and tortillas, ending with tortillas. Sprinkle with 1 cup Monterey Jack cheese.

4. Cover loosely with foil. Bake at 350° for 20 minutes. Add remaining 1 cup Monterey Jack; bake, uncovered, 10 more minutes. Let stand 10 minutes. Top with tomato, green onion, and avocado.

Mexican Lasagna

Black Beans with
Saffron Rice

editor's favorite

Black Beans with Saffron Rice

We started with canned beans and a packaged rice mix for convenience and then added characteristic Mexican flavors to create this colorful traditional side.

MAKES 10 TO 12 SERVINGS
PREP: 10 MIN.   COOK: 51 MIN.

1 (16-oz.) package saffron rice (we tested with Mahatma)
4 (15-oz.) cans black beans, divided
1 Tbsp. olive oil
1 medium onion, chopped
1 green bell pepper, chopped
1 jalapeño pepper, minced
3 garlic cloves, minced
1 (14.5-oz.) can diced tomatoes with green chiles (we tested with Del Monte)
1 (14-oz.) can chicken broth
1 Tbsp. tomato paste
1 Tbsp. fresh lime juice
2 Tbsp. chopped fresh cilantro
¼ tsp. salt
¼ tsp. pepper
Garnishes: additional chopped fresh cilantro, sour cream

1. Cook rice according to package directions; keep hot.
2. Rinse and drain 2 cans beans (do not drain remaining 2 cans).
3. Heat oil in a Dutch oven over medium-high heat. Add onion and next 3 ingredients; sauté 5 minutes or until tender. Stir in beans, tomatoes, and next 6 ingredients. Bring to a boil; reduce heat, and simmer, uncovered, 30 minutes, stirring occasionally. Serve over hot rice. Garnish, if desired.

editor's favorite · quick & easy

Mini Churros

Serve these crunchy strands with Hot Mocha (page 112), or dip them in chocolate fondue.

MAKES 30 CHURROS
PREP: 5 MIN.   COOK: 24 MIN.   OTHER: 1 MIN.

Vegetable oil
½   cup sugar
1¼ tsp. ground cinnamon
1   cup self-rising flour
3   Tbsp. sugar
3   Tbsp. butter
1   tsp. vanilla extract
2   large eggs

1. Pour oil into a Dutch oven to a depth of 3". Heat oil to 360°.
2. Meanwhile, whisk together ½ cup sugar and 1 tsp. cinnamon in a shallow bowl; set aside. Combine flour and remaining ¼ tsp. cinnamon in a bowl.
3. Place 1 cup water, 3 Tbsp. sugar, and butter in a medium saucepan. Bring to a boil; remove from heat, and add flour mixture, all at once, stirring vigorously until mixture leaves sides of pan and forms a ball. Let stand 1 minute. Add vanilla. Add eggs, 1 at a time, beating vigorously with a wooden spoon until smooth after each addition.
4. Spoon batter into a pastry bag fitted with a ⅜" star tip. Pipe batter, 5 (3" or 4" long) strips at a time, into hot oil. (Use a paring knife to release strips of batter from pastry tip into hot oil.) Fry 1 to 2 minutes on each side or until browned; drain on paper towels. Roll hot churros in reserved cinnamon-sugar mixture. Serve warm or at room temperature.

Mini Churros

Mexican Chocolate Bar Cookies with Bittersweet Chocolate Frosting

MAKES 12 SERVINGS
PREP: 19 MIN.   COOK: 34 MIN.

1   cup butter, divided
60   vanilla wafers, crushed (about 2½ cups)
1   Tbsp. vanilla extract, divided
2   (2-oz.) dark chocolate bars with chiles and nibs, chopped*
2   large eggs
¾   cup firmly packed light brown sugar
½   cup granulated sugar
1½   cups all-purpose flour
⅓   cup unsweetened cocoa
½   tsp. salt
1½   tsp. baking powder
1½   tsp. ground cinnamon
¾   tsp. ancho chile pepper (we tested with McCormick)*
1   cup powdered sugar
½   cup bittersweet chocolate morsels, melted
3   Tbsp. milk

1. Preheat oven to 350°. Grease a 13" x 9" pan; dust with flour, shaking out excess.
2. Place ¼ cup butter, cut into 4 pieces, in a medium microwave-safe bowl. Cover and microwave at HIGH 40 seconds or until melted. Stir in cookie crumbs and 1½ tsp. vanilla. Press crumb mixture firmly into prepared pan. Bake at 350° for 10 minutes or until browned around edges; set aside.
3. Combine remaining ¾ cup butter, cut into 12 pieces, and chopped chocolate in a small microwave-safe bowl. Cover and microwave at HIGH 1 minute until melted; stir until smooth.
4. Beat eggs, sugars, and remaining 1½ tsp. vanilla at medium speed with an electric mixer until blended. Whisk together flour and next 5 ingredients in a bowl; gradually add to egg mixture, beating at low speed. Stir in chocolate mixture. (Batter will be thick.) Spoon batter over prepared crust, spreading to edges of pan.
5. Bake at 350° for 22 minutes. Cool in pan on a wire rack.
6. Whisk together powdered sugar, melted chocolate morsels, and milk in a medium bowl until smooth. Spread frosting over cooled cookie. Let stand until frosting is set. Cut into 12 bars.

*We tested with Dagoba Xocolatl chocolate bars, which can be found at Whole Foods Market and www.dagobachocolate. com. You may substitute 1½ tsp. freshly ground black pepper for the ancho chile pepper, if desired.

Mexican Chocolate
Bar Cookies with
Bittersweet Chocolate
Frosting

editor's favorite • quick & easy

Pineapple Agua Fresca

Agua Fresca means fresh water. In Mexico on a hot summer day, you can purchase fresh fruit-flavored waters on nearly every street corner. We've chosen fresh pineapple, readily available at Christmastime, to flavor this thirst quencher for our spicy menu.

MAKES ABOUT 6½ CUPS
PREP: 24 MIN.

8½ cups cubed fresh pineapple (about 2 small)
1¼ cups sugar
 ¼ cup fresh lime juice
 3 cups cold water
Ice cubes (optional)
Garnishes: lime wedges on long skewers, fresh mint sprigs

1. Combine first 4 ingredients in a large bowl. Process pineapple mixture in a blender in 3 batches until smooth.
2. Pour pineapple mixture through a wire-mesh strainer into a pitcher, using back of a spoon to squeeze out liquid to measure 6½ cups. Cover and chill thoroughly. Serve over ice cubes, and garnish, if desired.

elf PARTY

Join the elf craze by hosting this fanciful party for little ones. Elf cookies, milkshakes, party bags, a whimsical centerpiece, and more will magically appear when you follow our easy game plan.

menu

FRUIT SKEWERS WITH STRAWBERRY DIP

TURKEY ROLL-UPS

HONEY-GLAZED MUNCHIE MIX

CRISPY COOKIE WANDS

ELF COOKIES

OATMEAL TURTLE BARS

PEPPERMINT MILKSHAKES

serves 10 to 12

For a colorful centerpiece, fill glass jars with holiday candies. Let little guests scoop candies into paper takeout boxes for party favors.

game plan

2 weeks ahead:

- [ ] Make grocery list. Shop for nonperishables.
- [ ] Plan table centerpiece and decorations.

1 day ahead:

- [ ] Prepare Honey-Glazed Munchie Mix; place in goodie bags.
- [ ] Prepare Oatmeal Turtle Bars.
- [ ] Prepare Crispy Cookie Wands.

3 hours ahead:

- [ ] Bake Elf Cookies.

2 hours ahead:

- [ ] Cut Oatmeal Turtle Bars.
- [ ] Prepare Fruit Skewers with Strawberry Dip.

1 hour ahead:

- [ ] Crush peppermints for Peppermint Milkshakes.
- [ ] Prepare Turkey Roll-Ups.

20 minutes ahead:

- [ ] Prepare milkshakes, but don't garnish. Store in freezer.

during party:

- [ ] Garnish and serve milkshakes.
- [ ] Decorate baked Elf Cookies with kids.

Fruit Skewers with Strawberry Dip

You can make the skewers up to 3 hours before the party. The pineapple juice keeps the apples from turning brown.

MAKES 12 SERVINGS
PREP: 20 MIN.

¼ cup pineapple juice
1 medium Braeburn apple, cut into small chunks
1 medium Granny Smith apple, cut into small chunks
12 seedless red grapes
12 seedless green grapes
12 large fresh strawberries, halved
12 (6") wooden skewers*
2 (6-oz.) containers strawberry cheesecake yogurt
(we tested with Yoplait)

1. Combine pineapple juice and 2 Tbsp. water in a large bowl. Add apple chunks to bowl, tossing with juice to coat fruit.
2. Thread 1 piece of each color apple, 1 of each grape, and 2 strawberry halves onto each skewer. Serve fruit skewers with yogurt for dipping.

*Plastic coffee stirrers can be substituted for wooden skewers if the points of skewers are a concern for young children.

Fruit Skewers with Strawberry Dip, Turkey Roll-Ups

make ahead

Turkey Roll-Ups

This recipe offers 3 different cheeses rolled up in deli-smoked turkey so there are options to suit everybody.

MAKES 26 ROLL-UPS
PREP: 11 MIN.

  8 thin slices deli white American cheese
 26 slices (about 1 lb.) thinly sliced deli smoked turkey
     (we tested with Sara Lee)
  8 thin slices deli orange American cheese
  1 (8-oz.) container cream cheese, softened

1. Place 1 slice white American cheese on 1 turkey slice; roll up tightly, and place, seam side down, on a cutting board. Repeat procedure with 7 more turkey slices and remaining white American cheese. Repeat procedure with 8 more turkey slices and orange American cheese slices; place roll-ups, seam side down, on cutting board.

2. Spread about 1 Tbsp. cream cheese onto each of remaining 10 turkey slices; roll up. (Reserve remaining cream cheese for another use.) Cut roll-ups in half diagonally, if desired. Arrange roll-ups on a serving platter. Cover and chill up to 24 hours.

editor's favorite · make ahead

Honey-Glazed Munchie Mix

This snack has just the right mix of ingredients to keep kids of all ages coming back for seconds.

MAKES 14 CUPS
PREP: 10 MIN.   COOK: 35 MIN.   OTHER: 10 MIN.

  3 cups sweet and salty honey-nut snack mix (we tested with Chex Mix)
  3 cups dark chocolate snack mix (we tested with Chocolate Chex Mix)
  2 cups fish-shaped pretzel crackers (we tested with Goldfish)
  2 cups honey-flavored bear-shaped graham crackers (we tested with Teddy Grahams)
  ¼ cup butter
  ¼ cup light corn syrup
  2 Tbsp. honey
  1 tsp. vanilla extract
Wax paper
  1 (13-oz.) package bear-shaped chewy candy (we tested with Gummy Bears)
  1 (14-oz.) package candy-coated chocolate pieces

1. Preheat oven to 325°. Combine first 4 ingredients in a large bowl.

2. Heat butter and next 3 ingredients in a small saucepan over medium-low heat, stirring until butter melts. Pour over snack mixture, stirring until well coated. Spread snack mix on a 15½" x 10½" jelly-roll pan.

3. Bake at 325° for 30 minutes, stirring every 10 minutes. Spread snack mix on wax paper; let cool 10 minutes. Add candy bears and chocolate pieces; toss well with fingers. Store in a large zip-top plastic freezer bag up to 1 week.

Honey-Glazed
Munchie Mix

make ahead

Crispy Cookie Wands

These cookie wands taste like a familiar rice cereal treat, but we've put them on sticks all decorated for little holiday elves.

MAKES 16 COOKIE WANDS
PREP: 16 MIN.   COOK: 25 MIN.

3 Tbsp. butter
1 (10-oz.) package large marshmallows
6 cups crisp rice cereal (we tested with Rice Krispies)
Wax paper
16 round white or holiday-colored craft sticks
4 oz. white chocolate, coarsely chopped
2 Tbsp. whipping cream
Colored sprinkles

1. Melt butter in a Dutch oven over medium-low heat. Add marshmallows; stir until completely melted. Remove from heat; add cereal, stirring until coated.
2. Using a lightly greased spoon, firmly pack cereal mixture into a lightly greased 13" x 9" pan. Cool completely in pan.
3. Cut cereal treats into 16 rectangles. Place rectangles on wax paper. Carefully push a craft stick into 1 short end of each rectangle.

4. Combine white chocolate and cream in top of a double boiler over hot, not simmering, water. Cook, stirring often, until smooth. Spoon white chocolate mixture into a 1-qt. zip-top plastic freezer bag. (Do not seal.) Snip 1 corner of bag with scissors to make a small hole. Pipe white chocolate over rectangles; decorate with sprinkles.

Note: Find craft sticks (the kind used to make lollipops) in the candy-making section of a hobby store.

make ahead

Prepare cookie wands up to 1 day ahead. Place on a tray between layers of wax paper. Cover tightly with aluminum foil, and store in refrigerator.

Elf Cookies

Start with store-bought cookie dough and an elf-themed cookie cutter and let the kids decorate cookies.

MAKES 2 DOZEN
PREP: 18 MIN.   COOK: 12 MIN. PER BATCH   OTHER: 15 MIN.

2 (19-oz.) packages sugar cookie dough sheets (we tested with Pillsbury)
Parchment paper
1 egg white, lightly beaten
Red and green coarse decorator sugars
1 (6.4-oz.) can white decorating icing (we tested with Betty Crocker)
48 milk chocolate or semisweet chocolate morsels

1. Preheat oven to 350°. Using an elf face-shaped cookie cutter, cut out dough (we used a 5" x 4" copper elf face cutter from www.thecookiecuttershop.com). Reroll trimmings to make additional cookies.
2. Place cutouts 1" apart on parchment paper-lined large baking sheets. Brush hats and bow ties of elves with egg white; sprinkle with decorator sugars.
3. Bake at 350° for 10 to 12 minutes or until edges are lightly browned. Cool 5 minutes on baking sheets; remove to wire racks to cool completely.
4. Squirt 2 drops of icing onto each cookie face for eyes. Top each drop of icing with a chocolate morsel.

Note: Find sugar cookie dough sheets in the dairy case of your grocery store during the holiday season.

Elf Cookies

Crispy Cookie Wands

editor's favorite · gift idea · make ahead

Oatmeal Turtle Bars

Here's a deluxe bar cookie for moms to nibble on while the kids enjoy some elf mischief.

MAKES 40 BARS
PREP: 29 MIN.   COOK: 1 HR., 2 MIN.   OTHER: 8 HR.

  Heavy-duty aluminum foil
  1 (14-oz.) package caramels
  1 (14-oz.) can sweetened condensed milk
  1½ cups unsalted butter, softened
  1½ cups granulated sugar
  1½ cups firmly packed brown sugar
  2 large eggs, lightly beaten
  1 tsp. vanilla extract
  3 cups all-purpose flour
  1 tsp. baking powder
  1 tsp. salt
  ½ tsp. baking soda
  2½ cups uncooked quick-cooking oats
  1 (12-oz.) package semisweet chocolate morsels
  1 (6-oz.) package semisweet chocolate morsels
  1 cup chopped pecans

1. Line a greased 13" x 9" pan with heavy-duty aluminum foil, allowing several inches of foil to extend over sides. Lightly grease foil.
2. Combine caramels and milk in a medium saucepan. Cook over low heat, stirring often, 22 minutes or until caramels melt and mixture is smooth. Set aside.
3. Preheat oven to 350°. Beat butter at medium speed with an electric mixer until creamy. Gradually add sugars, beating until smooth. Add eggs and vanilla, beating until blended.
4. Combine flour, baking powder, salt, and baking soda; gradually add to butter mixture, beating just until blended. Stir in oats.
5. Press 4 cups dough into prepared pan. Top with chocolate morsels and pecans. Pour caramel mixture over pecans. Crumble remaining dough over caramel.
6. Bake at 350° for 38 to 40 minutes or until golden. Cool completely in pan on a wire rack. Cover and chill 8 hours. Cut into small bars. Store in refrigerator up to 5 days.

editor's favorite

Peppermint Milkshakes

This yummy dessert drink appeals to all ages. Use less milk for really thick shakes.

MAKES 9¼ CUPS
PREP: 16 MIN.

  8 cups vanilla ice cream
  2 cups milk
  1 cup crushed hard peppermint round candies
    (about 45 to 50 candies)
  1 (8.5-oz.) can refrigerated instant whipped cream
    (we tested with Reddi-wip)
  Peppermint sticks

1. Process 4 cups ice cream, 1 cup milk, and ½ cup crushed candies in a blender until smooth, stopping to scrape down sides as needed. Pour into small serving glasses; top with whipped cream, and place a peppermint stick in each glass. Repeat with remaining ingredients.

Note: Process peppermint candies in a food processor for quick crushing.

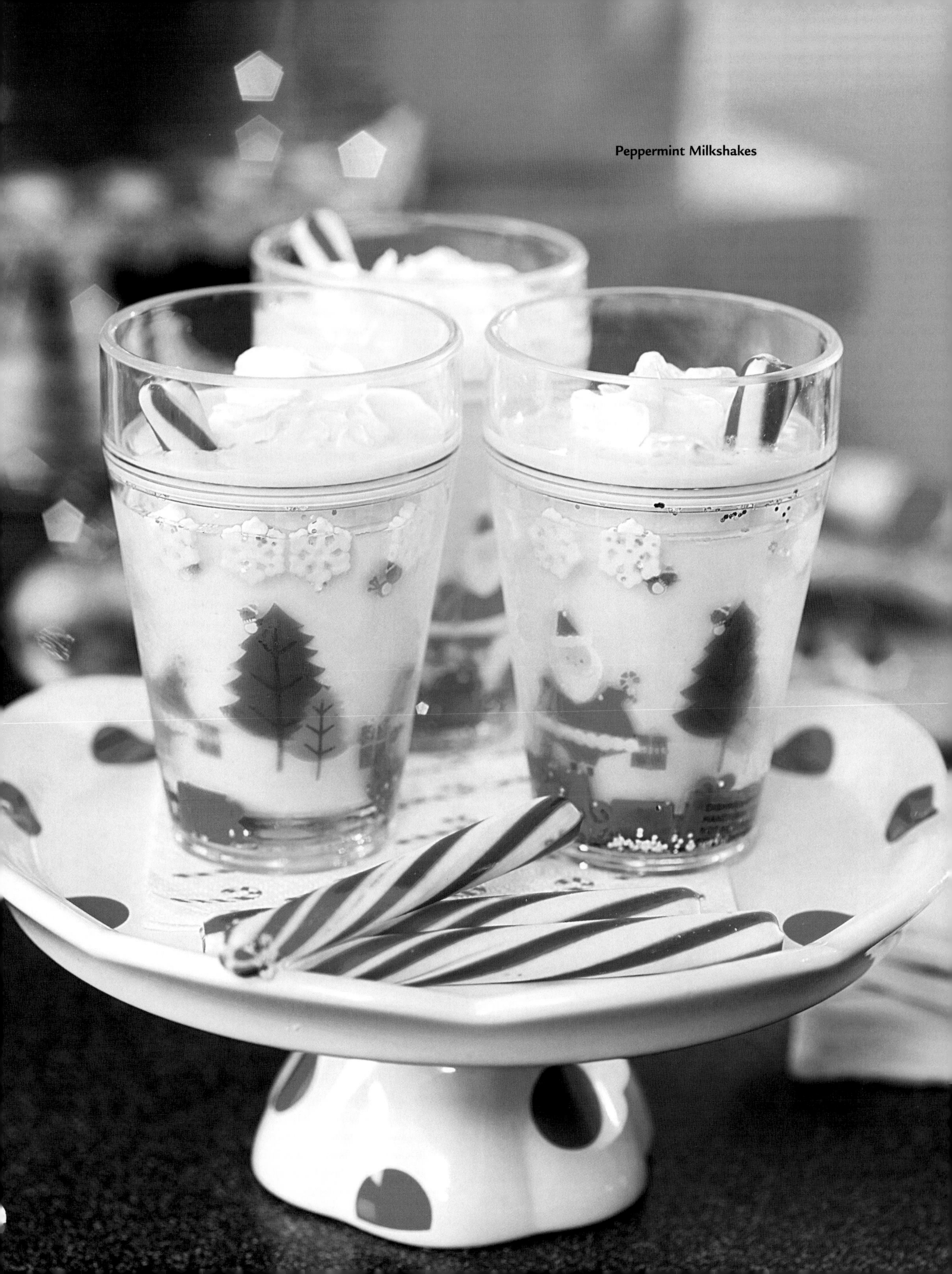

Peppermint Milkshakes

farmhouse HOLIDAY BREAKFAST

A hearty country breakfast in front of a crackling fire is a dream come true on any winter morning. Farm-fresh eggs enhanced with herbs, sugar-smoked bacon, fluffy biscuits, and homestyle charm are the highlights of this meal.

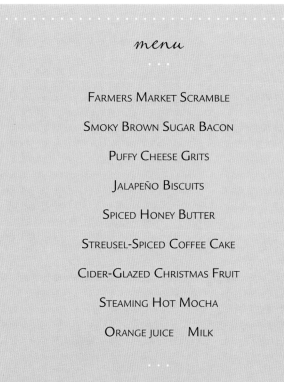

menu

FARMERS MARKET SCRAMBLE

SMOKY BROWN SUGAR BACON

PUFFY CHEESE GRITS

JALAPEÑO BISCUITS

SPICED HONEY BUTTER

STREUSEL-SPICED COFFEE CAKE

CIDER-GLAZED CHRISTMAS FRUIT

STEAMING HOT MOCHA

ORANGE JUICE   MILK

serves 12

game plan

2 weeks ahead:

- [ ] Make grocery list. Shop for nonperishables.
- [ ] Plan table centerpiece and/or decorations.

2 days ahead:

- [ ] Do remaining shopping.
- [ ] Prepare Spiced Honey Butter; cover and refrigerate.

1 day ahead:

- [ ] Mix together Streusel-Spiced Coffee Cake; cover and refrigerate unbaked.
- [ ] Prepare Cider-Glazed Christmas Fruit; cover and refrigerate.
- [ ] Measure out sugar and cocoa for Steaming Hot Mocha.

2 hours ahead:

- [ ] Prepare and bake Smoky Brown Sugar Bacon. Cool completely; cover loosely at room temperature.
- [ ] Bake coffee cake.
- [ ] Prepare and cut Jalapeño Biscuits dough; place on baking sheet.

1 hour ahead:

- [ ] Prepare Steaming Hot Mocha; cover and keep hot until ready to serve.

40 minutes ahead:

- [ ] Prepare and bake Puffy Cheese Grits.
- [ ] Gather ingredients for Farmers Market Scramble.

20 minutes ahead:

- [ ] Bake biscuits.
- [ ] Scramble eggs.
- [ ] Reheat Cider-Glazed Christmas Fruit.

quick & easy

Farmers Market Scramble

Hearty scrambled eggs get a punch of flavor with fresh herbs and tomato.

MAKES 12 SERVINGS
PREP: 10 MIN.   COOK: 14 MIN.

- 24 large eggs
- ½ cup milk
- ¼ cup whipping cream
- 1½ tsp. salt
- ½ tsp. freshly ground pepper
- ½ tsp. hot sauce
- ¼ cup butter, divided
- 1 large tomato, chopped and drained on a paper towel
- ⅓ cup chopped fresh chives
- ¼ cup chopped fresh flat-leaf parsley

1. Whisk together first 6 ingredients in a large bowl.
2. Melt 2 Tbsp. butter in a large nonstick skillet over medium heat; add half of egg mixture, and cook, without stirring, until eggs begin to set on bottom. Draw a spatula across bottom of skillet to form large curds. Cook until eggs are thickened but still moist. (Do not stir constantly.) Stir in half of tomato. Remove from heat, and transfer to a warm platter. Repeat procedure with remaining butter, egg mixture, and tomato. Sprinkle whole platter of eggs with chives and parsley; serve hot.

editor's favorite

Smoky Brown Sugar Bacon

This bacon takes a little while to prepare, but it's more than worth it. The aroma alone gets our highest rating.

MAKES 24 SLICES
PREP: 12 MIN.   COOK: 20 MIN. PER BATCH

- 3 cups firmly packed light brown sugar
- 24 slices applewood smoked bacon (we tested with Nueske's)*

1. Preheat oven to 425°. Spread brown sugar onto a large plate; dredge half of bacon in sugar, pressing to be sure plenty of sugar sticks to both sides of bacon. Place bacon in a single layer on a large baking rack on an aluminum foil-lined rimmed baking sheet. Bake at 425° for 18 to 20 minutes or until crisp. Remove bacon from rack to a serving platter or parchment paper to cool. Repeat with remaining bacon and brown sugar.

*For this recipe, we used 1½ (1-lb.) packages Nueske's applewood smoked bacon to yield the 24 slices; otherwise, any thick-cut bacon, smoked or not, would also work fine in this recipe.

Puffy Cheese Grits

This airy grits casserole stands tall as it finishes baking. Plan to bring it straight from the oven to the table.

MAKES 12 SERVINGS
PREP: 21 MIN.   COOK: 20 MIN.

  1 cup milk
  1 cup water
  1 tsp. salt
  1 cup uncooked quick-cooking grits
  ⅓ cup unsalted butter
  ¼ tsp. ground white pepper
  4 large egg yolks
1½ cups (6 oz.) shredded Monterey Jack cheese
  8 large egg whites
  ¼ tsp. cream of tartar

1. Preheat oven to 425°. Combine first 3 ingredients in a large saucepan. Bring to a boil; stir in grits. Reduce heat, and simmer 3 minutes or until thickened, stirring often. Remove from heat; add butter and pepper, stirring until butter melts. Stir in egg yolks, 1 at a time, and cheese.
2. Beat egg whites and cream of tartar at high speed with an electric mixer until stiff peaks form. Fold one-third of beaten egg whites into grits; fold in remaining egg whites. Pour into a lightly greased 13" x 9" baking dish. Bake at 425° for 20 minutes or until puffed and browned. Serve immediately.

Round out this menu's farmhouse theme by serving milk in old-fashioned, single-serving milk bottles.

Jalapeño Biscuits

If you prefer less heat in these big yummy biscuits, seed the jalapeños before chopping them.

MAKES 20 BISCUITS
PREP: 15 MIN. COOK: 18 MIN.

    4   cups all-purpose flour
    2   Tbsp. baking powder
    1   tsp. salt
    ⅔   cup butter, chilled and cut into pieces
    2   medium jalapeño peppers, minced (about ¼ cup)
 1½ to 1¾ cups buttermilk
        Melted butter (optional)

1. Preheat oven to 425°. Combine first 3 ingredients; cut in ⅔ cup butter with a pastry blender or 2 knives until crumbly. Stir in jalapeño. Add buttermilk, stirring just until dry ingredients are moistened.
2. Turn out dough onto a lightly floured surface, and knead lightly 3 or 4 times. Pat or roll dough to ½" thickness; cut with a 2½" round cutter. Place on a lightly greased baking sheet.
3. Bake at 425° for 16 to 18 minutes or until golden. Brush with melted butter, if desired, before serving.

make ahead · quick & easy

Spiced Honey Butter

Make this sweet and spicy butter in advance so the flavors have a chance to blend; it's wonderful spread over coffee cake or fresh-from-the-oven biscuits.

MAKES 1¼ CUPS
PREP: 9 MIN.

    1   cup unsalted butter, softened
    ¼   cup raw honey or regular processed honey
    ¼   tsp. freshly grated nutmeg
    ¼   tsp. ground cinnamon
        Pinch of ground cloves

1. Combine all ingredients in a bowl; beat at medium speed with a handheld electric mixer until blended. Serve at room temperature. Store in refrigerator.

make ahead

Streusel-Spiced Coffee Cake

MAKES 12 SERVINGS
PREP: 16 MIN. COOK: 35 MIN. OTHER: 8 HR.

    ¾   cup unsalted butter, softened
    1   cup granulated sugar
    2   large eggs
    1   cup sour cream
    2   cups all-purpose flour
    2   tsp. baking powder
    1   tsp. baking soda
    ½   tsp. ground cinnamon
    ½   tsp. grated nutmeg
    ½   tsp. salt
    ¾   cup firmly packed light brown sugar
    1   cup coarsely chopped pecans
    ½   tsp. ground cinnamon
    ¼   to ½ tsp. grated nutmeg

1. Beat butter at medium speed with an electric mixer until fluffy; gradually add granulated sugar, beating well. Add eggs, 1 at a time, beating until blended after each addition. Add sour cream, mixing well.
2. Combine flour and next 5 ingredients; add to butter mixture, beating well. Spread batter into a greased and floured 13" x 9" pan.
3. Combine brown sugar, pecans, ½ tsp. cinnamon, and ¼ to ½ tsp. nutmeg in a small bowl. Sprinkle evenly over batter. Cover and refrigerate 8 hours.
4. Preheat oven to 350°. Uncover; bake at 350° for 35 minutes or until a wooden pick inserted in center comes out clean.

Cider-Glazed Christmas Fruit

An apple cider reduction and two kinds of apples create layers of flavor in this buttery glazed fruit that is equally good served over waffles, pancakes, or ice cream.

MAKES 6 CUPS
PREP: 7 MIN. COOK: 25 MIN.

    1   cup apple cider
    6   Tbsp. unsalted butter, divided
    ¾   tsp. ground cinnamon
    1   Tbsp. brown sugar
    3   Granny Smith apples, peeled, cored, and sliced
    3   Braeburn apples, unpeeled, if desired, cored, and sliced
    ½   cup granulated sugar
    2   cups fresh cranberries

1. Pour apple cider into a medium skillet. Cook over medium-high heat 14 minutes or until syrupy. Remove from heat, and stir in 2 Tbsp. butter and cinnamon. Set aside.

2. Melt remaining ¼ cup butter in a large deep skillet over medium-high heat. Stir in brown sugar. Add apple slices, tossing to coat. Sprinkle apples with granulated sugar, and cook, stirring often, 8 minutes or until apples are mostly tender. Transfer apples to a serving bowl using a slotted spoon.

3. Add cranberries to buttery drippings in skillet. Cook, stirring constantly, 2 minutes or until cranberries begin to pop. Stir in apple cider reduction, and cook 1 minute. Pour cranberry mixture over apples in serving bowl, and fold in gently. Serve warm.

make ahead

You can prepare Cider-Glazed Christmas Fruit up to 1 day ahead. Cover and refrigerate; reheat in microwave until warm.

quick & easy

Steaming Hot Mocha

Coffee combines with hot chocolate for a bracing drink to be enjoyed on the coldest of mornings.

MAKES 15½ CUPS
PREP: 4 MIN.   COOK: 20 MIN.

   2 cups sugar
1½ cups unsweetened cocoa
   ¼ tsp. salt
   7 cups milk
   7 cups strong brewed coffee
   1 Tbsp. vanilla extract
Marshmallow crème (optional)

1. Combine first 3 ingredients in a Dutch oven. Whisk in milk and coffee until smooth. Cook mixture over medium heat, stirring often, 20 minutes or just until bubbles appear (do not boil); remove from heat. Stir in vanilla. Top each serving with marshmallow crème, if desired.

Steaming Hot Mocha, Streusel-Spiced Coffee Cake

COMPANY BRUNCH

Who could ask for more than this luscious meal sparkling with color, fresh flavors, and healthy, wholesome goodness all on the same holiday table?

menu

· · ·

BASIL MARY

BACON, TOMATO, AND EGG GRATIN

HERB BUTTERMILK BISCUITS

GRIDDLED GRITS WITH CILANTRO OIL

SPINACH SALAD WITH CORNBREAD CROUTONS

FRUIT SALAD WITH LEMON-MINT SYRUP

COFFEE   JUICE

· · ·

serves 16

game plan

2 days ahead:

- [ ] Set frozen O'Brien potatoes in the refrigerator to thaw. (It takes more than one day.)

1 day ahead:

- [ ] Make grits for Griddled Grits with Cilantro Oil; cool and cut into triangles. Stack triangles on aluminum foil and seal edges of foil. Refrigerate.
- [ ] Make Cilantro Oil for grits; cover and refrigerate.
- [ ] Make custard for Bacon, Tomato, and Egg Gratin. Store in refrigerator.
- [ ] Make syrup for Fresh Fruit Salad with Lemon-Mint Syrup; cool. Chop mango slices and place them and the cooled syrup back in the bottle the mango came in. Refrigerate.
- [ ] Make cornbread croutons; cool and store in a zip-top plastic bag.

the morning of:

- [ ] Roast tomatoes; assemble and bake Bacon, Tomato, and Egg Gratin.
- [ ] Cut up fruit for Fresh Fruit Salad. Combine fruit and syrup in a serving bowl; cover and chill.
- [ ] Place spinach for Spinach Salad with Cornbread Croutons in salad spinner to keep fresh. Slice onions, and store in a zip-top plastic bag in the refrigerator. Measure out cranberries and bacon, and store in another zip-top plastic bag in the refrigerator.
- [ ] Prepare Basil Mary.

30 minutes ahead:

- [ ] Prepare and bake Herb Buttermilk Biscuits; remove biscuits from oven. Reduce oven heat to 300°. Add gratin to oven, and bake for 20 minutes to reheat. Turn off oven; keep gratin in oven and return biscuits to oven to keep warm.
- [ ] Cook grits triangles; reheat Cilantro Oil in microwave. Place grits on ovenproof serving platter; drizzle with oil. Cover with foil, and keep warm in oven.
- [ ] Assemble spinach salad. Add salad dressing just before serving, or serve on the side.
- [ ] Arrange gratin, fruit salad, and spinach salad on buffet. Add warm biscuits and grits as guests arrive.

quick & easy

Basil Mary

You'll love the fresh basil flavor in this classic cocktail. We liked it without vodka, but if you prefer a spirited version, add 3 cups of chilled vodka to the pitcher before serving.

MAKES 16 (½-CUP) SERVINGS
PREP: 14 MIN.

- 8 cups low-sodium tomato juice
- 1 cup packed fresh basil leaves
- ½ cup fresh lemon juice
- ¼ cup Worcestershire sauce
- 1 Tbsp. hot sauce
- ½ to 1 tsp. freshly ground black pepper
- ¼ tsp. celery seeds
- Garnish: fresh basil

1. Place 1 cup tomato juice and 1 cup basil in a blender, and pulse until basil is pureed. Add lemon juice and next 4 ingredients. Add remaining tomato juice as needed to fill blender, and pulse to blend. Pour mixture into a serving pitcher; stir in remaining tomato juice.
2. Fill glasses half-full with crushed ice. Pour drink to fill glasses. Garnish, if desired.

Bacon, Tomato, and Egg Gratin

Look for O'Brien potatoes (diced potatoes with onions and peppers) in the freezer section of the supermarket.

MAKES 16 SERVINGS
PREP: 5 MIN.   COOK: 1 HR., 5 MIN.

- 2 pints grape tomatoes
- 1 (28-oz.) bag frozen O'Brien potatoes, thawed (we tested with Ore-Ida)
- ¼ cup chopped fresh chives
- 12 large eggs
- 2 tsp. coarse-grained Country Dijon mustard
- 1 tsp. salt
- ¼ tsp. freshly ground pepper
- 1 (16-oz.) carton egg substitute
- ½ cup 1% low-fat milk
- 8 fully cooked bacon slices, chopped
- ¼ cup shredded Parmesan cheese

1. Preheat oven to 400°. Place tomatoes on a lightly greased rimmed baking sheet. Roast at 400° for 20 minutes or until tomatoes collapse and begin to brown.

2. Reduce oven temperature to 350°. Place potatoes in a lightly greased 13" x 9" baking dish. Sprinkle with roasted tomatoes and chives; toss gently.

3. Combine 1 egg, mustard, salt, and pepper in a large bowl; whisk until blended. Add remaining 11 eggs, egg substitute, and milk; whisk until blended. Pour over potatoes in dish. Sprinkle with bacon and Parmesan.

4. Bake, uncovered, at 350° for 45 minutes or until set.

Herb Buttermilk Biscuits

Sometimes known as "angel biscuits," this type of biscuit is made with yeast, which makes the end result extra light and tender. You can find fresh poultry herbs (a mixture of thyme, sage, rosemary, and marjoram) packaged together in many produce sections along with other fresh herbs. Or, you can blend your own herbs as desired.

MAKES 20 BISCUITS
PREP: 17 MIN. COOK: 15 MIN. OTHER: 1 HR.

- 1 (¼-oz.) package active dry yeast
- ½ cup warm water (100° to 110°)
- 4½ cups all-purpose flour
- ½ cup yellow cornmeal
- ¼ cup sugar
- 1 tsp. baking powder
- 1 tsp. baking soda
- 1 tsp. salt
- 9 Tbsp. butter, divided
- 2 cups low-fat buttermilk
- ¼ cup finely chopped fresh poultry herbs
- Butter-flavored cooking spray

1. Combine yeast and warm water (100° to 110°) in a 1-cup glass measuring cup; let stand 5 minutes.

2. Preheat oven to 450°. Whisk together flour and next 5 ingredients in a large bowl. Cut 1 stick of butter into small pieces. Cut into flour mixture with a pastry blender until mixture resembles coarse meal. Add yeast mixture, buttermilk, and herbs; stir with a fork just until dry ingredients are moistened. Cover and chill dough for 1 hour.

3. Turn out dough onto a floured surface; knead lightly 5 times. Roll dough to ½" thickness; cut with a 2½" round biscuit cutter. Place biscuits on 2 large baking sheets coated with cooking spray. Melt remaining 1 Tbsp. butter; brush lightly over biscuits.

4. Bake at 450° for 12 to 15 minutes or until golden.

Basil Mary

Bacon, Tomato, and Egg Gratin;
Griddled Grits with Cilantro Oil,
page 152

make ahead

Griddled Grits with Cilantro Oil

(pictured on pages 149 and 151)

MAKES 16 SERVINGS
PREP: 12 MIN.   COOK: 26 MIN.   OTHER: 2 HR.

- 1 (14-oz.) can low-sodium fat-free chicken broth
- 2 cups uncooked quick-cooking grits
- 1 tsp. salt
- ½ tsp. freshly ground black pepper
- 2 oz. fontina cheese, diced
- Butter-flavored cooking spray
- 2 thin green onions, cut into 1" pieces
- ½ cup packed fresh cilantro leaves
- ½ cup canola oil
- 2 tsp. sherry vinegar or white wine vinegar

1. Bring 4 cups water and broth to a boil in a 4-qt. saucepan. Stir in grits, salt, and pepper. Bring to a boil, and cook, uncovered, 8 minutes or until very thick. Add cheese, stirring until it melts. Remove from heat, and pour grits into a 13" x 9" pan coated with cooking spray. Set aside to cool completely.

2. While grits cool, process green onions and cilantro in a small food processor until minced. With processor running, slowly add oil, and process until well blended. Pour cilantro oil into a small saucepan; set aside.

3. Cut cooled grits into 8 rectangles. Cut each rectangle into 2 triangles. Place a 12" cast-iron skillet over medium-high heat until hot; coat skillet with cooking spray. Add half of grits rectangles to skillet, taking care to keep rectangles together for easier turning. Cook 3 minutes; coat tops with cooking spray. Turn and cook on other side 3 minutes or until golden. Transfer grits to a serving platter, separating rectangles into triangles, and keep warm. Repeat procedure with remaining grits rectangles.

4. Heat oil mixture over medium heat just until warm. Remove from heat, and stir in vinegar. Drizzle 1 tsp. oil evenly over each triangle; serve with remaining oil, if desired.

make ahead

Cut cooled grits as directed above. Cover and store in refrigerator. Brown grits and prepare herb oil just before serving.

quick & easy

Spinach Salad with Cornbread Croutons

This salad is simple to assemble and sports the holiday color of cranberries.

MAKES 16 SERVINGS
PREP: 5 MIN.   COOK: 6 MIN.

- 3 (6-oz.) packages fresh baby spinach, thoroughly washed
- 1 cup thinly sliced red onion (about 1 medium)
- 1 cup dried cranberries
- ½ cup fat-free red wine vinaigrette (we tested with Girard's)
- 8 fully cooked bacon slices, crumbled
- Cornbread Croutons

1. Combine first 3 ingredients in a salad bowl. Add vinaigrette, and toss to coat. Sprinkle with bacon and Cornbread Croutons before serving.

Cornbread Croutons

Prepare croutons up to a day ahead, and store them in a zip-top plastic bag until ready to serve.

MAKES 5 CUPS CROUTONS
PREP: 11 MIN.   COOK: 10 MIN.   OTHER: 1 HR., 4 MIN.

- 1 (8½-oz.) package corn muffin mix (we tested with Jiffy)
- 1 large egg
- ⅓ cup 1% low-fat milk

1. Preheat oven to 400°. Stir together all ingredients in a bowl just until moistened; let stand 4 minutes. Using a spatula, spread corn muffin batter into an 8" x 9" rectangle in a lightly greased, parchment paper-lined jelly-roll pan.

2. Bake at 400° for 10 minutes or until golden; turn oven off, and remove cornbread. Cool. Cut cornbread into 1" cubes. Return cornbread to warm (turned-off) oven. Let stand in oven, with door closed, 1 hour or until the croutons are dry and crunchy.

Fruit Salad with Lemon-Mint Syrup

MAKES 16 SERVINGS
PREP: 27 MIN.   COOK: 2 MIN.

1 (24-oz.) jar sliced mangos in light syrup
1 large lemon
5 fresh mint leaves, crushed
4 large kiwifruit, peeled, halved lengthwise, and sliced
3 cups seedless red grapes
1 cup seedless green grapes
1 pomegranate, seeds removed and reserved
Garnish: fresh mint

1. Drain mangos, reserving 1 cup syrup. Peel 3 strips of lemon rind with a vegetable peeler; juice lemon to measure 3 Tbsp. Combine reserved syrup, lemon rind, lemon juice, and crushed mint leaves in a small microwave-safe bowl. Cover and microwave at HIGH 2 minutes or until syrup begins to bubble. Cover and cool completely; chill.

2. Cut mango slices into cubes, and place in a large bowl; add kiwifruit, grapes, and pomegranate seeds. Remove lemon rind and mint from syrup with a slotted spoon. Pour syrup over fruit; toss. Cover and chill until ready to serve. Garnish, if desired.

make ahead

Prepare the syrup up to 1 day ahead, and refrigerate it until ready to assemble the salad.

Crescent City CLASSICS

Enjoy an elegant menu that pays homage to New Orleans with its piquant Cajun and refined French accents. Let the good times roll!

menu

SAZERAC MARTINI

CREAMY OYSTER-AND-ARTICHOKE SOUP WITH
ROASTED RED PEPPER OIL

CAJUN FRIED TURKEY

ANDOUILLE-CHEESE GRITS DRESSING WITH CRAWFISH GRAVY

ROASTED HARICOTS VERTS WITH CREOLE MUSTARD SAUCE

MAQUE CHOUX

SWEET POTATO BISCUITS

BLACK-AND-WHITE BREAD PUDDING WITH BOURBON SAUCE

BANANAS FOSTER CAKE

serves 8

game plan

2 weeks ahead:

- [ ] Make grocery list. Shop for nonperishables.
- [ ] Plan table centerpiece and/or decorations.

1 week ahead:

- [ ] Prepare sugar syrup for Sazerac Martinis.
- [ ] Prepare Roasted Red Pepper Oil; chill.
- [ ] Prepare spice rub mixture for Cajun Fried Turkey; store in an airtight container.

3 or 4 days ahead:

- [ ] Finish remaining shopping.
- [ ] Place turkey in refrigerator to thaw, if frozen.
- [ ] Cube bread for bread pudding. Seal bread in a zip-top plastic bag.

2 days ahead:

- [ ] Prepare and chill grits for Andouille-Cheese Grits Dressing.
- [ ] Make cake layers for Bananas Foster Cake, wrap in plastic wrap, and refrigerate.

1 day ahead:

- [ ] Inject turkey; cover and chill overnight.
- [ ] Prepare dressing, and spoon into a baking dish; cover and chill, unbaked, overnight.
- [ ] Prepare Creamy Oyster-and-Artichoke Soup up to before adding oysters; cover and chill.
- [ ] Make Brown Sugar Rum Glaze and frosting for cake. Assemble cake, cover loosely with plastic wrap, and chill.
- [ ] Make White Chocolate Bourbon Sauce for bread pudding; cover and chill.

4 hours ahead:

- [ ] Heat oil in turkey fryer.
- [ ] Rub turkey with spice rub mixture; place on fryer rod to drain.
- [ ] Let dressing come to room temperature.
- [ ] Prepare and bake bread pudding.

2 hours ahead:

- [ ] Fry turkey; let stand covered with aluminum foil.
- [ ] Bake Andouille-Cheese Grits Dressing; keep warm.
- [ ] Prepare Maque Choux; keep warm.
- [ ] Prepare Sweet Potato Biscuits.

45 minutes ahead:

- [ ] Prepare Crawfish Gravy.
- [ ] Reheat soup.
- [ ] Prepare Roasted Haricots Verts with Creole Mustard Sauce.
- [ ] Take cake out of refrigerator and garnish.
- [ ] Reheat Black-and-White Bread Pudding and White Chocolate Bourbon Sauce.

10 minutes ahead:

- [ ] Add oysters to soup.

Sazerac Martini

MAKES 8 SERVINGS
PREP: 5 MIN. COOK: 2 MIN.

- ½ cup sugar
- ¼ cup absinthe
- Ice cubes
- 1½ cups rye whisky
- 8 dashes of bitters

1. Stir together sugar and ¼ cup water in a small saucepan. Cook over medium heat, stirring often, until sugar dissolves. Remove from heat; cool. Cover and chill.
2. Coat each of 8 chilled martini glasses with 1½ tsp. absinthe. Fill a martini shaker half full of ice. Add sugar mixture, whisky, and bitters. Cover with lid, and shake until thoroughly chilled. Remove lid, and strain into prepared glasses. Serve drink immediately.

Creamy Oyster-and-Artichoke Soup with Roasted Red Pepper Oil

MAKES 16 CUPS
PREP: 11 MIN. COOK: 1 HR., 3 MIN. OTHER: 4 HR.

- 2 (14-oz.) cans quartered artichoke hearts, drained
- 2½ tsp. salt, divided
- 1½ tsp. freshly ground pepper, divided
- ¼ cup butter
- 1 medium onion, finely chopped
- 3 celery ribs, finely chopped
- 4 garlic cloves, minced
- 1 cup all-purpose flour
- 2 (8-oz.) bottles clam juice
- 6 cups heavy cream
- ¼ tsp. ground red pepper
- 1 (1-qt.) container fresh standard oysters
- 3 Tbsp. butter
- Roasted Red Pepper Oil*

1. Preheat oven to 375°. Place artichokes in a single layer on a lightly greased large baking sheet. Sprinkle with 1 tsp. salt and ½ tsp. pepper. Bake at 375° for 18 minutes or until lightly browned.
2. Melt ¼ cup butter in a large Dutch oven over medium heat. Add onion, celery, and garlic; sauté 4 minutes. Stir in flour. Cook, stirring constantly, 1 minute. Gradually stir in clam juice, cream, remaining 1½ tsp. salt, remaining 1 tsp. pepper, artichokes, and ground red pepper; cook over medium heat, stirring often, 28 minutes or until thickened.
3. Add oysters and their liquid; cook 10 more minutes. Stir in 3 Tbsp. butter. Ladle soup into bowls; drizzle each serving with about ½ tsp. Roasted Red Pepper Oil.

*You may substitute oil from sun-dried tomatoes packed in oil or from red peppers packed in oil for the Roasted Red Pepper Oil, if desired.

Roasted Red Pepper Oil

MAKES 1 CUP
PREP: 1 MIN. COOK: 2 MIN. OTHER: 4 HR.

- ½ cup diced drained roasted red bell peppers
- 1 cup extra virgin olive oil

1. Place both ingredients in a small saucepan. Cook over medium-high heat 2 minutes or until thoroughly heated. Remove from heat; cover and let stand 4 hours.
2. Pour oil mixture through a wire-mesh strainer into sterilized decorative bottles, discarding solids. Seal bottles, and store in refrigerator.

Cajun Fried Turkey

It's easier to insert the thermometer into the thigh if the turkey is lowered into the hot oil upside down.

MAKES 8 SERVINGS
PREP: 11 MIN.   COOK: 25 MIN.   OTHER: 8 HR., 25 MIN.

 1   (12½-lb.) turkey
 ¼   cup chicken broth
 ¼   cup butter, melted
 2   Tbsp. fresh lemon juice
 1   Tbsp. hot sauce
 2   tsp. garlic salt
 3   Tbsp. paprika
 2   tsp. salt
 2   tsp. garlic powder
 2   tsp. onion powder
 1   tsp. ground red pepper
 1   tsp. dried thyme leaves
 1   tsp. dried oregano
 1   tsp. coarsely ground pepper
 3   to 4 gal. peanut oil

1. Remove giblets and neck from turkey; rinse with cold water. Drain well; pat dry.
2. Combine chicken broth and next 4 ingredients. Inject mixture into turkey using a meat injector. Cover and chill 8 hours.
3. Combine paprika and next 7 ingredients in a small bowl; rub in cavities and over surface of turkey. Place turkey, legs up, on fryer rod; allow liquid to drain for 20 to 30 minutes.
4. Meanwhile, pour oil into a deep propane turkey fryer 10" to 12" from top; heat oil to 375° over a medium-low flame according to manufacturer's instructions.
5. Carefully lower turkey into hot oil with rod attachment. Fry turkey 2 to 2½ minutes per lb. or until a meat thermometer inserted in thigh registers 170°. (Keep oil temperature at 350°.)
6. Remove turkey from oil; drain well, and let cool slightly before slicing.

Andouille-Cheese Grits Dressing with Crawfish Gravy

To jump-start this recipe, prepare and chill the grits up to 2 days ahead.

MAKES 8 SERVINGS
PREP: 4 MIN.   COOK: 1 HR., 21 MIN.

 3½   cups chicken broth
 1½   cups uncooked quick-cooking grits
 ¼   tsp. ground red pepper
 1   cup shredded sharp Cheddar cheese
 1   Tbsp. olive oil
 12   oz. andouille sausage, cut into bite-size pieces
       (2½ cups)
 2   celery ribs, chopped
 2   garlic cloves, minced
 1   onion, chopped
 1   small red bell pepper, chopped
 ¼   cup chopped fresh flat-leaf parsley
 2   tsp. fresh thyme leaves
 1   large egg, lightly beaten
Crawfish Gravy

1. Bring broth and 1 cup water to a boil in a large saucepan. Gradually stir in grits. Cover, reduce heat, and simmer 7 minutes or until thickened, stirring twice. Add ground red pepper and cheese, stirring until cheese melts. Remove from heat.
2. Spoon grits into a greased 13" x 9" baking dish. Cover and chill until firm.
3. Preheat oven to 450°. Unmold grits onto a large cutting board, sliding a knife or a spatula under grits to loosen them from dish. Cut grits into ¾" cubes. Place cubes in a single layer on a greased large rimmed baking sheet or jelly-roll pan.
4. Bake at 450° for 20 minutes; turn grits cubes, and bake 10 to 12 more minutes or until crisp and browned. Reduce oven temperature to 350°.
5. Meanwhile, heat oil in a large skillet over medium-high heat; add sausage and cook 3 minutes or until browned. Using a slotted spoon, remove sausage from skillet, reserving drippings in pan; drain on paper towels.
6. Reduce heat to medium. Cook celery and next 3 ingredients in hot drippings over medium heat 3 to 4 minutes or until tender. Combine sausage, vegetable mixture, grits cubes, parsley, and thyme in a large bowl. Gradually add egg, stirring gently to coat. Spoon dressing loosely into a greased 13" x 9" baking dish.
7. Bake, uncovered, at 350° for 35 minutes or until browned. Serve with Crawfish Gravy.

Crawfish Gravy

Crawfish Gravy

MAKES 4 CUPS
PREP: 6 MIN.   COOK: 13 MIN.

  6 Tbsp. butter
  1 lb. cooked, peeled crawfish tails, chopped
  1 large shallot, minced
  2 garlic cloves, minced
  ¼ cup all-purpose flour
 2½ cups chicken broth
  1 tsp. Cajun seasoning
  1 bay leaf
  2 tsp. fresh thyme leaves
  ¼ tsp. freshly ground pepper

1. Melt butter in a large saucepan or Dutch oven over medium-high heat. Add crawfish; sauté 3 to 4 minutes or until browned. Remove crawfish with a slotted spoon, reserving drippings in pan. Sauté shallot and garlic in hot drippings 1 minute or until shallot is tender. Whisk in flour. Reduce heat to medium, and cook 2 minutes or until bubbly and golden brown.

2. Gradually stir in chicken broth. Add Cajun seasoning, bay leaf, thyme, pepper, and crawfish. Bring to a boil; reduce heat, and simmer, uncovered, 7 minutes or until thickened. Remove and discard bay leaf. Serve Crawfish Gravy over Andouille-Cheese Grits Dressing.

Roasted Haricots Verts with Creole Mustard Sauce

Slender French green beans are treated with Louisiana flair in this highly rated side.

MAKES 8 SERVINGS
PREP: 2 MIN.   COOK: 35 MIN.

- 4 (8-oz.) packages trimmed haricots verts or thin green beans
- 2 Tbsp. olive oil
- ¼ tsp. freshly ground pepper
- 3 garlic cloves, thinly sliced
- 4 bacon slices
- ⅔ cup chopped onion
- 2 garlic cloves, minced
- 1½ Tbsp. chopped fresh thyme
- 1½ cups chicken broth
- 2 Tbsp. Creole mustard
- 1 Tbsp. sherry vinegar

1. Preheat oven to 475°. Toss together first 4 ingredients in a large bowl until beans are coated. Spread beans evenly in a single layer in 2 large rimmed baking sheets. Bake at 475° for 14 minutes or until browned.
2. Meanwhile, cook bacon in a large skillet over medium heat 7 to 8 minutes or until crisp; remove bacon, and drain on paper towels, reserving drippings in skillet. Crumble bacon.
3. Sauté onion and garlic in hot drippings 4 minutes or until onion is tender; stir in thyme and broth. Bring to a boil over medium-high heat; boil 5 minutes or until liquid is reduced to 1 cup. Stir in mustard and vinegar; cook 4 minutes or until liquid almost evaporates.
4. Place beans in a large bowl. Pour the sauce over the beans, tossing to coat. Sprinkle with crumbled bacon. Serve hot.

Maque Choux

Omitting the whipping cream makes the vegetables in this dish more vibrant. We liked it both ways.

MAKES 8 SERVINGS
PREP: 5 MIN.   COOK: 34 MIN.

- 10 bacon slices
- 1½ cups chopped onion
- ½ cup coarsely chopped green bell pepper
- ½ cup coarsely chopped red bell pepper
- 2 (16-oz.) packages frozen baby gold and white corn (we tested with Birds Eye)
- 1 Tbsp. Creole seasoning
- 1 cup chicken broth
- 1 cup whipping cream
- 1½ cups grape tomatoes, halved
- ½ cup sliced green onions
- Garnish: sliced green onions

1. Cook bacon in a large skillet over medium heat 15 minutes or until crisp; remove bacon, and drain on paper towels, reserving 2 Tbsp. drippings in skillet. Crumble bacon.
2. Sauté onion in hot drippings over medium heat 5 minutes or until almost tender. Add bell peppers; sauté 3 minutes or until peppers are almost tender. Stir in crumbled bacon, reserving 2 Tbsp. Stir in corn, Creole seasoning, and broth. Increase heat to medium-high; cook 6 minutes or until corn is tender. Stir in whipping cream, and cook 3 minutes or until creamy and thickened. Stir in tomato and ½ cup green onions. Increase heat to high; cook 2 minutes or just until tomato begins to soften. Sprinkle with reserved bacon, and garnish, if desired.

editor's favorite

Sweet Potato Biscuits

Baking the sweet potato in a hot oven for about 1 hour for these fluffy biscuits creates a sweet, caramelized flavor you won't get if you microwave it.

MAKES 3 DOZEN
PREP: 17 MIN.   COOK: 15 MIN.

¾ cup cooked mashed sweet potato
    (about 1 medium)
½ cup butter, melted
3 Tbsp. light brown sugar
¼ tsp. ground cinnamon
2 cups all-purpose flour
2 tsp. baking powder
1 tsp. salt
½ tsp. baking soda
¾ cup buttermilk

1. Preheat oven to 400°. Combine sweet potato, butter, brown sugar, and cinnamon; beat at medium speed with an electric mixer until blended.
2. Combine flour, baking powder, and salt; stir well. Stir soda into buttermilk. Combine sweet potato mixture, flour mixture, and buttermilk mixture in a large bowl, stirring just until dry ingredients are moistened. Turn dough out onto a lightly floured surface, and knead gently 4 to 6 times.
3. Roll dough to ½" thickness; cut with a 1½" biscuit cutter. Place on ungreased baking sheets; bake at 400° for 12 to 15 minutes or until golden brown.

'Tis the season of Réveillon, an old French dining tradition that has become a mainstay in New Orleans. Typically it refers to one long dinner or party held on the evening preceding Christmas Day. It comes from the word réveil (meaning "waking") because it involves staying up until dawn.

editor's favorite

Black-and-White Bread Pudding with Bourbon Sauce

Soft semi-melted chunks of dark chocolate are nestled inside the pudding, while a bourbon-splashed white chocolate sauce is spooned over each serving.

MAKES 8 SERVINGS
PREP: 25 MIN.   COOK: 55 MIN.   OTHER: 10 MIN.

- 1 (12-oz.) loaf French bread, cubed and toasted
- 1 (11.5-oz.) package semisweet chocolate chunks
- 3 cups milk
- 1 cup heavy cream
- ¾ cup sugar
- 6 oz. white chocolate baking bar, chopped (we tested with Ghirardelli)
- 4 large eggs, lightly beaten
- 1 Tbsp. vanilla bean paste
- White Chocolate Bourbon Sauce

1. Preheat oven to 350°. Place bread cubes in a buttered 13" x 9" baking dish. Sprinkle chocolate chunks over bread.
2. Cook milk, cream, and sugar in a heavy nonaluminum saucepan over medium heat, stirring often, 6 minutes or just until bubbles appear (do not boil); remove from heat. Add white chocolate, stirring until chocolate melts. Gradually stir about one-fourth of hot chocolate mixture into eggs; add egg mixture to remaining hot mixture, stirring constantly. Stir in vanilla bean paste. Pour over bread; let stand 10 minutes.
3. Bake at 350° for 45 minutes or until set. Serve warm with White Chocolate Bourbon Sauce.

White Chocolate Bourbon Sauce

MAKES 1⅓ CUPS
PREP: 4 MIN.   COOK: 2 MIN.

- ¾ cup heavy cream
- 6 oz. white chocolate baking bar, chopped
- 1 Tbsp. butter
- ⅛ tsp. salt
- 2 Tbsp. bourbon

1. Cook cream in a heavy nonaluminum saucepan over medium heat, stirring often, 2 minutes or just until bubbles appear (do not boil); remove from heat. Whisk in chocolate, butter, and salt until chocolate melts. Whisk in bourbon.

Both dark and white chocolates take this traditional New Orleans dessert to new heights.

editor's favorite

Bananas Foster Cake

We loved the glaze for this moist cake because it contributes all the luscious flavors of traditional Bananas Foster. The cake's also delicious without the glaze.

MAKES 16 SERVINGS
PREP: 21 MIN.   COOK: 30 MIN.   OTHER: 15 MIN.

Cake

- 1 cup butter, softened
- 1 cup granulated sugar
- 1 cup firmly packed light brown sugar
- 5 large eggs
- 3 cups all-purpose flour
- 1 tsp. baking soda
- ¼ tsp. salt
- 1 cup milk
- 3 ripe bananas, mashed
- 1 tsp. vanilla extract
- Cooking spray for baking
- 2 firm ripe bananas, sliced

Brown Sugar Rum Glaze

- 6 Tbsp. light brown sugar
- 1 Tbsp. light corn syrup
- 1 Tbsp. butter
- 2 Tbsp. dark rum
- ¼ tsp. ground cinnamon

Cream Cheese Frosting

- 1 (8-oz.) package cream cheese, softened
- ½ cup butter, softened
- 1 (16-oz.) package powdered sugar, sifted
- 1 Tbsp. milk
- 2 tsp. vanilla extract
- Garnishes: cinnamon sticks, store-bought pralines

1. Prepare cake: Preheat oven to 350°. Beat butter and sugars at medium speed with an electric mixer until fluffy. Add eggs, 1 at a time, beating until blended after each addition.

2. Combine flour, baking soda, and salt; add to butter mixture alternately with milk, beginning and ending with flour mixture. Beat at low speed until blended after each addition, stopping to scrape bowl as needed. Stir in mashed banana and vanilla. Pour batter into 3 (8") round cake pans coated with cooking spray for baking.

3. Bake at 350° for 25 minutes or until a wooden pick inserted in center comes out clean. Run a sharp knife around edges of pan. Cool cake layers in pans on wire racks 5 minutes; remove from pans to wire racks, and cool completely (about 1 hour).

4. Meanwhile, prepare glaze: Bring brown sugar, corn syrup, and 3 Tbsp. water to a boil in a small saucepan, stirring constantly. Cook, stirring constantly, 1 minute or until sugar dissolves. Stir in butter, rum, and cinnamon.

5. Prepare Cream Cheese Frosting: Beat cream cheese and butter at medium speed with an electric mixer until smooth. Gradually add powdered sugar, beating until smooth; stir in milk and vanilla.

6. Pierce cake layers with a wooden pick; drizzle with Brown Sugar Rum Glaze. Let stand for at least 10 minutes.

7. Spread ¼ cup Cream Cheese Frosting on 1 cake layer; arrange half of banana slices over frosting. Repeat procedure with a second cake layer, ¼ cup frosting, and remaining half of banana slices. Top with third cake layer. Frost top and sides of cake with remaining frosting. Garnish, if desired.

family CELEBRATION

Host a crowd of loved ones with this bounteous meal that begins with a beautiful cocktail and ends with two luscious sweets. And the dinner plate will win raves in between.

Serve sparkling Prosecco Splash in stemless champagne flutes on a metal tray. Cheers!

menu

Prosecco Splash

Roasted Root Vegetable Bisque

Ham with Bourbon, Cola, and Cherry Glaze

Holiday Potato Bake

Roasted Brussels Sprouts and Cauliflower
with Bacon Dressing

Pear and Pecan Frangipane Galette

Chocolate-Orange Velvet Tart

serves 12

game plan

up to 1 week ahead:

- [ ] Prepare Roasted Root Vegetable Bisque (up to the point of sautéing onion); freeze.

1 day ahead:

- [ ] Prepare Holiday Potato Bake, but don't bake. Chill overnight.
- [ ] Cut up vegetables for Roasted Brussels Sprouts and Cauliflower. Chill overnight.
- [ ] Prepare Chocolate-Orange Velvet Tart. Chill overnight.

5 hours ahead:

- [ ] Prepare and bake Ham with Bourbon, Cola, and Cherry Glaze.
- [ ] Prepare Pear and Pecan Frangipane Galette, but don't bake.

1 hour ahead:

- [ ] Thaw bisque in microwave, if frozen, and complete recipe.
- [ ] Bake potato casserole.
- [ ] Bake and finish preparing Brussels sprouts and cauliflower.

30 minutes ahead:

- [ ] Prepare and serve Prosecco Splash.
- [ ] Bake galette.

editor's favorite • quick & easy

Prosecco Splash

(pictured on page 166)

Dress up Prosecco, an Italian sparkling wine, with a splash of pomegranate liqueur and a few frozen berries for a festive cocktail.

MAKES 18 SERVINGS
PREP: 10 MIN.

3⅓ cups pomegranate liqueur (we tested with PAMA)
2 (750-milliliter) bottles Prosecco, chilled
Frozen blackberries and raspberries

1. Spoon 3 Tbsp. pomegranate liqueur into each of 18 champagne flutes. Pour Prosecco into each flute, filling two-thirds full. Drop a frozen blackberry and raspberry into each glass. Serve immediately.

make ahead

Roasted Root Vegetable Bisque

This appetizer soup will get your family gathering off to a delicious start. It's a thick puree of winter's best ingredients, blended with cream and Cajun seasoning.

MAKES 17 CUPS
PREP: 35 MIN.   COOK: 1 HR., 38 MIN.

6 parsnips, peeled and chopped (1 lb.)
4 small turnips, peeled and chopped (1 lb.)
2 medium celeriac, peeled and chopped (1 lb.)
1 large butternut squash, peeled and chopped (2 lb.)
¼ cup olive oil
10 cups chicken broth, divided
¼ cup butter
1 large onion, chopped (about 2 cups)
4 garlic cloves, minced
3 Tbsp. all-purpose flour
3 Tbsp. tomato paste
2 tsp. Cajun seasoning
1 cup heavy whipping cream
½ tsp. salt

1. Preheat oven to 450°. Combine parsnips and next 4 ingredients in a large bowl; toss to coat. Transfer vegetables into a large roasting pan, spreading into 1 layer.
2. Roast at 450° for 1 hour to 1 hour and 10 minutes or until very tender and browned. Process half of roasted vegetables and 3 cups chicken broth in a blender until smooth. Pour vegetable puree into a large pot. Repeat with remaining roasted vegetables and 3 cups chicken broth; set aside.
3. Melt butter in a large skillet over medium-high heat; add onion and garlic, and sauté 7 minutes. Reduce heat to medium. Add flour; cook, stirring constantly, 3 minutes or until browned. Stir in tomato paste and Cajun seasoning; cook, stirring often, 3 minutes. Process onion mixture and remaining 4 cups chicken broth in blender until smooth. Transfer to pot with vegetable mixture. Stir in cream and salt. Bring to a boil over medium heat; reduce heat to medium-low, and simmer, stirring often, 15 minutes.

make ahead

Prepare this soup up to the point of sautéing the onion. Freeze the pureed vegetable mixture in zip-top plastic freezer bags up to 1 month.

editor's favorite

Ham with Bourbon, Cola, and Cherry Glaze

This holiday ham sizzles with Southern comfort. Pick a ham with a fat layer intact that will crisp up when baked and show off its pepper and clove crust.

MAKES 12 TO 14 SERVINGS
PREP: 11 MIN.   COOK: 3 HR., 48 MIN.   OTHER: 1 HR.

  1 (12- to 14-lb.) fully cooked, bone-in ham shank
  1 Tbsp. black peppercorns
 30 whole cloves
  1 (12-oz.) can cola soft drink, divided
  ¼ cup bourbon, divided
  6 Tbsp. firmly packed brown sugar, divided
  1 (13-oz.) jar cherry preserves, divided (we tested with Bonne Maman)
     Garnishes: kumquats, cherries

1. Preheat oven to 350°. Remove skin from ham; trim fat to ¼" thickness. Make shallow cuts in fat 1" apart in a diamond pattern. Place peppercorns in a small zip-top plastic freezer bag. Tap peppercorns with a meat mallet or small heavy skillet until coarsely crushed. Rub peppercorns over surface of ham; insert cloves in centers of diamonds. Insert a meat thermometer into ham, making sure it does not touch fat or bone. Place ham in a lightly greased 13" x 9" pan; set aside.
2. Combine ¼ cup cola, 2 Tbsp. bourbon, and 2 Tbsp. brown sugar; set aside. Combine remaining cola, bourbon, and brown sugar; pour over ham.
3. Bake at 350° for 2 hours, basting with cola mixture every 15 minutes. Remove ham from oven; leave oven on.

Ham with Bourbon, Cola, and Cherry Glaze

4. Meanwhile, combine reserved cola mixture and ⅔ cup cherry preserves in a medium saucepan. Cook over medium heat 3 minutes or until glaze is hot and sugar dissolves; brush ham with glaze. Return ham to oven; bake at 350° for 1 hour and 45 more minutes or until thermometer registers 140°. (Cover ham with aluminum foil during the last hour, if necessary, to prevent excessive browning.) Let ham stand 1 hour before carving.
5. Transfer baked ham to a serving platter; cover with foil. Remove fat from drippings in pan. Whisk remaining ½ cup cherry preserves into drippings in pan. Transfer mixture to a saucepan, if desired, or continue cooking in roasting pan placed over 2 burners on the stovetop. Bring to a boil; reduce heat, and simmer until slightly thickened (8 to 10 minutes). Serve glaze with ham. Garnish ham, if desired.

make ahead

Holiday Potato Bake

Simple mashed potatoes get dressed up in this comfort food dish inspired by twice-baked potatoes.

MAKES 10 TO 12 SERVINGS
PREP: 24 MIN.   COOK: 1 HR., 10 MIN.

  6 large baking potatoes, peeled and cut into chunks
  ¼ cup butter
  1 cup chopped green onions
  4 garlic cloves, minced
  2 cups milk
  2 cups (8 oz.) shredded extra-sharp Cheddar cheese, divided
  2 tsp. salt
  1 (12-oz.) jar roasted red bell peppers, drained and finely chopped
  4 oz. cream cheese, softened
  2 large eggs, lightly beaten

1. Preheat oven to 375°. Cook potatoes in boiling water to cover 15 to 20 minutes or until tender; drain well.
2. Meanwhile, melt butter in a large skillet over medium-high heat; add green onions and garlic. Sauté 5 minutes or until tender.
3. Combine potatoes and green onion mixture in a large bowl; mash using a potato masher. Add milk, 1 cup cheese, and next 4 ingredients; mash. Spoon into a lightly greased 13" x 9" baking dish. Top with remaining 1 cup cheese.
4. Bake at 375° for 45 to 50 minutes or until browned and bubbly.

Roasted Brussels Sprouts and Cauliflower with Bacon Dressing

This is one of the best side dish offerings of the holiday season. Brussels sprouts and cauliflower develop a nutty flavor once roasted, and the bacon vinaigrette adds a smoky hit.

MAKES 12 SERVINGS
PREP: 29 MIN.   COOK: 48 MIN.

1½   lb. fresh Brussels sprouts
  2   medium heads cauliflower (about 2 lb. each),
       cut into florets
  ¼   cup olive oil
  2   Tbsp. sugar
 10   bacon slices
  2   Tbsp. white wine vinegar
  1   Tbsp. olive oil
  2   garlic cloves, minced
  1   tsp. salt
  ½   tsp. pepper
  ¾   cup pitted kalamata olives, coarsely chopped
  1   Tbsp. chopped fresh parsley
  1   tsp. chopped fresh thyme

1. Preheat oven to 450°. Rinse Brussels sprouts thoroughly; remove any discolored leaves. Trim stem ends; cut in half lengthwise. Combine sprouts and next 3 ingredients in a large roasting pan; toss to coat. Spread into 1 layer. Roast at 450° for 45 to 48 minutes or until vegetables are tender and browned, stirring after 30 minutes.
2. Meanwhile, cook bacon in a large skillet over medium-high heat 15 minutes or until crisp; remove bacon, and drain on paper towels, reserving 2 Tbsp. drippings. Crumble bacon. Whisk together drippings, vinegar, and next 4 ingredients.
3. Drizzle vinaigrette over roasted vegetables. Add crumbled bacon, olives, parsley, and thyme; toss to coat.

make ahead

Cut vegetables up to 1 day ahead, and store them in airtight containers in refrigerator.

Pear and Pecan Frangipane Galette

Chocolate-Orange
Velvet Tart

Pear and Pecan Frangipane Galette

Frangipane is a pastry filling made thick with ground almonds. This Southern version of a French-inspired dish couldn't be easier.

MAKES 12 SERVINGS
PREP: 1 HR.   COOK: 45 MIN.   OTHER: 20 MIN.

- 2¼ cups all-purpose flour
- ½ tsp. salt, divided
- ⅓ cup turbinado sugar
- 1 cup butter, softened and divided
- 3 egg yolks
- 1 cup pecan halves
- ½ cup granulated sugar
- 1 tsp. freshly ground cinnamon*
- ¼ tsp. freshly grated nutmeg*
- 6 firm Bartlett pears, peeled and sliced (about 2 lb.)
- 1 Tbsp. turbinado sugar
- 1 Tbsp. fresh lemon juice
- Parchment paper
- Garnish: unsweetened whipped cream

1. Whisk together flour, ¼ tsp. salt, and ⅓ cup turbinado sugar in a large bowl. Add ½ cup butter and egg yolks. Using your hands, gently combine mixture until it resembles small peas and dough is crumbly. Add 3 Tbsp. water until dough forms a smooth ball. (It's crucial to use your hands in this step, so you can feel the texture of the dough.) Flatten dough into a 1"-thick disk; wrap in plastic wrap, and chill 20 minutes.

2. While dough chills, process pecans, 6 Tbsp. butter, ½ cup granulated sugar, cinnamon, nutmeg, and remaining ¼ tsp. salt in a food processor 30 seconds. Scrape down sides; process 30 more seconds or until smooth. Set aside.

3. Preheat oven to 400°. Place remaining 2 Tbsp. butter in a large microwave-safe bowl. Microwave at HIGH 20 seconds or until melted. Add pear slices, 1 Tbsp. turbinado sugar, and lemon juice to butter, tossing until pears are coated.

4. Unwrap dough and place in center of a 16" x 15" piece of parchment paper. Cover dough with a 16" piece of plastic wrap. Roll out dough to a 16" circle. (Rolled dough will overhang edges of parchment ½" on each side.) Remove plastic wrap and carefully transfer parchment with dough onto a large baking sheet. Spread pecan filling over dough, leaving a 1" border around edges. Arrange pear mixture over filling to within 2" of edges. Fold a 2" border of dough over pears. Bake at 400° for 40 to 45 minutes or until well browned. Serve warm or at room temperature. Garnish, if desired.

*We tested with McCormick Cinnamon Grinder. Substitute ground cinnamon and nutmeg for the freshly ground and grated spices, if desired.

Chocolate-Orange Velvet Tart

This luxurious tart is more like a truffle than a pie.
Serve slivers or slices; coffee's a must.

MAKES 8 TO 12 SERVINGS
PREP: 27 MIN.   COOK: 15 MIN.   OTHER: 4 HR.

1¼ cups cinnamon-flavored graham cracker crumbs
     (about 8 sheets)
  3 Tbsp. brown sugar
  ¼ cup butter, melted
  ¾ cup heavy whipping cream
  ½ cup milk
  ¼ cup turbinado sugar
  1 Tbsp. orange zest
  1 tsp. ground cinnamon
  3 (4-oz.) semisweet chocolate baking bars, coarsely
     chopped (we tested with Ghirardelli)
   Garnishes: sweetened whipped cream, orange zest

1. Preheat oven to 375°. Combine first 3 ingredients; press firmly into a lightly greased 9" pie plate.
2. Bake at 375° for 11 minutes or until lightly browned. Remove from oven; let cool.
3. Combine cream and next 4 ingredients in a saucepan. Bring to a simmer over medium-low heat. Remove from heat; add chocolate, and stir until chocolate is melted and mixture is smooth. Pour filling into baked crust. Refrigerate 4 hours or until firm. Garnish, if desired.

impressive table touches

Here are three ideas for freshening up the holiday table.
• **Chandelier Cranberries.** For a beautiful addition to your table décor, fill bottoms of glass globes with fresh cranberries and add small candles (top right); suspend globes from your chandelier with sturdy ribbon. Light candles during the meal.
• **Button Napkin Rings.** Tuck a sprig of seeded eucalyptus or other Christmas greenery into a large-button napkin ring at each place setting (middle right).
• **Fancy Menu Display.** Use a dry erase pencil to write and display your holiday menu on a porcelain memo board (bottom right).

make-ahead PROGRESSIVE DINNER

A progressive dinner lets hosts divide and conquer. Setting the scene and mastering a single dish is all that's required before the party moves to the next home on the menu.

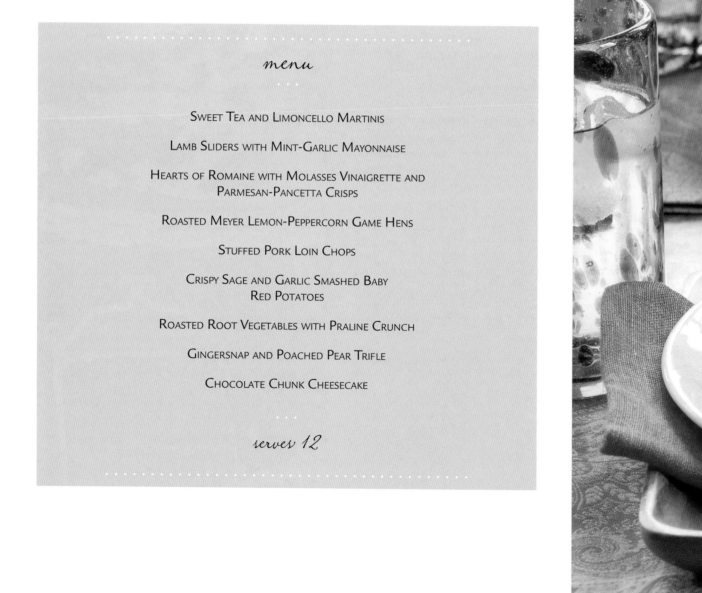

menu

SWEET TEA AND LIMONCELLO MARTINIS

LAMB SLIDERS WITH MINT-GARLIC MAYONNAISE

HEARTS OF ROMAINE WITH MOLASSES VINAIGRETTE AND PARMESAN-PANCETTA CRISPS

ROASTED MEYER LEMON-PEPPERCORN GAME HENS

STUFFED PORK LOIN CHOPS

CRISPY SAGE AND GARLIC SMASHED BABY RED POTATOES

ROASTED ROOT VEGETABLES WITH PRALINE CRUNCH

GINGERSNAP AND POACHED PEAR TRIFLE

CHOCOLATE CHUNK CHEESECAKE

serves 12

game plan

up to 1 week ahead:

- [ ] Prepare Molasses Vinaigrette; cover and chill.
- [ ] Chop vegetables for Roasted Root Vegetables with Praline Crunch and store in a large airtight container.
- [ ] Prepare Praline Crunch; store in an airtight container.

2 days ahead:

- [ ] Prepare, cover, and chill Mint-Garlic Mayonnaise.
- [ ] Prepare and brine game hens.
- [ ] Cook and mash red potatoes; cover and chill.
- [ ] Prepare poached pears for Gingersnap and Poached Pear Trifle; cover and chill.

1 day ahead:

- [ ] Combine and chill ingredients for Sweet Tea and Limoncello Martinis.
- [ ] Prepare patties for Lamb Sliders; cover and chill.
- [ ] Prepare Parmesan-Pancetta Crisps; store in an airtight container.
- [ ] Prepare trifle; cover and chill.
- [ ] Prepare Chocolate Chunk Cheesecake; cover loosely with plastic wrap, and chill.

4 hours ahead:

- [ ] Remove hens from brine. Tie with strings and arrange on baking sheets; chill.

2 hours ahead:

- [ ] Prepare Roasted Meyer Lemon-Peppercorn Game Hens. Cover and keep warm.
- [ ] Stuff pork loin chops.

1 hour ahead:

- [ ] Prepare Lamb Sliders.
- [ ] Prepare Roasted Root Vegetables.

30 minutes ahead:

- [ ] Fry sage and garlic for Crispy Sage and Garlic Smashed Baby Red Potatoes.

10 minutes ahead:

- [ ] Arrange Hearts of Romaine salads on serving plates.
- [ ] Reheat potatoes in microwave.

when guests arrive:

- [ ] Finish Stuffed Pork Loin Chops.

*This game plan is set up as if the menu is being prepared at one location. For a progressive-style dinner, assign and prepare recipes accordingly.

---

make ahead · quick & easy

Sweet Tea and Limoncello Martinis

MAKES 12 SERVINGS
PREP: 4 MIN.   OTHER: 2 HR.

- 6 cups cold sweetened tea
- 3 cups vodka
- 1½ cups limoncello
- Garnish: lemon twists

1. Combine first 3 ingredients in a large pitcher. Cover and chill thoroughly. Serve in chilled martini glasses.

2. For each serving, fill a martini shaker half full of crushed ice. Add ¾ cup tea mixture. Cover with lid, and shake until thoroughly chilled. Remove lid, and strain into a chilled martini glass. Garnish, if desired, and serve immediately.

editor's favorite · make ahead

Lamb Sliders

Regular slider buns were too big for these tiny sandwiches, so we used dinner rolls instead.

MAKES 2 DOZEN
PREP: 23 MIN.   COOK: 4 MIN.

- 1 large egg
- 1 lb. ground lamb
- ½ cup soft, fresh white-wheat breadcrumbs (1 slice)
- 3 Tbsp. chopped fresh flat-leaf parsley
- ½ tsp. kosher salt
- ½ tsp. freshly ground pepper
- 2 garlic cloves, minced
- 2 shallots, minced
- 1 English cucumber
- 24 (2½") dinner rolls, halved and toasted
- Mint-Garlic Mayonnaise

1. Preheat broiler with oven rack 3" from heat. Whisk egg in a medium bowl. Add lamb and next 6 ingredients; combine, using hands. Shape mixture into 24 (2") patties. Place patties on a lightly greased jelly-roll pan. Broil 3 to 4 minutes or until done.

2. Meanwhile, cut 24 thin slices from cucumber, reserving remaining cucumber for another use.

3. Spread cut sides of rolls with Mint-Garlic Mayonnaise. Place patties on bottoms of rolls; top with cucumber slices and roll tops.

Sweet Tea and
Limoncello Martinis,
Lamb Sliders

Mint-Garlic Mayonnaise

MAKES ABOUT ½ CUP
PREP: 5 MIN.

- ½ cup mayonnaise
- 1½ Tbsp. minced fresh mint
- 1½ tsp. fresh lemon juice
- ½ tsp. lemon zest
- ¼ tsp. kosher salt
- ⅛ tsp. ground red pepper
- 2 garlic cloves, minced

1. Stir together all ingredients in a small bowl. Cover and chill until ready to use.

make ahead

Cover and chill slider patties up to 24 hours ahead. Prepare, cover, and chill Mint-Garlic Mayonnaise up to 2 days ahead.

editor's favorite · make ahead

Hearts of Romaine with Molasses Vinaigrette and Parmesan-Pancetta Crisps

MAKES 12 SERVINGS
PREP: 29 MIN.   COOK: 15 MIN.   OTHER: 30 MIN.

6   romaine lettuce hearts
Ice water
Molasses Vinaigrette
Parmesan-Pancetta Crisps

1. Cut lettuce hearts in half lengthwise, leaving stem intact. Plunge into ice water to cover; let stand 30 minutes. Drain well, and pat dry with paper towels. Cover and chill until ready to serve.

2. Trim 3" from stem end of each lettuce heart half, and arrange on each of 12 serving plates. Drizzle with desired amount of Molasses Vinaigrette, and serve immediately with Parmesan-Pancetta Crisps.

make ahead

The lettuce, vinaigrette, and crisps can be prepared a day ahead, if desired. Prepare the vinaigrette while the lettuce stands in the ice water. Assemble salad just before serving.

Molasses Vinaigrette

MAKES 2½ CUPS
PREP: 5 MIN.

½   cup sherry vinegar
½   cup chopped fresh flat-leaf parsley
¼   cup light molasses
2   tsp. salt
1   tsp. freshly ground pepper
3   shallots, minced
1   cup extra virgin olive oil

1. Combine first 6 ingredients in a medium bowl; gradually whisk in olive oil. Cover and chill up to 1 week.

Parmesan-Pancetta Crisps

MAKES 2 DOZEN
PREP: 15 MIN.   COOK: 15 MIN.

2   oz. (⅛"-thick) slices pancetta, minced
    (about 6 Tbsp.)
4   oz. Parmesan cheese, grated
Parchment paper

1. Preheat oven to 400°. Cook pancetta in a large nonstick skillet over medium-high heat 7 minutes or until crisp, stirring occasionally; remove pancetta, and drain on paper towels.

2. Spoon cheese by about 1 Tbsp. into 24 portions 2" apart on large baking sheets lined with parchment paper; flatten each portion slightly, and sprinkle with pancetta. Bake at 400° for 5 to 8 minutes or until lightly browned and crisp. Immediately transfer crisps to a wire rack, using a spatula; let cool completely.

Roasted Meyer Lemon-Peppercorn Game Hens

MAKES 12 SERVINGS
PREP: 15 MIN.   COOK: 1 HR., 25 MIN.   OTHER: 8 HR., 15 MIN.

These succulent little birds are worth the wait; the overnight brining makes them tender and juicy.

  1 cup kosher salt
  1 cup sugar
  2 Meyer lemons, thinly sliced
  2 tsp. freshly ground mixed peppercorns*
  4 bay leaves
  3 qt. ice water
12 (1½-lb.) Cornish hens
  2 Tbsp. Meyer lemon zest
  2 Tbsp. freshly ground mixed peppercorns
  ¼ cup butter, melted

1. Bring 1 qt. water, kosher salt, and next 4 ingredients to a boil in a large stockpot over medium-high heat. Reduce heat, and simmer 30 minutes. Stir in 3 qt. ice water. Rinse hens; pat dry, and add to brine. Cover and chill 8 hours or overnight.

2. Preheat oven to 425°. Remove hens from brine; pat dry. Tuck wing tips under. Tie legs together with string. Stir together lemon zest and 2 Tbsp. mixed peppercorns; rub spice mixture on all sides of hens. Arrange hens on racks in 2 large foil-lined rimmed baking sheets. Brush with melted butter.

3. Bake at 425° for 50 minutes or until hens are done. Cover and let stand 15 minutes before serving.

*We tested with Alessi Tip N' Grind Whole Mixed Peppercorns.

make ahead

Brine hens up to 2 days ahead. Remove from brine; pat dry, and prepare for baking. Cover and chill until ready to bake.

Stuffed Pork Loin Chops

editor's favorite • make ahead

Stuffed Pork Loin Chops

MAKES 8 SERVINGS
PREP: 10 MIN.   COOK: 46 MIN.   OTHER: 1 HR.

    1 Tbsp. oil from sun-dried tomatoes
    8 sun-dried tomatoes in oil, drained and minced
    2 garlic cloves, minced
    1 tsp. salt, divided
    1 tsp. freshly ground pepper, divided
    2 tsp. minced fresh thyme, divided
    ½ cup Japanese breadcrumbs (panko)
    ½ cup (4 oz.) crumbled goat cheese
    2 Tbsp. shredded Parmesan cheese
    8 (1"-thick) boneless pork loin chops
    2 Tbsp. olive oil, divided
    2 cups chicken broth
    2 tsp. lemon zest
    4 tsp. Dijon mustard
    2 Tbsp. fresh lemon juice
    2 Tbsp. butter

1. Heat sun-dried tomato oil in a large nonstick skillet; add tomatoes, garlic, ½ tsp. salt, ½ tsp. pepper, and 1 tsp. thyme. Sauté 2 minutes; transfer tomato mixture to a bowl. Stir in breadcrumbs and cheeses.

2. Cut a slit (about 2" deep and 3" long; do not cut in half) in thick side of each pork chop to form a pocket. Spoon 2 Tbsp. goat cheese mixture in each pocket. Pinch edges to seal. Sprinkle pork with remaining ½ tsp. salt and ½ tsp. pepper. Cover and chill 1 hour.

3. Preheat oven to 450°. Heat 1 Tbsp. olive oil in a large nonstick skillet over medium-high heat. Add half of pork; cook 2 minutes on each side. Place pork on a cooling rack in a rimmed baking sheet. Repeat procedure with remaining oil and pork. Bake at 450° for 25 minutes or until a thermometer inserted in center registers 155°.

4. Meanwhile, stir together remaining 1 tsp. thyme, 2 cups chicken broth, and next 3 ingredients in a small bowl; add to pan, stirring to loosen browned bits. Bring to a boil; reduce heat, and simmer 7 minutes or until slightly thickened. Stir in butter. Serve pork with sauce.

make ahead

Prepare and chill pork chops as directed, setting drippings aside. When guests arrive, place pork in oven to bake. Reheat drippings while pork bakes; finish sauce.

editor's favorite • make ahead

Crispy Sage and Garlic Smashed Baby Red Potatoes

(pictured on page 179)

MAKES 12 SERVINGS
PREP: 17 MIN.   COOK: 27 MIN.   OTHER: 10 MIN.

    6 lb. small red potatoes, halved (about 40 potatoes)
    2 cups milk
    ⅓ cup butter, melted
    2 tsp. kosher salt
  1½ tsp. freshly ground pepper
    4 garlic cloves, minced
    ½ cup extra virgin olive oil
   12 large garlic cloves, thinly sliced
   20 large fresh sage leaves

1. Cook potatoes in boiling salted water to cover in a large Dutch oven 20 minutes or until potato is tender. Drain; return potatoes to pan.

2. Combine milk and next 4 ingredients in a 4-cup glass measuring cup. Microwave at HIGH 2 to 3 minutes or until butter melts. Add milk mixture to potato; mash with a potato masher to desired consistency. Cover and keep warm.

3. Heat oil in a small skillet over medium-low heat; add garlic slices, and fry 2 to 3 minutes or until lightly browned. Remove garlic from oil, using a slotted spoon; drain on paper towels.

4. Increase heat to medium; add half of sage leaves. Fry 45 seconds or until crisp and browned. Remove sage leaves from oil, using a slotted spoon. Drain on paper towels. Repeat procedure with remaining half of sage leaves. Remove pan from heat; let oil cool 10 minutes.

5. Crumble sage leaves slightly. Before serving, drizzle oil over potatoes; sprinkle with sage leaves and garlic slices.

make ahead

Cook and mash potato as directed up to 2 days ahead. Cover and chill. Just before serving, reheat potato in microwave, and fry garlic slices and sage leaves to complete recipe as directed.

editor's favorite

Roasted Root Vegetables with Praline Crunch

(pictured on page 179)

MAKES 12 SERVINGS
PREP: 13 MIN.   COOK: 45 MIN.   OTHER: 35 MIN.

2   lb. carrots, peeled, halved lengthwise, and cut into
    2" pieces
2   lb. parsnips, peeled, halved lengthwise, and cut into
    2" pieces
2   large red onions, halved lengthwise and cut into
    1" wedges
½   cup extra virgin olive oil
1   Tbsp. kosher salt
½   tsp. freshly ground pepper
    Praline Crunch

1. Preheat oven to 425°. Combine first 6 ingredients in a large bowl, tossing to coat vegetables. Arrange in a single layer on 2 foil-lined rimmed baking sheets. Bake at 425° for 30 minutes. Stir and bake for 10 more minutes. Remove from oven. Sprinkle with Praline Crunch.

Praline Crunch

MAKES ABOUT 2 CUPS
PREP: 5 MIN.   COOK: 5 MIN.   OTHER: 35 MIN.

1   cup sugar
¾   cup chopped pecans
1   tsp. kosher salt

1. Lightly grease a large baking sheet. Combine sugar and ¼ cup water in a medium skillet; cook over medium-high heat 8 minutes or until sugar caramelizes, tipping pan to incorporate mixture.
2. Stir in pecans and salt; remove from heat. Quickly spread mixture onto prepared pan. Cool completely. Peel Praline Crunch off baking sheet, break into large pieces, and chop. Store in an airtight container for up to 1 week.

make ahead

Chop vegetables and store in a large airtight container in the refrigerator up to 3 days ahead. Prepare and store Praline Crunch.

---

make ahead

Gingersnap and Poached Pear Trifle

This dessert offers ample make-ahead opportunities, leaving simple assembly to be done shortly before your guests arrive.

MAKES 10 SERVINGS
PREP: 13 MIN.   COOK: 19 MIN.   OTHER: 11 HR.

6   large ripe pears, peeled, cored, and cut into 1" cubes
2   cups Chardonnay or other dry white wine
½   cup sugar
1   (3") cinnamon stick
1   vanilla bean, split lengthwise
1   whole clove
1   (4.6-oz.) package vanilla-flavored cook-and-serve
    pudding mix
3   cups milk
1½ cups heavy cream
3   Tbsp. sugar
1   (1-lb.) package gingersnaps (we tested with Murray)

1. Bring pears and next 5 ingredients to a boil in a large saucepan over medium heat; reduce heat, and simmer 14 minutes or until pears are tender, stirring occasionally. Remove from heat. Transfer pears to a medium bowl, using a slotted spoon. Reserve pear syrup, discarding cinnamon stick and clove. Cover and chill syrup and pears 8 hours.
2. Prepare pudding mix according to package directions, using 3 cups milk. Place plastic wrap directly onto warm pudding (to prevent a film from forming), and chill thoroughly.
3. Scrape vanilla bean seeds into chilled pears, discarding vanilla bean.
4. Beat cream and 3 Tbsp. sugar in a medium bowl at high speed with an electric mixer until stiff peaks form.
5. Arrange one-fourth of gingersnaps in a 3-qt. trifle bowl, dipping each cookie quickly into pear syrup. Sprinkle with one-third of pears. Top with one-third of vanilla pudding and ½ cup sweetened whipped cream. Repeat layers twice, ending with gingersnaps and remaining sweetened whipped cream. Cover and chill 3 to 8 hours.

fix it faster

Save time by using instant vanilla pudding mix or pre-packaged vanilla pudding. You'll need 3 cups pudding.

Gingersnap and Poached Pear Trifle

Assemble Gingersnap and Poached Pear Trifle in
individual trifle bowls for a pretty presentation.
Parfait glasses also work well for this dessert.

editor's favorite • make ahead

Chocolate Chunk Cheesecake

This highly rated dessert will satisfy chocolate and cheesecake lovers alike with its creamy chocolate filling and bursts of chocolate chunks.

MAKES 12 SERVINGS
PREP: 14 MIN.   COOK: 1 HR., 12 MIN.   OTHER: 9 HR., 5 MIN.

- 24   chocolate wafer cookies
- 2   Tbsp. sugar
- ¼   cup butter, melted
- 2½   (4-oz.) semisweet chocolate baking bars, divided*
- 3   (8-oz.) packages cream cheese, softened
- ½   cup sour cream, at room temperature
- 1   tsp. vanilla extract
- 1   cup sugar
- 3   Tbsp. all-purpose flour
- 5   large eggs
- 1   (11.5-oz.) package chocolate chunks, divided*
- ¾   cup whipping cream

1. Preheat oven to 350°. Process cookies and 2 Tbsp. sugar in a food processor until cookies are coarsely crushed. With processor running, pour butter through food chute; process until cookies are finely crushed. Press mixture firmly on bottom of a lightly greased 9" springform pan. Place springform pan in a shallow baking pan. Bake at 350° for 10 minutes; let cool. Reduce oven temperature to 325°.

2. Break 1 baking bar into squares, and place in a microwave-safe bowl. Microwave at HIGH 1 minute; stir until smooth. Beat cream cheese, sour cream, and vanilla at low speed with an electric mixer until creamy. Gradually beat in melted chocolate; beat in 1 cup sugar and flour. Add eggs, 1 at a time, beating just until yellow disappears. Stir in 1 cup chocolate chunks.

3. Pour batter into baked crust; sprinkle with remaining chocolate chunks. Bake at 325° for 1 hour or until set.

4. Remove cheesecake from oven; gently run a knife around outer edge of cheesecake to loosen from sides of pan; cool completely on a wire rack. Cover and chill 8 hours.

5. Remove sides and bottom of pan; place cheesecake on a serving plate.

6. Chop remaining 1½ baking bars, and place in a microwave-safe bowl. Add whipping cream, and microwave at HIGH 1 minute. Stir until blended and smooth; let stand 5 minutes.

7. Pour ganache over chilled cheesecake, allowing ganache to spill over edges of cheesecake; smooth ganache with an offset spatula. Chill at least 1 hour before serving.

*We tested with Ghirardelli baking bars and Nestlé Toll House chocolate chunks.

You can prepare this cheesecake a day ahead. Just cover it loosely with plastic wrap, and chill.

cozy CHRISTMAS EVE DINNER

Set an intimate table for two and toast the season with this Mediterranean-inspired meal at fireside.

menu

CREAMY TURNIP SOUP WITH BACON, CARAMELIZED PEARS, AND ONIONS

ROAST PORK WITH PROVENÇAL BREADCRUMB CRUST AND SHERRY GLAZE

GREENS WITH GOAT CHEESE, PECANS, AND SHERRY VINAIGRETTE

BROCCOLI WITH ROASTED GARLIC AND TOMATOES

MINI CHOCOLATE-CHERRY LAYER CAKES

serves 2

game plan

1 day ahead:

- [ ] Prepare Mini Chocolate-Cherry Layer Cakes; chill.
- [ ] Prepare Creamy Turnip Soup (but not the bacon, pear, and onion topping); chill.
- [ ] Prepare and chill Sherry Glaze.
- [ ] Prepare and chill salad dressing.
- [ ] Roast and chill garlic for broccoli.

2 hours ahead:

- [ ] Prepare breadcrumb crust, and roast the pork.

30 minutes ahead:

- [ ] Reheat soup; keep warm.
- [ ] While pork roasts, prepare bacon, caramelized pear, and onion topping for soup.
- [ ] While pork stands, roast broccoli and prepare salad.
- [ ] Plate the meal; pour wine and light a fire.

editor's favorite · make ahead

Creamy Turnip Soup with Bacon, Caramelized Pears, and Onions

Right before serving, prepare the bacon, pear, and onion topping.

MAKES ABOUT 2 CUPS
PREP: 11 MIN. COOK: 44 MIN.

2 Tbsp. butter, divided
1 cup thinly sliced leek (about 1 small)
½ lb. turnips, peeled and diced ½" (1½ cups)
1 cup low-sodium fat-free chicken broth
3 Tbsp. whipping cream
¼ tsp. salt
¼ tsp. ground white pepper
1 bacon slice
½ firm pear, peeled and thinly sliced
½ small onion, halved and thinly sliced
2 tsp. sugar

1. Melt 1 Tbsp. butter in a medium-size heavy saucepan over medium heat. Add leeks; sauté 5 minutes or until tender. Add turnips, chicken broth, and ½ cup water; bring to a boil. Cover, reduce heat, and simmer 20 minutes or until turnips are very tender.

2. Process soup, in batches, in a blender or food processor until smooth, stopping to scrape down sides as needed. Return to saucepan; stir in cream, salt, and pepper. Set aside, and keep warm.

3. Cook bacon in a large skillet over medium heat 5 minutes or until crisp; remove bacon, and drain on paper towels. Crumble bacon; set aside. Wipe skillet clean with a paper towel. Melt remaining 1 Tbsp. butter in skillet over medium-high heat. Add pear and onion; sprinkle with sugar. Sauté 9 to 11 minutes or until golden brown.

4. To serve, ladle soup into bowls, and top with crumbled bacon and pear mixture.

editor's favorite

Roast Pork with Provençal Breadcrumb Crust

A French-inspired crusting gives this roast an incredible aroma in the oven. Ask your butcher to french the roast for you. If you do it yourself, be sure to cut all the fat from the rib bones and scrape them clean to make a beautiful presentation.

MAKES 2 TO 3 SERVINGS
PREP: 6 MIN. COOK: 55 MIN. OTHER: 15 MIN.

⅓ cup fresh breadcrumbs
¼ cup freshly grated Parmesan cheese
3 Tbsp. finely chopped pitted kalamata olives
1½ Tbsp. finely chopped fresh thyme
2 garlic cloves, pressed
3 Tbsp. olive oil, divided
1 (3-rib) (1¼- to 1½-lb.) pork loin roast, frenched
Salt and freshly ground pepper
3 Tbsp. Sherry Glaze

1. Preheat oven to 350°. Combine first 5 ingredients in a small bowl; stir in 2 Tbsp. oil.

2. Place pork roast, bone side down, in a small greased roasting pan. Rub remaining 1 Tbsp. oil over meaty top side of roast; sprinkle with desired amount of salt and pepper, and pat breadcrumb mixture over oil to adhere.

3. Bake at 350° for 45 to 55 minutes or until a thermometer inserted into thickest portion registers 155°. Let stand 15 minutes or until thermometer registers 160°. Carve roast between bones into 3 chops. Drizzle each serving with Sherry Glaze.

Sherry Glaze

Reserve 1 Tbsp. of this glaze for the next recipe.

MAKES ¼ CUP
PREP: 1 MIN.   COOK: 18 MIN.

2 cups cream sherry

1. Bring sherry to a boil in a medium saucepan over medium-high heat; boil until syrupy and reduced to ¼ cup. Remove from heat; let cool.

Note: To make a nonalcoholic reduction, substitute 1 cup apple cider for cream sherry. Bring cider to a boil over medium-high heat in a small saucepan; boil 15 minutes or until reduced to ¼ cup.

quick & easy

Greens with Goat Cheese, Pecans, and Sherry Vinaigrette

MAKES 2 SERVINGS
PREP: 4 MIN.

1 Tbsp. Sherry Glaze (see recipe above)
1½ tsp. sherry vinegar
¼ tsp. salt
¼ tsp. freshly ground pepper
1½ Tbsp. extra virgin olive oil
3 cups mixed baby greens
1 oz. goat cheese, crumbled
¼ cup sugared pecans (we tested with Hoody's)

1. Combine first 4 ingredients in a small bowl, stirring with a wire whisk; gradually whisk in oil.
2. Place greens on 2 salad plates. Sprinkle salads with goat cheese and pecans; drizzle with vinaigrette.

Broccoli with Roasted Garlic and Tomatoes

Roasted broccoli and tomatoes make a festive pairing for pork.

MAKES 2 SERVINGS
PREP: 5 MIN.   COOK: 42 MIN.

Heavy-duty aluminum foil
4 large garlic cloves
3 cups broccoli florets (7 oz.)
1 Tbsp. olive oil
1 cup grape tomatoes
2 Tbsp. unsalted butter, softened
¼ tsp. salt
¼ tsp. freshly ground pepper
3 Tbsp. freshly grated Parmesan cheese (optional)

1. Preheat oven to 425°. Fold a sheet of foil in half, creasing it to form a double sheet. Place garlic in center; drizzle with 1 tsp. water. Fold foil to seal. Bake at 425° for 20 minutes or until lightly browned and tender. Transfer to a small bowl; mash garlic with a fork. Increase oven temperature to 450°.
2. Combine garlic, broccoli, and oil in a lightly greased cast-iron skillet. Spread vegetables in a single layer.
3. Roast at 450° for 10 minutes or until broccoli begins to brown. Add tomatoes and next 3 ingredients to skillet, tossing to combine. Roast 12 more minutes or until tomato skins begin to split. Sprinkle with cheese, if desired.

make ahead

Mini Chocolate-Cherry Layer Cakes

Share one of these tender-rich chocolate mousse cakes with your sweetie, and freeze the other up to 2 weeks.

MAKES 4 SERVINGS
PREP: 13 MIN.   COOK: 20 MIN.   OTHER: 2 HR., 55 MIN.

Parchment paper
¼ cup all-purpose flour
¼ cup unsweetened cocoa
¼ tsp. salt
3 large eggs, at room temperature
½ cup sugar
2 tsp. hot water
2 Tbsp. unsalted butter, melted
Cherry Syrup
Chocolate Mousse
Chocolate Glaze
Garnish: cherries with stems

1. Preheat oven to 400°. Grease an 8" square cake pan. Line bottom of pan with parchment paper; flour edges of pan. Set aside.
2. Sift ¼ cup flour, cocoa, and salt into a small bowl. Combine eggs, sugar, and hot water in a small, deep bowl; beat at medium-high speed with an electric mixer 5 minutes or until thick and pale. Sift half of flour mixture over egg mixture; gently fold into egg mixture. Repeat procedure with remaining flour mixture. Drizzle butter over batter; fold butter into batter. (Do not overmix.) Pour batter into prepared pan.
3. Bake at 400° for 17 to 20 minutes or until a wooden pick inserted in center comes out clean. Cool in pan on a wire rack 10 minutes; remove from pan to a wire rack to cool completely.
4. Brush Cherry Syrup over cake. Cut cake into 4 squares. Spoon Chocolate Mousse onto 2 cake squares, spreading to edges. Place remaining 2 squares on top of mousse, and press gently to adhere. Chill 30 minutes.
5. Pour Chocolate Glaze over cakes, spreading to cover tops and sides. Chill 2 to 24 hours before serving. Garnish, if desired.

Cherry Syrup

MAKES 3 TBSP.
PREP: 4 MIN.

3 Tbsp. cherry preserves
2 tsp. cherry brandy or ¼ tsp. almond extract

1. Press preserves through a fine wire-mesh strainer into a bowl using the back of a spoon to yield 2 Tbsp. sieved preserves; stir in liqueur.

Chocolate Mousse

MAKES ¾ CUP
PREP: 3 MIN.   COOK: 1 MIN.

1½ oz. bittersweet chocolate, finely chopped
     (about ⅓ cup)
⅓   cup whipping cream

1. Microwave chocolate in a small microwave-safe bowl at HIGH 30 seconds or until chocolate melts; stir until smooth. While chocolate is warm, beat whipping cream with an electric mixer until stiff peaks form; beat in chocolate.

Chocolate Glaze

MAKES ½ CUP
PREP: 1 MIN.   COOK: 3 MIN.   OTHER: 15 MIN.

⅓   cup whipping cream
1   Tbsp. light corn syrup
2   oz. bittersweet chocolate, finely chopped
     (about ½ cup)
2   tsp. cherry brandy or ¼ tsp. almond extract

1. Bring whipping cream and corn syrup to a boil in a small saucepan. Remove from heat; stir in chocolate and liqueur. Stir until smooth. Cool 15 minutes or until mixture is thickened but still pourable.

Christmas FAMILY GATHERING

This bountiful menu delivers great flavor and evokes nostalgia for a simpler time. Pass these hearty dishes around the table family-style for some old-fashioned togetherness.

Set a Unique Place

Usher your family and friends to the holiday table with these ultra cute, miniature chalkboard trugs (shallow wooden gardening baskets) as place cards. Clip variegated holly, pine, Leyland cypress, and pepper berry to fill each trug. No floral foam or water is needed; these materials will stay fresh for several days. Write names on chalkboard strips.

menu

Two Herb-Roasted Turkey with Bourbon Gravy

Country Ham and Sage Dressing

Cranberry Chutney (page 215)

Roasted Brussels Sprout Salad

Roasted Apples and Sweet Potatoes in Honey-Bourbon Glaze

Old-Fashioned Green Beans

Creamed Cauliflower with Farmhouse Cheddar

Dinner rolls

Coconut Cake

serves 12

game plan

2 weeks ahead:

- ☐ Make grocery list. Shop for nonperishables.
- ☐ Plan table centerpiece and/or decorations.

3 or 4 days ahead:

- ☐ Finish remaining shopping.
- ☐ Place turkey in refrigerator to thaw, if frozen.

2 days ahead:

- ☐ Make cake layers, wrap in plastic wrap, and refrigerate.
- ☐ Cook cauliflower. Transfer to zip-top plastic bag; chill.
- ☐ Bake sweet potatoes; cool and chill.

1 day ahead:

- ☐ Make frosting, assemble Coconut Cake, cover loosely with plastic wrap, and chill.
- ☐ Prepare Sage Dressing, and spoon into a baking dish; cover and chill, unbaked, overnight.
- ☐ Make sauce for Creamed Cauliflower with Farmhouse Cheddar, assemble dish, cover, and chill.
- ☐ Make dressing for Roasted Brussels Sprout Salad.
- ☐ Prepare and chill Cranberry Chutney (page 215).

5 hours ahead:

- ☐ Assemble and bake Roasted Apples and Sweet Potatoes.

4 hours ahead:

- ☐ Prepare Two Herb-Roasted Turkey; bake. Cover with aluminum foil.

2 hours ahead:

- ☐ Cook giblets and neck for Bourbon Gravy.
- ☐ Roast Brussels sprouts.
- ☐ Let dressing come to room temperature.
- ☐ Let cauliflower casserole come to room temperature.
- ☐ Cook Old-Fashioned Green Beans.

1½ hours ahead:

- ☐ Assemble Brussels sprout salad (don't add dressing).
- ☐ Bake cauliflower casserole.
- ☐ Bake Country Ham and Sage Dressing.

45 minutes ahead:

- ☐ Reheat Roasted Apples and Sweet Potatoes.
- ☐ Finish making Bourbon Gravy.
- ☐ Bake dinner rolls.
- ☐ Take cake out of refrigerator.

10 minutes ahead:

- ☐ Dress Brussels sprout salad.

Two Herb-Roasted Turkey with Bourbon Gravy

This tender and juicy bird is prepared with a traditional technique and has classic flavor. A bourbon-splashed gravy makes it extra-special. Be sure to set aside half of the gravy for the kids before adding bourbon.

MAKES 12 TO 14 SERVINGS
PREP: 23 MIN.   COOK: 3 HR.   OTHER: 15 MIN.

- 1 (12- to 14-lb.) fresh or frozen turkey, thawed
- 6 Tbsp. unsalted butter, softened
- 1½ Tbsp. minced fresh sage or 1½ tsp. rubbed sage
- 1½ Tbsp. fresh thyme leaves or 1½ tsp. dried thyme
- 2 tsp. salt
- 1 tsp. pepper
- 1 large onion, cut into wedges
- 2 celery ribs, coarsely chopped
- 3 garlic cloves, halved
- Garnishes: fresh sage, fresh flat-leaf parsley
- Bourbon Gravy

1. Remove giblets and neck from turkey; place in refrigerator for use in gravy, if desired. Rinse turkey with cold water; pat dry with paper towels. Place turkey, breast side up, on a rack in a lightly greased roasting pan. Lift wing tips up and over back, and tuck under bird.

2. Preheat oven to 325°. Combine butter and next 4 ingredients in a small bowl; rub 2 Tbsp. seasoned butter inside turkey cavity. Place onion, celery, and garlic inside turkey cavity. Rub remaining 4 Tbsp. seasoned butter all over outside of turkey, legs and all. Tie ends of legs together with heavy string, or tuck under flap of skin around tail.

3. Bake, uncovered, at 325° for 2½ to 3 hours or until a meat thermometer inserted into the meaty part of thigh registers 170°. Shield turkey with aluminum foil towards end of cooking, if necessary, to prevent overbrowning.

4. Transfer turkey to a serving platter, reserving pan drippings for Bourbon Gravy. Let turkey stand, covered with foil, at least 15 minutes before carving. Garnish platter, if desired. Serve turkey with Bourbon Gravy.

editor's favorite

Bourbon Gravy

MAKES ABOUT 3 CUPS
PREP: 5 MIN. COOK: 1 HR., 8 MIN.

Giblets and neck reserved from turkey
Pan drippings from turkey
½ cup all-purpose flour
½ tsp. garlic powder
2 Tbsp. bourbon

1. Combine giblets, neck, and 3 cups water in a saucepan. Bring to a boil; cover, reduce heat, and simmer 45 minutes to 1 hour or until giblets are tender. Strain, reserving broth. Discard turkey neck. Coarsely chop giblets; set aside.
2. Add reserved broth (2 cups) to turkey pan drippings; stir until browned bits are loosened from bottom of roasting pan.

3. Transfer broth and drippings to a saucepan, if desired, or continue cooking in roasting pan placed over 2 burners on the stovetop. Stir in chopped giblets, if desired. Bring to a boil; reduce heat, and simmer, uncovered, 3 to 5 minutes.
4. Combine flour and ½ cup water, stirring until blended; gradually stir into gravy. Bring to a boil; boil 1 minute or until thickened. Set aside some plain gravy, if desired. Stir garlic powder and bourbon into remaining gravy. Serve hot.

fix it faster

Substitute canned chicken broth instead of making home-made broth, if desired.

make ahead

Country Ham and Sage Dressing

This dressing is good any time of year. Serve it alongside roast chicken or pork.

MAKES 12 SERVINGS
PREP: 25 MIN.   COOK: 1 HR., 13 MIN.

1   (1½-lb.) loaf firm-textured white bread, cut into
    ¾" cubes
½   cup unsalted butter, divided
½   lb. country ham, cubed
2   medium onions, chopped (about 4 cups)
4   celery ribs, chopped (about 2 cups)
6   garlic cloves, minced
2   cups chicken broth
1   large egg, beaten
1   tsp. pepper
⅔   cup chopped fresh flat-leaf parsley
3   Tbsp. minced fresh sage
1   Tbsp. minced fresh thyme

1. Preheat oven to 350°. Spread bread cubes in a single layer on 2 large baking sheets. Bake at 350° for 10 minutes or until toasted. Let cool, and transfer to a very large bowl.
2. Increase oven temperature to 400°. Melt 1 Tbsp. butter in a large deep skillet over medium-high heat; add country ham, and sauté 2 to 3 minutes. Add ham to bread in bowl.
3. Melt remaining butter in same skillet over medium heat; add onion and celery, and sauté 8 minutes. Add garlic, and sauté 2 minutes. Remove from heat; add to bread in bowl. Combine broth, egg, and pepper. Add broth mixture to bread, tossing well. Stir in fresh herbs. Spoon dressing into a lightly greased 13" x 9" baking dish.
4. Bake, covered, at 400° for 30 minutes. Uncover and bake 15 to 20 more minutes or until top is browned and crusty.

make ahead

Roasted Brussels Sprout Salad

This vibrant holiday salad can be served warm or even made ahead and served at room temperature.

MAKES 12 TO 16 SERVINGS
PREP: 20 MIN.   COOK: 30 MIN.

1   Tbsp. Dijon mustard
1   large garlic clove, finely minced
2   to 3 Tbsp. white wine vinegar
½   tsp. sugar
½   tsp. salt
¼   tsp. pepper
½   cup olive oil
3   lb. Brussels sprouts
⅓   cup olive oil
1   tsp. salt
½   tsp. pepper
2   cups grape or cherry tomatoes, halved
⅔   cup minced green onions
¼   cup minced fresh flat-leaf parsley

1. Preheat oven to 450°. Whisk together first 6 ingredients; gradually whisk in ½ cup oil until blended. Set aside.
2. Rinse Brussels sprouts thoroughly, and remove any discolored leaves. Trim stem ends; cut in half lengthwise. Combine Brussels sprouts and next 3 ingredients in a large bowl; toss to coat. Transfer Brussels sprouts to 1 or 2 large rimmed baking sheets, spreading into 1 layer.
3. Roast at 450° for 25 to 30 minutes or until tender and browned, stirring once. Transfer roasted Brussels sprouts to a serving bowl, and cool slightly. Add tomatoes, green onions, and parsley; toss to blend. Add desired amount of dressing, and toss to coat. Serve warm or at room temperature.

make ahead

Prepare dressing a day ahead. Store dressing, unbaked, in refrigerator. The next day, let dressing stand at room temperature 30 minutes and bake as directed. Reheat briefly just before serving.

3. Peel cooled potatoes, and slice ⅓" thick. Arrange potatoes and apples alternately in a greased 13" x 9" baking dish. Pour remaining lemon juice over potatoes and apples.

4. Combine brown sugar and next 6 ingredients in a saucepan, stirring well. Bring to a boil over medium heat, stirring occasionally; boil 2 minutes or until slightly thickened. Pour glaze over potatoes and apples. Bake, uncovered, at 400° for 30 minutes.

5. Remove from oven; baste with glaze in bottom of dish, and sprinkle nuts across top. Bake 14 to 15 more minutes or until apples look roasted. Baste with glaze just before serving.

Old-Fashioned Green Beans

These beans are simmered long and slow with premium double-smoked bacon to develop that trademark "Southern-style" goodness. Red pepper flakes add a nice punch to the dish.

MAKES 12 SERVINGS
PREP: 12 MIN.   COOK: 1 HR.

- ½ lb. double-smoked bacon, diced*
- 1 medium onion, chopped
- 3 lb. green beans, trimmed
- 1 tsp. dried crushed red pepper
- 1 tsp. salt
- 2 Tbsp. unsalted butter, softened
- 2 to 3 Tbsp. cider vinegar

1. Cook bacon in a Dutch oven over medium heat 10 minutes or until browned and crisp. Add onion, and sauté 5 minutes or until tender. Stir in green beans, red pepper, and salt. Add enough water to cover green beans. Bring to a boil; cover, reduce heat, and simmer 40 to 45 minutes or until beans are very tender. Drain beans, and transfer to a bowl. Add butter and vinegar; toss well. Serve hot.

*We discovered 2 great online sources for the specialty bacon: Schaller and Weber from www.germandeli.com and www. nodinesmokehouse.com. Regular bacon is an option too but contributes a milder flavor.

Roasted Apples and Sweet Potatoes in Honey-Bourbon Glaze

editor's favorite · make ahead

Roasted Apples and Sweet Potatoes in Honey-Bourbon Glaze

MAKES 12 SERVINGS
PREP: 32 MIN.   COOK: 1 HR., 47 MIN.   OTHER: 45 MIN.

- 5 large sweet potatoes (about 5 lb.)
- 3 Golden Delicious apples
- ¼ cup fresh lemon juice
- ⅔ cup firmly packed brown sugar
- ½ cup honey
- 6 Tbsp. unsalted butter
- ¼ cup bourbon
- 1 tsp. ground cinnamon
- ½ tsp. ground ginger
- ½ tsp. salt
- ⅔ cup coarsely chopped pecans

1. Preheat oven to 400°. Wash sweet potatoes, and place on a baking sheet; prick with a fork. Bake at 400° for 1 hour or until almost tender. Remove from oven. Let stand 45 minutes or until cooled.

2. Meanwhile, peel and core apples. Slice apples into ⅓"-thick wedges; toss with lemon juice in a bowl.

editor's favorite • make ahead

Creamed Cauliflower with Farmhouse Cheddar

MAKES 12 TO 14 SERVINGS
PREP: 12 MIN. COOK: 58 MIN.

2 large heads cauliflower (about 2½ lb. each), cut into florets
3 Tbsp. unsalted butter
½ cup minced green onions
2 large garlic cloves, minced
3 Tbsp. all-purpose flour
2 cups milk
2 cups heavy whipping cream
½ tsp. salt
½ tsp. freshly grated nutmeg
¼ tsp. black pepper
¼ tsp. ground red pepper
1 cup (4 oz.) shredded Farmhouse Cheddar cheese or sharp Cheddar cheese
1½ cups fresh breadcrumbs*
¼ cup freshly grated Parmesan cheese
½ tsp. salt
¼ tsp. black pepper
3 Tbsp. unsalted butter, melted

1. Bring 4 qt. salted water to a boil in a large Dutch oven over high heat. Add cauliflower; cook just until crisp-tender, stirring often. Drain; rinse under cold water. Let cool in colander.
2. Preheat oven to 400°. Melt 3 Tbsp. butter in a large skillet over medium heat; add green onions and garlic, and sauté 3 minutes. Whisk in flour until smooth. Cook 1 minute, whisking constantly. Gradually whisk in milk and cream; cook over medium heat, whisking constantly, until mixture is thickened and bubbly. Stir in ½ tsp. each salt and nutmeg and ¼ tsp. each black pepper and ground red pepper. Add cheese, stirring until cheese melts. Remove from heat; add cauliflower, stirring to coat well. Spoon cauliflower into a greased 13" x 9" baking dish.
3. Combine breadcrumbs and next 3 ingredients in a small bowl; sprinkle over cauliflower. Drizzle with melted butter. Bake, uncovered, at 400° for 35 minutes or until browned and bubbly.

*To make 1½ cups homemade breadcrumbs, place 3 slices bread, torn, in a mini chopper. Cover and pulse just until you have fine crumbs.

Note: Farmhouse Cheddar gets its distinction, in part, because it's made on a farmer's property, using only milk from his cows. We tested with Keen's.

Coconut Cake

MAKES 1 (2-LAYER) CAKE
PREP: 10 MIN. COOK: 25 MIN. OTHER: 5 MIN.

1¼ cups unsalted butter, softened
1½ cups sugar
4 large eggs
3 cups all-purpose flour
2 tsp. baking powder
½ tsp. salt
1 cup coconut milk
1 tsp. vanilla extract
1 tsp. coconut extract
   Coconutty-Pecan Frosting

1. Preheat oven to 350°. Grease 2 (9") round cake pans with shortening, line pans with wax paper, and grease paper. Dust with flour, shaking out excess.
2. Beat butter at low speed with an electric mixer 2 minutes or until creamy. Gradually add sugar, beating at medium speed 5 minutes or until light and fluffy. Add eggs, 1 at a time, beating just until yellow disappears.
3. Combine flour, baking powder, and salt in a medium bowl. With mixer at low speed, add dry ingredients alternately with coconut milk, beginning and ending with dry ingredients. Add extracts. Pour batter into prepared pans.
4. Bake at 350° for 23 to 25 minutes or until a wooden skewer inserted in center comes out clean. Cool layers in pans on wire racks 5 minutes; remove from pans, and cool completely on wire racks. Cake layers can be wrapped and chilled up to 2 days, if desired.
5. Spread Coconutty-Pecan Frosting between layers and on top of cake; let ooze down sides.

Coconutty-Pecan Frosting

MAKES 4¼ CUPS
PREP: 5 MIN. COOK: 10 MIN.

1 (12-oz.) can evaporated milk
1½ cups sugar
¾ cup butter
4 egg yolks, lightly beaten
2½ cups unsweetened organic coconut flakes
1½ cups chopped pecans
2 tsp. vanilla extract

1. Combine milk, sugar, butter, and egg yolks in a 3-qt. heavy saucepan. Bring to a simmer over medium heat; cook 8 to 10 minutes or until frosting is thickened, stirring occasionally. Remove from heat. Stir in coconut, pecans, and vanilla. Let cool.

Coconut Cake

Christmas DINNER WITH A TWIST

We've taken holiday classics and given them a new spin—a surprising flavor, an unusual method, or a novel companion. You may never go back to the traditional versions!

menu

CORNBREAD AND SAUSAGE DRESSING-STUFFED MUSHROOMS

PERSIMMON-AND-POMEGRANATE SALAD

PISTACHIO-CRUSTED BEEF WELLINGTON

PAN-ROASTED PORK TENDERLOIN

GARLIC AND GINGER GREEN BEANS

HORSERADISH MASHED POTATOES

ROASTED BABY PUMPKINS WITH JARLSBERG AND HAZELNUTS

DATE-NUT GALETTE

PUMPKIN PIE WITH CRYSTALLIZED GINGER

serves 6

game plan

up to 1 month ahead:

- ☐ Prepare Crystallized Ginger; store in an airtight container.

1 day ahead:

- ☐ Prepare and chill dressing for salad.
- ☐ Prepare beef for Pistachio-Crusted Beef Wellington up to Madeira sauce step; cover and chill.
- ☐ Prepare and marinate pork tenderloin in a large zip-top plastic freezer bag overnight.
- ☐ Prepare Pumpkin Pie; cover with plastic wrap, and chill overnight.

4 hours ahead:

- ☐ Prepare filling for Cornbread and Sausage Dressing-Stuffed Mushrooms; cover and chill.
- ☐ Cook green beans for Garlic and Ginger Green Beans; plunge in ice water. Place in a large zip-top plastic bag; chill.
- ☐ Prepare baby pumpkins, but don't bake.
- ☐ Prepare galette, but don't bake.
- ☐ Prepare sweetened whipped cream for galette; store in an airtight container in refrigerator.

2 hours ahead:

- ☐ Prepare and finish Pistachio-Crusted Beef Wellington.
- ☐ Bake Date-Nut Galette.

1 hour ahead:

- ☐ Prepare Pan-Roasted Pork Tenderloin.
- ☐ Prepare Horseradish Mashed Potatoes.
- ☐ Bake Roasted Baby Pumpkins with Jarlsberg and Hazelnuts.

30 minutes ahead:

- ☐ Bake Cornbread and Sausage Dressing-Stuffed Mushrooms.
- ☐ Arrange Persimmon-and-Pomegranate Salad on serving plates.

10 minutes ahead:

- ☐ Finish green beans.

editor's favorite

Cornbread and Sausage Dressing-Stuffed Mushrooms

The filling for these mushrooms will remind you of Grandma's turkey dressing, so you can enjoy the taste of the holidays without slaving over a big meal.

MAKES 1½ DOZEN
PREP: 14 MIN.   COOK: 27 MIN.

- 18 large fresh mushrooms
- 5 Tbsp. butter, melted and divided
- 4 oz. sage-flavored breakfast sausage (we tested with Jimmy Dean)
- ½ cup finely chopped onion
- ½ cup finely chopped celery
- 2 garlic cloves, minced
- 1½ cups (6 oz.) sharp Cheddar cheese, shredded and divided
- 1 cup fine cornbread crumbs (about 1 corn muffin)*
- 1 slice white bread, torn into small pieces
- 1 large egg, lightly beaten
- ½ tsp. salt
- ⅛ tsp. pepper
- Garnish: fresh rosemary or other herbs

1. Preheat oven to 400°. Remove and chop mushroom stems. Brush mushroom caps on all sides with 3 Tbsp. butter, and place on a 15" x 10" jelly-roll pan.

2. Cook mushroom stems, sausage, and next 3 ingredients in a large skillet over medium-high heat until browned, stirring to crumble sausage. Stir together remaining 2 Tbsp. butter, sausage mixture, 1 cup cheese, cornbread crumbs, and next 4 ingredients in a large bowl. Spoon filling into mushroom caps.

3. Bake at 400° for 15 minutes; top with remaining ½ cup cheese. Bake 5 more minutes or until cheese melts. Garnish platter, if desired.

*You can use a leftover homemade corn muffin or purchase a single muffin from your local bakery or cafeteria.

editor's favorite · quick & easy

Persimmon-and-Pomegranate Salad

Choose persimmons that are a deep orange color and that give slightly when gently pressed; otherwise they will be bitter.

MAKES 8 SERVINGS
PREP: 18 MIN.

　3　Tbsp. extra virgin olive oil
　2　Tbsp. honey
　2　Tbsp. pomegranate juice (we tested with POM)
　2　Tbsp. sherry vinegar
　1　Tbsp. Dijon mustard
　½　tsp. salt
　⅛　tsp. freshly ground pepper
　12　cups sweet baby greens
　2　ripe Fuyu persimmons, peeled and cut into wedges
　½　cup pomegranate seeds*
　½　cup coarsely chopped hazelnuts, toasted

1. Whisk together first 7 ingredients in a small bowl. Divide greens among 8 salad plates; top greens with persimmon wedges, and sprinkle with pomegranate seeds. Drizzle dressing over salads, and sprinkle with hazelnuts. Serve immediately.

*Look for pomegranate seeds in the produce department of your supermarket.

editor's favorite · make ahead

Pistachio-Crusted Beef Wellington

To make this delectable entrée more family friendly and economical, we've substituted duxelles, a rich herbed mushroom mixture, for the traditional pâté. If you're a member of a wholesale club, purchase your tenderloin there to make this holiday splurge even more affordable.

MAKES 8 TO 10 SERVINGS
PREP: 30 MIN.   COOK: 1 HR., 13 MIN.   OTHER: 1 HR., 20 MIN.

1	(4-lb.) beef tenderloin, trimmed
¾	tsp. salt, divided
¾	tsp. freshly ground pepper, divided
¼	cup butter, divided
2	Tbsp. olive oil, divided
¾	cup Japanese breadcrumbs (panko)
½	cup pistachios
¼	cup Dijon mustard
2	garlic cloves
2	large shallots, quartered
4	(8-oz.) packages sliced fresh mushrooms
1	tsp. fresh thyme leaves
1	cup Madeira
1	(14-oz.) can beef broth
4	tsp. cornstarch
20	thin slices prosciutto
1	(17.3-oz.) package frozen puff pastry sheets, thawed
1	egg yolk

1. Cut tenderloin in half; tuck narrow end under, if necessary, to create an even thickness in each portion. Sprinkle beef with ½ tsp. salt and ½ tsp. pepper.

2. Heat 2 Tbsp. butter and 1 Tbsp. oil in a large skillet over medium-high heat until butter melts. Add beef; cook 3 minutes on each side until browned. Remove from pan; let cool 10 minutes.

3. Meanwhile, process breadcrumbs and pistachios in a food processor until nuts are finely chopped. Place pistachio mixture in a large shallow dish. Brush beef with mustard and dredge in pistachio mixture. Cover and chill 30 minutes.

4. Meanwhile, with processor running, drop garlic through food chute; process until minced. Add shallots; process until chopped. Heat remaining 2 Tbsp. butter and 1 Tbsp. oil in a large skillet over medium heat until butter melts. Add shallot mixture; cook, stirring occasionally, while processing half of mushrooms until finely chopped. Stir chopped mushrooms into shallot mixture. Process remaining half of mushrooms until finely chopped; stir into shallot mixture. Add remaining ¼ tsp. salt, remaining ¼ tsp. pepper, and thyme. Cook 15 minutes or until liquid evaporates, stirring often. Remove mushroom mixture from pan, and cool to room temperature. Add Madeira and broth to hot pan. Combine cornstarch and 1 Tbsp. water, stirring until smooth. Whisk cornstarch mixture into broth mixture. Cook, whisking constantly, over medium-high heat 1 minute or until thickened. Set aside.

5. On a work surface, overlap a couple of sheets of plastic wrap to create 2 rectangles, long and wide enough to wrap each portion of beef. Overlap 10 prosciutto slices on each plastic wrap rectangle to create a rectangle large enough to completely wrap around 1 prepared beef portion. Spread half of mushroom mixture over each prosciutto rectangle. Place a beef portion on mushroom mixture lengthwise next to a long edge of each rectangle. Using plastic wrap to help, roll up each portion of beef with mushroom-lined prosciutto. Chill 30 minutes.

6. Preheat oven to 425°. Roll each sheet of puff pastry into a 14" x 12" rectangle (or large enough to completely wrap 1 prepared beef portion in dough). Carefully unwrap each beef portion and place in center of a dough rectangle. Wrap each portion with dough, pressing to seal. Place wrapped beef, seam side down, on a large lightly greased baking sheet. Using a sharp knife, slash tops of dough in a decorative pattern. (Do not cut completely through dough.)

7. Whisk together egg yolk and 1 tsp. water. Brush dough on all sides with egg wash. Bake at 425° for 50 minutes or until desired degree of doneness, shielding with aluminum foil after 25 to 30 minutes, if necessary, to prevent excessive browning.

8. While beef bakes, reheat Madeira sauce. Let beef stand 10 minutes before slicing. Serve with Madeira sauce.

make ahead

You can prepare beef through Step 5 up to 1 day ahead.

Let the beef Wellington stand 10 minutes before slicing.

Pistachio-Crusted Beef Wellington

editor's favorite · make ahead

Pan-Roasted Pork Tenderloin

Canned green peppercorns resemble capers. You'll find them with the pickles and olives at your supermarket. Be sure to rinse them before adding to the sauce— they're packed in brine, which would make the sauce too salty.

MAKES 8 SERVINGS
PREP: 6 MIN.   COOK: 41 MIN.   OTHER: 8 HR., 10 MIN.

¼ cup olive oil
2 Tbsp. fresh lemon juice
1 Tbsp. minced fresh thyme
1 tsp. salt
½ tsp. freshly ground pepper
3 garlic cloves, minced
3 (1-lb.) pork tenderloins, trimmed
1 Tbsp. olive oil
2 Tbsp. butter
¼ cup minced shallots
1½ Tbsp. green peppercorns, rinsed and drained
½ cup brandy
¼ cup chicken broth (we tested with Swanson's)
2 cups heavy whipping cream
½ tsp. salt

1. Combine first 6 ingredients in a large zip-top plastic freezer bag. Add pork; seal bag. Marinate in refrigerator 8 hours.
2. Remove pork from marinade, discarding marinade.
3. Heat 1 Tbsp. olive oil in a large nonstick skillet over medium-high heat; add pork. Cook 12 minutes or until browned, turning occasionally. Add ½ cup water to pan, stirring to loosen browned bits. Cover, reduce heat, and simmer 13 minutes or until a meat thermometer inserted in thickest portion registers 155° and liquid has evaporated. Remove pork, reserving drippings in pan; cover loosely with foil. Let stand 10 minutes or until thermometer registers 160°.
4. Add butter to drippings in pan; cook over medium heat until melted. Add shallots and peppercorns; cook 1 minute. Remove pan from heat; add brandy, stirring to loosen brown bits. Carefully ignite the fumes just above mixture with a long match or long multipurpose lighter. Let flames die down. Stir in chicken broth. Bring to a boil; boil 1 minute. Stir in whipping cream. Bring to a boil; reduce heat, and simmer 12 to 14 minutes or until slightly thickened. Stir in ½ tsp. salt.
5. Cut pork diagonally across grain into ½"-thick slices. Serve with peppercorn sauce.

**Pan-Roasted Pork Tenderloin, Roasted Baby
Pumpkins with Jarlsberg and Hazelnuts,
Garlic and Ginger Green Beans**

Garlic and Ginger Green Beans

Simple green beans get spruced up with fresh ginger and garlic. When buying ginger, be sure to pick a root that is firm and smooth.

MAKES 8 SERVINGS
PREP: 7 MIN. COOK: 12 MIN.

- 1½ lb. green beans, trimmed
- 2 Tbsp. unsalted butter
- 1 Tbsp. olive oil
- 2 large garlic cloves, minced
- 1 Tbsp. grated fresh ginger
- ¾ tsp. salt
- ½ tsp. freshly ground pepper
- 3 Tbsp. minced fresh flat-leaf parsley

1. Cook green beans in boiling salted water to cover 7 minutes or until crisp-tender; drain. Plunge beans into a bowl of ice water to stop the cooking process; drain.
2. Heat butter and oil in a large skillet over medium heat; add garlic and ginger; sauté 1 minute or until golden. Stir in green beans, salt, and pepper; sauté 4 minutes or until beans are thoroughly heated. Sprinkle with parsley just before serving.

Horseradish Mashed Potatoes

Microwaving the half-and-half for 1 minute or until very warm before adding it to the cooked potatoes ensures that they will be fluffy when mashed.

MAKES 6 SERVINGS
PREP: 10 MIN. COOK: 18 MIN.

- 2 lbs. Yukon gold potatoes, peeled and cut into ¾" cubes
- ¼ cup butter, softened
- ⅔ cup warm half-and-half
- 1½ Tbsp. prepared horseradish
- 1 tsp. salt
- 1 tsp. stone-ground mustard
- ½ tsp. freshly ground pepper
- 3 green onions, thinly sliced (optional)

1. Cook potatoes in boiling water to cover in a large saucepan 18 minutes or until tender. Drain potatoes, and return to pan. Add butter and next 5 ingredients; mash with a potato masher to desired consistency. Sprinkle with green onions, if desired.

Roasted Baby Pumpkins with Jarlsberg and Hazelnuts

Microwaving the pumpkins for a few minutes before removing the tops makes them easier to prepare.

MAKES 8 SERVINGS
PREP: 20 MIN. COOK: 54 MIN.

- 2 Tbsp. butter
- 1 medium onion, chopped
- 1 tsp. salt, divided
- ¼ tsp. freshly ground pepper
- 1¼ cups (6 oz.) shredded Jarlsberg cheese
- ¾ cup chopped hazelnuts, toasted
- 1 tsp. hot sauce (we tested with Tabasco)
- 8 (8-oz.) baby pumpkins*
- 1 cup whipping cream

1. Preheat oven to 350°. Melt butter in a medium nonstick skillet over medium-high heat. Add onion, ½ tsp. salt, and pepper; cook 3 minutes or until tender, stirring often. Place onion mixture in a bowl. Stir in cheese, hazelnuts, and hot sauce.
2. Pierce pumpkins several times with a small sharp knife. Microwave at HIGH 6 minutes. Cut tops off pumpkins, reserving tops; remove and discard seeds. Sprinkle insides of pumpkins with remaining ½ tsp. salt. Spoon cheese mixture into pumpkins; top evenly with cream, and replace tops. Place pumpkins on a baking sheet coated with cooking spray.
3. Bake at 350° for 45 minutes or until pumpkins are tender.

*You may substitute 4 (1-lb.) acorn squash for the pumpkins. Preheat oven to 350°. Pierce squash; microwave at HIGH 8 minutes. Cut in half vertically; remove and discard seeds. Spoon cheese mixture into squash halves; place on a large rimmed baking sheet. Cover with aluminum foil, and bake at 350° for 1 hour or until squash are tender.

Dress down for dinner by omitting the tablecloth and letting the rustic wood of your table contrast with the glistening silver, china, and crystal.

Date-Nut Galette

Pumpkin Pie with
Crystallized Ginger

Date-Nut Galette

Make a quick-and-easy crème anglaise for this dessert by simply melting a rich French vanilla ice cream and drizzling it over each serving, if desired.

MAKES 8 SERVINGS
PREP: 16 MIN.   COOK: 45 MIN.

1   (15-oz.) package refrigerated piecrusts
Parchment paper
2   large eggs
⅓   cup dark corn syrup
2   Tbsp. butter, melted
1   tsp. vanilla extract
1   tsp. orange zest
¼   tsp. salt
1   cup chopped walnuts
1   (8-oz.) package chopped dates
1   egg white
Sweetened whipped cream
Garnish: orange zest strips

1. Preheat oven to 425°. Unroll 1 piecrust, and place on a parchment paper-lined baking sheet; lightly brush top of crust with water. Unroll remaining crust; place over bottom crust. Gently roll or press crusts together to form a 12" circle.
2. Whisk together eggs and next 5 ingredients; stir in walnuts and dates. Spoon date filling into center of prepared crust, spreading to within 2" of edges. Fold a 2" border of dough over filling, overlapping edges. Whisk together egg white and 1 tsp. water in a small bowl. Brush border of dough with egg white mixture.
3. Bake on lowest oven rack at 425° for 10 minutes. Reduce oven temperature to 350°, and bake 35 minutes or until pastry is browned. Cool on a wire rack before serving with dollops of sweetened whipped cream. Garnish, if desired.

editor's favorite · make ahead

Pumpkin Pie with Crystallized Ginger

MAKES 1 (9") PIE
PREP: 17 MIN.   COOK: 2 HR., 5 MIN.   OTHER: 2 HR.

Crystallized Ginger
½   (15-oz.) package refrigerated piecrusts
3   large eggs
1   (15-oz.) can pumpkin
1   tsp. pumpkin pie spice
1   tsp. vanilla extract
1   cup half-and-half
Sweetened whipped cream

1. Prepare Crystallized Ginger, reserving excess sugar.
2. Preheat oven to 425°. Fit piecrust into a 9" pie plate according to package directions; fold edges under, and crimp. Chill until ready to use.
3. Whisk eggs and 1 cup reserved excess sugar together in a large bowl; whisk in pumpkin, pumpkin pie spice, and vanilla. Gradually whisk in half-and-half. Pour filling into prepared piecrust.
4. Bake at 425° for 15 minutes. Reduce oven temperature to 350°; bake 38 more minutes or until set. Cool completely on a wire rack. Chill at least 2 hours. Serve with dollops of sweetened whipped cream and a generous sprinkling of Crystallized Ginger.

editor's favorite · great gift · make ahead

Crystallized Ginger

Sprinkle chopped Crystallized Ginger on stewed fruit, stir into muffin or cake batter, or dip slices in dark chocolate to accompany espresso.

MAKES 1½ CUPS
PREP: 6 MIN.   COOK: 1 HR., 12 MIN.

½   lb. fresh ginger, peeled and cut into ⅛" slices (about 1¾ cups)
2   cups sugar, divided

1. Cook ginger in boiling water to cover 20 minutes or until tender; drain and let dry on a wire rack.
2. Combine ginger, 1 cup sugar, and 2 Tbsp. water in a 12" skillet. Cook, uncovered, over medium-low heat 52 minutes or until thick, syrupy, and beginning to crystallize, stirring occasionally to separate slices. (Do not let sugar caramelize.) Using a slotted spoon, transfer ginger to a wire rack set over paper towels. Cool completely.
3. Place remaining 1 cup sugar in a large bowl. Add ginger slices, tossing to coat. Spoon sugared ginger into a wire-mesh sieve; shake excess sugar back into bowl, and reserve for other uses in place of regular sugar. Store Crystallized Ginger and excess sugar in airtight containers up to 1 month.

Package Crystallized Ginger in cellophane bags tied with ribbon to give as gifts.

a quick & easy CHRISTMAS DINNER

When it comes to the big Christmas meal, timing is everything: Follow our step-by-step game plan and kitchen tips to host the most relaxed and enjoyable holiday possible.

menu

POINSETTIA SIPPER

PIMIENTO CHEESE PINWHEELS

SLICED PEARS WITH RÉMOULADE DOLLOP

SWEET APPLE AND MUSTARD-GLAZED TURKEY

CRANBERRY CHUTNEY

MOIST CORNBREAD DRESSING WITH SPICY CRAWFISH

CANDIED YAMS

WILTED COLLARDS WITH BACON AND ONION

BREAD PUDDING WITH RUM SAUCE OR PUMPKIN PIE ICE CREAM FANTASY

serves 12

Glazed Turkey
Chutney
with Spicy Crawfish
Yams
Bacon and Onion

game plan

1 week ahead:

- Assemble serving pieces; label what goes with what.

3 days ahead:

- Grocery shop.
- Make Cranberry Chutney. Put into serving dish; cover and refrigerate.
- Tear bread for bread pudding. Seal bread in zip-top plastic bag.

1 day ahead:

- Chill juices for Poinsettia Sipper.
- Prep lettuce for Sliced Pears with Rémoulade Dollop.
- Prepare collards; transfer to a foil pan, cover, and refrigerate. Refrigerate reserved bacon separately.
- Assemble Candied Yams; cover and refrigerate.

3 to 4 hours ahead:

- Roast turkey, adding glaze near the end.
- Prepare and bake bread pudding.

1 to 2 hours ahead:

- Assemble Pimiento Cheese Pinwheels; place on baking sheet. Bake when oven is free.
- Prep pears for salad.
- Make Rum Sauce.

30 minutes ahead:

- Stir together Poinsettia Sipper.
- Assemble pear salad; cover with plastic wrap.
- Reheat Wilted Collards in oven. Add reserved bacon after reheating and prior to serving.
- Bake Candied Yams.
- Prepare Moist Cornbread Dressing.
- Carve Sweet Apple and Mustard-Glazed Turkey.
- Freeze baked pumpkin pie for 1 hour.

when guests arrive:

- Serve Poinsettia Sipper.
- Put salads on the table.
- Allow the guests who want to help you…help you.
- Have helper put hot food into designated serving dishes.
- Warm up Bread Pudding and Rum Sauce.

after dinner:

- Assemble Pumpkin Pie Ice Cream Fantasy.

---

quick & easy

Poinsettia Sipper

Mix this nonalcoholic aperitif right before serving.

MAKES 16½ CUPS
PREP: 8 MIN.

- 1 (64-oz.) bottle 100% cranberry juice, chilled
- 1 cup thawed orange juice concentrate
- 1 (1-liter) bottle lemon-lime soft drink, chilled
- 1 lime, thinly sliced
- ½ cup fresh cranberries

1. Stir together first 3 ingredients in a large pitcher; garnish with lime slices and cranberries.

quick & easy

Pimiento Cheese Pinwheels

Here's an easy appetizer recipe to help occupy the kids (pressing out dough and rolling it into logs) on a buzzing holiday.

MAKES 20 APPETIZERS
PREP: 10 MIN.   COOK: 10 MIN.

- 2 (8-oz.) packages reduced-fat refrigerated crescent rolls (we tested with Pillsbury)
- 1 cup pimiento cheese*

1. Preheat oven to 400°. Unroll crescent rolls on a lightly floured surface, and pat into 2 rectangles; press perforations to seal. Spread ½ cup pimiento cheese onto each rectangle, spreading to edges. Roll up each dough rectangle, starting at 1 long end; cut each into 10 even slices. Place pinwheels on a lightly greased baking sheet. Bake at 400° for 10 minutes or until browned.

*Use your favorite brand of pimiento cheese, your own recipe, or the widely available 5-oz. jars of sharp process cheese spread (Old English).

Easy Table Ideas

Here are three ideas for impressive and easy-to-create table decorations. Each can be made ahead.

Gift Box Centerpiece

Select an empty box to use as the centerpiece. Set a jar or small vase on top of box; trace diameter of jar or vase onto center of box, and cut hole in box to match size. Wrap box. Add ribbon, using double-sided tape. Set the jar or vase filled with flowers and greenery into box hole. Another really quick idea is to just place a small potted plant into the hole of the wrapped box.

Mum Balls

To make 6 mum balls, buy 3 bunches of Kermit mums and 6 florist foam balls (5" to 6" in diameter). Trim mums, leaving 1½" of stems. Stick mums into water-soaked florist foam, covering it completely. Spritz with water to keep fresh up to 5 days.

Candy Cane Easels

For each easel, hot glue 2 candy canes together side by side (as if making an easel). Break a third candy cane halfway down the stem; hot glue it in place to serve as the back of the easel. Display holiday menu or place card on each easel.

Sliced Pears with Rémoulade Dollop

quick & easy

Sliced Pears with Rémoulade Dollop

Rémoulade is a classic French sauce often served with seafood, but we love it in this recipe spooned over ripe pears.

MAKES 12 SERVINGS
PREP: 21 MIN.

  6 firm ripe red pears, sliced
  1 cup orange juice
 12 Bibb lettuce leaves
  ¾ cup rémoulade dressing (we tested with Louisiana)
  1 cup crumbled blue cheese
  1 cup chopped pecans or pecan pieces

1. Combine pears and orange juice in a bowl.
2. Place lettuce leaves on salad plates. Remove pear slices from bowl with a slotted spoon, pat dry, and arrange over lettuce. Spoon dressing over pears. Sprinkle cheese and pecans over each salad.

fix it faster

For an easier salad, use fresh or canned pear halves and spoon dressing and toppings in center of each.

Sweet Apple and Mustard-Glazed Turkey

This year at Christmas, if convenience is key, try a ready-to-cook turkey and apply our simple glaze for dazzling results. You'll love the convenience of the oven-ready bird. Otherwise, you can buy a fresh or frozen turkey and visit www.myrecipes.com for basic prep and roasting instructions.

MAKES 12 SERVINGS
PREP: 4 MIN.   COOK: 3 HR., 45 MIN.

  1 (12-lb.) ready-to-cook frozen turkey (we tested with Jennie-O)
  1 (18-oz.) jar apple jelly
  2 Tbsp. yellow mustard

1. Follow package directions carefully for baking turkey (while still frozen), allowing last 30 minutes of baking for adding glaze. (A 12-lb. frozen turkey should take 3½ to 4 hours to reach 170° in the breast.)

2. Combine jelly and mustard in a small saucepan, stirring well. Bring glaze mixture to a boil; boil 1 minute or until jelly is melted. Remove from heat. Set aside 1 cup glaze for serving.
3. When ready to apply glaze to turkey, carefully cut open top of oven bag, watching out for hot steam and juices. Pull bag away from top of turkey. Brush remaining ⅔ cup glaze over turkey in 2 additions during last 30 minutes of baking. Serve turkey with reserved 1 cup glaze.

make ahead · quick & easy

Cranberry Chutney

Prepare this dressed-up cranberry sauce up to 3 days ahead, and chill it.

MAKES 3½ CUPS
PREP: 5 MIN.

  2 (16-oz.) cans whole-berry cranberry sauce
  2 Tbsp. mango chutney (we tested with Major Grey)
  2 tsp. orange liqueur (we tested with Grand Marnier)

1. Combine all ingredients in a bowl; stir well. Serve chilled or at room temperature.

quick & easy

Moist Cornbread Dressing with Spicy Crawfish

To best enjoy this moist, quick stovetop dressing, make it just before sitting down to the big meal. Find frozen crawfish tails in the seafood department of some larger grocery stores or in local seafood markets. We recommend using crawfish tails harvested in the United States.

MAKES 12 SERVINGS
PREP: 6 MIN.   COOK: 10 MIN.

  ¾ cup butter, divided
  ¾ cup chopped onion
  ¾ cup chopped celery
 2½ cups chicken broth
  1 (16-oz.) package frozen cooked peeled crawfish tails, thawed and drained
  ¼ to ½ tsp. ground red pepper
  1 (16-oz.) package seasoned cornbread stuffing (we tested with Pepperidge Farm)

1. Melt ½ cup butter in a large deep skillet or Dutch oven. Sauté onion and celery 4 to 5 minutes or until crisp-tender. Add chicken broth, crawfish tails, remaining ¼ cup butter, and red pepper; bring to a boil. Remove from heat. Add cornbread stuffing; gently toss and fluff with a fork until stuffing is moistened.

make ahead

Wilted Collards with Bacon and Onion

Prepare these greens a day ahead, and reheat before serving. Don't stir in the crisp bacon until ready to serve.

MAKES 12 TO 15 SERVINGS
PREP: 10 MIN.   COOK: 38 MIN.

    5   thick bacon slices, chopped
    2   cups chopped onion
    ½   cup chopped celery
    1   Tbsp. bottled minced garlic
    1   (14-oz.) can chicken broth
    3   (16-oz.) packages frozen chopped collard greens
    2   tsp. seasoned salt
    ½   tsp. black pepper

1. Cook bacon in a Dutch oven over medium-high heat 8 to 10 minutes or until crisp; remove bacon, and drain on paper towels, reserving drippings in pan. Set bacon aside.
2. Sauté onion and celery in hot drippings until crisp-tender. Add garlic, chicken broth, and next 3 ingredients. Cover and cook over low heat 25 minutes or until greens are wilted and tender. Stir bacon into greens just before serving.

fix it faster

Forego the thick-cut bacon and use fully cooked bacon slices, which reheat in a hot skillet or microwave in 1 minute or less. You'll want to use 8 slices of fully cooked bacon since it's thinner. Use 3 Tbsp. vegetable oil in place of bacon drippings to sauté onion and celery. And you can use prechopped onion and celery.

Candied Yams

High heat caramelizes these yams. The s'more-like topping is optional, but kids will love it.

MAKES 8 TO 12 SERVINGS
PREP: 6 MIN.   COOK: 25 MIN.   OTHER: 10 MIN.

    3   (40-oz.) or 4 (29-oz.) cans cut yams, well drained (we tested with Sugary Sam sweet potatoes in syrup)
    1   cup firmly packed light brown sugar
    ¼   cup butter, melted
    1   Tbsp. vanilla extract or vanilla bean paste
    1   tsp. ground cinnamon
   12   large marshmallows (optional)

1. Preheat oven to 425°. Arrange yams in a lightly greased 13" x 9" baking dish. Sprinkle brown sugar over yams. Combine butter and next 2 ingredients. Drizzle over yams. Bake, uncovered, at 425° for 20 minutes. Sprinkle marshmallows over yams, if desired, and bake 5 more minutes. Let stand 10 minutes before serving.

editor's favorite

Bread Pudding with Rum Sauce

Day-old bread is best for soaking up the liquid in this comforting dessert. The easy rum sauce makes each serving luscious.

MAKES 12 SERVINGS
PREP: 15 MIN.   COOK: 50 MIN.

    4   large eggs
   1½   cups sugar
    3   (12-oz.) cans evaporated milk
    ½   cup butter, melted
    1   Tbsp. vanilla extract
    2   tsp. ground cinnamon
    6   cups torn, packed French bread
    1   large Granny Smith apple, peeled and chopped
    1   cup chopped walnuts, toasted
    ½   cup golden raisins
        Rum Sauce

1. Preheat oven to 350°. Whisk eggs in a large bowl. Whisk in sugar and next 4 ingredients. Fold in bread and next 3 ingredients, stirring until bread is moistened. Pour into a 13" x 9" baking dish coated with cooking spray. Bake, uncovered, at 350° for 50 minutes or until set. Serve warm with Rum Sauce.

Rum Sauce

MAKES 2½ CUPS
PREP: 2 MIN.   COOK: 3 MIN.

    2   (14-oz.) cans sweetened condensed milk
    2   Tbsp. dark rum
    1   Tbsp. vanilla extract

1. Pour condensed milk into a small saucepan; heat over medium heat until hot, stirring often. Remove from heat, and stir in rum and vanilla. Serve warm.

Pumpkin Pie Ice Cream Fantasy

Two holiday dessert classics are swirled with caramel and pecans—what's not to love?

MAKES 12 SERVINGS
PREP: 10 MIN. OTHER: 1 HR., 8 MIN.

1 baked pumpkin pie*
½ gal. premium vanilla ice cream (we tested with
   Blue Bell)
Caramel topping (we tested with Smucker's)
Toasted pecan halves

1. Place pie in freezer for 1 hour; remove pie from freezer, and chop ¾ of pie into 1" chunks. Allow ice cream to stand about 8 to 10 minutes to slightly soften. "Chunk up" ice cream into a large bowl. Gently fold in pie chunks until blended.
2. To serve, scoop each serving into a wine glass or dessert bowl. Drizzle with caramel topping, and top with pecans.

*We tested with a Mrs. Smith's frozen pumpkin pie, baked according to package directions. We let it cool completely on a wire rack, then froze it briefly for easy chopping. You can use any type of pumpkin pie here—a deli baked pie or, better yet, a homemade pumpkin pie. (This idea would also work with a baked pecan pie. Just omit the toasted pecan halves.)

New Year's Eve DESSERT PARTY

Resolve to get the New Year off to a sweet start with a decadent menu of inspired cocktails and confectionary delights.

menu

SPARKLING COSMOPOLITAN

POM-APPLE-GRAPE MOCKTAIL

VANILLA COFFEE

WHITE CHOCOLATE-KEY LIME CHEESECAKE SQUARES

PETITE PERSIMMON PUFFS

CRANBERRY PISTACHIO TARTLETS

CHOCOLATE BROWN SUGAR CAKE WITH CARAMEL FILLING
AND PECAN FLORENTINE

serves 16

game plan

1 week ahead:

- [ ] Prepare Vanilla Bean Syrup.
- [ ] Prepare and bake tart shells for Cranberry Pistachio Tartlets; place in zip-top plastic freezer bags. Seal and freeze.

2 days ahead:

- [ ] Prepare White Chocolate-Key Lime Cheesecake Squares; cover loosely with plastic wrap and chill.
- [ ] Prepare persimmon filling; cover and chill.
- [ ] Make cake layers, wrap in plastic wrap, and refrigerate.

1 day ahead:

- [ ] Combine and chill ingredients for Sparkling Cosmopolitan except for sparkling wine.
- [ ] Prepare garnish for Sparkling Cosmopolitan.
- [ ] Bake puff pastry cups for Petite Persimmon Puffs; cool and store in an airtight container.
- [ ] Make Pecan Florentine, Caramel Filling, and frosting for cake. Assemble Chocolate Brown Sugar Cake, except for garnish, cover loosely with plastic wrap, and chill.

4 hours ahead:

- [ ] Prepare Cranberry Pistachio Tartlets.

1 to 2 hours ahead:

- [ ] Assemble Petite Persimmon Puffs.
- [ ] Garnish Chocolate Brown Sugar Cake.

30 minutes ahead:

- [ ] Set up coffee bar.

10 minutes ahead:

- [ ] Brew coffee.
- [ ] Prepare Pom-Apple-Grape Mocktail.

---

editor's favorite · quick & easy

Sparkling Cosmopolitan

(pictured on page 219)

Traditional cosmopolitans get a face-lift with the addition of bubbly Champagne—we suggest having a few extra bottles on hand for guests who prefer a higher ratio of Champagne to cranberry mixture.

MAKES 16 SERVINGS
PREP: 3 MIN.

3 cups cranberry juice
1 cup vodka
1 cup triple sec
⅓ cup fresh lime juice
2 (750-ml.) bottles sparkling wine or Champagne
Garnish: sugared cranberries*

1. Stir together first 4 ingredients in a large pitcher. Chill until ready to serve.

2. Pour about ⅓ cup cranberry mixture into each of 16 champagne glasses. Fill each glass with sparkling wine. Garnish, if desired.

*Roll fresh cranberries in light corn syrup; remove from syrup with a fork, shaking off excess. Dredge in sugar, and let dry on a wire rack. Thread several sugared cranberries on a wooden pick, and place in each glass.

quick & easy

Pom-Apple-Grape Mocktail

The flavors of both the sparkling apple cider and the white grape juice in this nonalcoholic refresher were great, but we preferred the clarity of the apple cider.

MAKES 6 SERVINGS
PREP: 3 MIN.

2 cups sparkling apple cider* or white grape juice, chilled
½ cup pomegranate juice*, chilled
Pomegranate seeds

1. Pour ⅓ cup cider or grape juice in each of 6 champagne glasses. Divide pomegranate juice among the glasses. Drop a few pomegranate seeds in each glass. Serve immediately.

*We tested with Martinelli's Sparkling Apple Cider and POM pomegranate juice.

Vanilla Coffee

Vanilla Coffee

Vanilla Bean Syrup is a delightful alternative to sugar to sweeten after-dinner coffee. Make your coffee bar a festive affair by offering whipped topping and a variety of flavorings, sweeteners, creamers, and spirits.

MAKES 1 SERVING
PREP: 4 MIN.   COOK: 6 MIN.

Vanilla Bean Syrup
1   cup hot brewed coffee
Half-and-half
1   Tbsp. vanilla-flavored vodka (optional)
Shaved bittersweet chocolate

1. Stir 1 Tbsp., or desired amount, of Vanilla Bean Syrup into hot coffee. Stir in desired amount of half-and-half and vanilla vodka, if desired. Sprinkle with shaved bittersweet chocolate.

Vanilla Bean Syrup

MAKES 2½ CUPS
PREP: 2 MIN.   COOK: 6 MIN.

2   cups sugar
1   vanilla bean, split lengthwise

1. Combine 2 cups water and sugar in a medium saucepan; cook over medium heat until sugar dissolves, stirring frequently. Scrape vanilla bean seeds into sugar syrup; add vanilla bean pod to syrup. Remove from heat, and let cool completely. Remove and discard vanilla bean pod.

make ahead

Prepare Vanilla Bean Syrup up to 1 week ahead. Cover and store in the refrigerator.

White Chocolate-Key Lime Cheesecake Squares

Velvety white chocolate and tart Key lime are paired together in these luscious squares.

MAKES 16 SQUARES
PREP: 42 MIN.   COOK: 1 HR., 5 MIN.   OTHER: 10 MIN.

½ cup butter, softened
¼ cup firmly packed light brown sugar
1 tsp. vanilla extract
1 cup all-purpose flour
1 (8-oz.) package cream cheese, softened
1½ cups powdered sugar
1 large egg
1 tsp. lime zest
1 tsp. vanilla extract
3 oz. white chocolate, melted
4 large egg yolks
¾ cup sugar
1 Tbsp. cornstarch
¼ cup bottled Key lime juice
2 tsp. lime zest
2 Tbsp. butter
Garnish: lime slices

1. Preheat oven to 325°. Beat first 2 ingredients at medium speed with an electric mixer until creamy; add 1 tsp. vanilla, beating until blended. Add flour; beat at low speed until blended. Press dough into a lightly greased 8" square pan. Bake at 325° for 25 minutes or until golden brown. Let cool on a wire rack.
2. While crust bakes, beat cream cheese and powdered sugar at medium speed until creamy. Add egg, 1 tsp. lime zest, and 1 tsp. vanilla; beat well. Add melted white chocolate; beat until combined. Cover and chill filling.
3. While cream cheese filling chills, make lime curd. Combine egg yolks, ¾ cup sugar, and cornstarch in a medium saucepan; gradually stir in ¾ cup water and lime juice. Cook over medium-low heat, stirring constantly, until mixture thickens and coats the back of a metal spoon. Remove from heat; stir in 2 tsp. lime zest and 2 Tbsp. butter. Remove from heat, and let cool 10 minutes.
4. Spread chilled cream cheese filling over cooled crust. Pour lime curd over cream cheese filling. Bake at 325° for 40 minutes or until edges are lightly browned. Let cool completely on a wire rack. Cut into squares. Garnish with lime slices, if desired. Store in refrigerator.

Petite Persimmon Puffs

MAKES 3 DOZEN
PREP: 35 MIN.   COOK: 30 MIN.   OTHER: 30 MIN.

½ (17.3-oz.) package frozen puff pastry sheets, thawed
1 egg white, lightly beaten
1 Tbsp. turbinado sugar
3 Fuyu persimmons, peeled and chopped (about ¾ lb.)*
3 Tbsp. apricot preserves
2 tsp. sugar
2 tsp. butter
2 tsp. honey
Powdered sugar

1. Preheat oven to 400°. Unfold puff pastry sheet; roll into an 11" square. Cut into 36 squares. Place each puff pastry square in lightly greased miniature muffin cups. Press each square gently into cups, letting corners extend slightly over edges of cups. Lightly brush each pastry cup with egg white, and sprinkle turbinado sugar on corners of pastry.
2. Bake at 400° for 10 minutes or until lightly puffed and golden. Remove from oven; immediately press the end of the handle of a wooden spoon into center of each cup to form a hole. Remove puff pastry cups from muffin pans; cool completely on a wire rack.
3. Meanwhile, combine persimmons and next 4 ingredients in a medium saucepan. Bring to a boil, reduce heat, and simmer 20 minutes or until persimmons are very soft, stirring occasionally. Mash persimmon mixture with a potato masher until consistency of fruit jam. Cover and chill 30 minutes.
4. Spoon about ½ tsp. persimmon filling into each puff pastry shell; sprinkle each shell with powdered sugar.

*Fuyu persimmons are a nonastringent persimmon variety and the best choice for these delicate morsels because they won't surprise you with a bitter experience should you select fruit that isn't perfectly ripe. They can be eaten when very firm or very soft, but we preferred fruit that had a slight "give" when lightly pressed.

make ahead

Bake puff pastry cups up to 1 day ahead; cool completely and store in an airtight container. Persimmon filling may also be made up to 2 days ahead and stored, covered, in the refrigerator.

Petite Persimmon Puffs,
White Chocolate-Key Lime
Cheesecake Squares

editor's favorite • make ahead

Cranberry Pistachio Tartlets

The filling for these tiny pies is similar to that of pecan pie with a chewy, nutty topping of cranberries and pistachios.

MAKES 2 DOZEN
PREP: 30 MIN. COOK: 24 MIN. OTHER: 1 HR., 5 MIN.

Pistachio Pastry Shells

⅓ cup butter, softened
1 (3-oz.) package cream cheese, softened
1 cup all-purpose flour
⅓ cup finely chopped pistachios
2 Tbsp. powdered sugar

Cranberry Pistachio Filling

2 large eggs
⅔ cup sugar
⅓ cup light corn syrup
2 Tbsp. butter, melted
1 tsp. vanilla extract
⅓ cup coarsely chopped sweetened dried cranberries
   (we tested with Craisins)
⅓ cup chopped pistachios
Garnishes: Sweetened whipped cream, finely chopped
   pistachios, and chopped sweetened dried cranberries

1. Prepare Pistachio Pastry Shells: Beat butter and cream cheese at medium speed with an electric mixer until smooth. Add flour, pistachios, and powdered sugar, beating well. Shape dough into a ball; wrap in wax paper, and chill 1 hour.
2. Divide dough into 24 balls. Place balls in 2 lightly greased (12-cup) miniature muffin pans. Press balls into bottom and up sides of pans. Chill until ready to fill.
3. Prepare Cranberry Pistachio Filling: Preheat oven to 350°. Whisk eggs in a medium bowl; whisk in sugar and next 3 ingredients. Add cranberries and pistachios, stirring well.
4. Remove pastry shells from refrigerator. Spoon filling into shells. Bake at 350° for 24 minutes or just until set. Let cool in pans 5 minutes. Remove from pans, and cool completely on wire racks. Garnish, if desired.

make ahead

Prepare, bake, and cool tartlets. Carefully place in zip-top plastic freezer bags; seal bags, and freeze up to 1 week. Thaw at room temperature.

Miniature muffin pans are the perfect size for these tasty tartlets.

editor's favorite · make ahead

Chocolate Brown Sugar Cake with Caramel Filling and Pecan Florentine

This showstopper is as decadent as it is stunning. It offers the whole dessert package: moist, chocolaty layers; gooey caramel filling; soft swirls of rich frosting; all topped with delicate, crunchy Pecan Florentine.

MAKES 16 SERVINGS
PREP: 30 MIN.   COOK: 1 HR., 3 MIN.   OTHER: 15 MIN.

Cake

- ½ cup butter, softened
- 2 cups firmly packed light brown sugar
- 3 large eggs
- 1 tsp. vanilla extract
- 2 (1-oz.) squares unsweetened chocolate, melted
- 2¼ cups all-purpose flour
- 1 tsp. baking soda
- ½ tsp. salt
- 1 cup buttermilk
- Cooking spray for baking

Pecan Florentine

- 6 Tbsp. sugar
- 6 Tbsp. heavy cream
- 2 Tbsp. butter
- 1 Tbsp. all-purpose flour
- 1½ cups finely chopped pecans
- Parchment paper

Caramel Filling

- 1 cup firmly packed light brown sugar
- 3 Tbsp. all-purpose flour
- 1 cup evaporated milk
- 2 egg yolks, lightly beaten
- 2 Tbsp. butter, softened

Chocolate Buttercream Frosting

- ½ cup semisweet chocolate morsels
- ½ cup milk, divided
- ¾ cup butter, softened
- 2 tsp. vanilla extract
- 5 cups powdered sugar
- ¾ cup unsweetened cocoa
- ¼ tsp. salt

1. Prepare cake: Preheat oven to 350°. Beat butter at medium speed with an electric mixer until creamy; gradually add sugar, beating well. Add eggs, 1 at a time, beating until blended after each addition. Stir in vanilla and chocolate.

2. Combine flour, baking soda, and salt; add to butter mixture alternately with buttermilk, beginning and ending with flour mixture. Beat at low speed until blended after each addition, stopping to scrape bowl as needed.

3. Pour batter into 2 (8") square cake pans coated with cooking spray for baking. Bake at 350° for 25 to 30 minutes or until a wooden pick inserted in center comes out clean. Cool in pans on wire racks 5 minutes; remove from pans to wire racks, and cool completely (about 1 hour).

4. Meanwhile, prepare Pecan Florentine: Preheat oven to 300°. Combine first 3 ingredients in a small saucepan; bring to a boil over medium-high heat. Remove from heat, and stir in flour and pecans. Pour onto a parchment paper-lined baking sheet, pressing into a single layer using the back of a spoon. Bake at 300° for 28 minutes or until bubbly and golden. Cool on pan 10 minutes. Cut into desired shapes with a pizza cutter, or break into shards. Cool completely.

5. Meanwhile, prepare Caramel Filling: Combine sugar and flour in a small saucepan; gradually whisk in evaporated milk. Bring to a boil over medium heat, whisking constantly. Boil, whisking constantly, 1 minute; remove from heat. Gradually whisk about one-fourth of hot mixture into egg yolks, whisking constantly; add yolk mixture to remaining hot caramel mixture, whisking constantly. Cook over medium heat 1 minute, whisking constantly. Remove from heat; whisk in butter until melted. Cool completely.

6. Prepare Chocolate Buttercream Frosting: Combine chocolate morsels and ¼ cup milk in a small saucepan; cook over low heat, stirring often until smooth. Remove from heat; cool to room temperature.

7. Beat butter at low speed with a heavy-duty stand mixer until creamy; gradually add chocolate mixture, beating until smooth. Add remaining ¼ cup milk, vanilla, and remaining ingredients; beat until smooth.

8. Spread Caramel Filling between cake layers; reserve ¼ cup for garnish.

9. Spread Chocolate Buttercream Frosting on top and sides of cake. Garnish with reserved Caramel Filling and desired amount of Pecan Florentine. Serve any remaining Pecan Florentine as snacks.

make ahead

Fill and frost cake and prepare Pecan Florentine 1 day ahead. Garnish with reserved Caramel Filling and Pecan Florentine before serving.

ideas for DECORATING

AS YOUR THOUGHTS TURN TO CHRISTMAS,
LET THE IDEAS ON THESE PAGES INSPIRE
TERRIFIC HOLIDAY TRIMMINGS.

welcoming STYLE

Greet friends and family with outdoor decorations that show your unique style. The ideas on these pages suggest ways to express holiday cheer from the front door, the garden, and even the mailbox.

Garden-fresh Greetings

"Plant" a wreath that will bring a hint of spring to your front door. Line a wire wreath form (photo 1) with sheet moss, leaving open areas in the moss. Tuck small plants such as pansies, lettuce, and herbs through the openings to decorate the front of the wreath (photo 2). Fill in behind the plants with potting soil, and cover the soil with sheet moss. Attach the back of the wreath form to the wreath. Mist or water the wreath as needed to keep the plants fresh.

Have plenty of natural materials, pretty ribbons, and sparkly ornaments on hand to make holiday decorating a breeze.

Pinecone Pizzazz

Extra-large sugar pinecones are striking on their own, but when you pair them with a pretty hanging vase filled with bright berries and greenery, you've got a stunning door decoration (facing page). Use wire to hold the separate elements together. In lieu of a hanging vase, you can use elongated finial-style ornaments and wire snips of greenery and berries at the tops of the ornaments. Wire a bow to the top of the arrangement and trail lengths of ribbons so they fall gracefully alongside the pinecones.

Simple Style

You can put this easy ornament decoration together in minutes (top right). After you make one for the front door, make smaller versions to hang from the mantel. Use a variety of large and small ornaments. Glue strips of ribbons around the ornaments, as desired. Loop rickrack or ribbon through the ornament hangers, and use a large safety pin to secure the ends. Pin or wire a bow at the top. Use the safety pin as a hanger.

Wintry Welcome

You can have a white Christmas even in the South (bottom right). Lay an evergreen wreath on the porch, and set tall glass vases in varying heights in the center. Fill the vases about half full with artificial snow. Place long twigs in each vase, anchoring the twigs in the snow. Sprinkle snow on the wreath, and tie ribbons around the vases. Look for long twigs at home decorating and crafts stores, or gather them from your backyard.

Chic and Classic

Greet family and friends with a distinctive Southern accent. Magnolia leaves—a time-honored regional favorite for holiday decorating—come together in a simple swag that's the essence of elegance. If you're lucky enough to have a magnolia tree or a friendly neighbor who does, clip enough branches to form a swag that's the right size for your door.

here's how

Start with a longer branch that can act as the backing for your arrangement. It will give a good base for attaching the other branches. Use paddle wire to bind the branches together, wrapping the wire around each branch, then wrapping the entire bundle. Turn some of the branches over so the warm bronze underside shows. Wire in stems of berries and curly willow, as desired. Tie a bow at the top of the swag.

Two for One

For a double-door entry, consider this idea for a two-piece wreath. Start with a regular wreath that has a sturdy base so it will hold its shape. A fresh evergreen wreath was used here, but a permanent wreath or grapevine wreath will work as well. Cut the wreath in half lengthwise. The type of wreath you have will determine what tool is needed to cut the wreath. Sturdy wire clippers should work in most cases. Use thin, flexible wire to attach evergreen clippings, fruits, and ribbons to the wreath. Securely hang one half wreath on each door so the two halves meet in the center when the doors are closed. Frame the entrance with a garland and pots of greenery. Place tall topiary forms in the pots for a dramatic addition.

Cottage Christmas

Play up your home's unique style with holiday decorations that complement its most appealing qualities. Boost the charm using objects that share a common look, like the garden-inspired pieces pictured on these pages that work together to convey a cozy welcome. Rustic aluminum containers on the door, porch, and stairs offer casual appeal in keeping with the relaxed architecture. Fill planters with herbs, and use bright accents, such as red amaryllis blooms, berries, ornaments, and gardening accessories, to cheer a neutral setting.

To keep the bucket decoration on the front door fresh, line the bucket with a zip-top plastic freezer bag, then fill it with moistened floral foam. Stick berry stems and evergreen cuttings into the foam. In addition to prolonging the life of the arrangement, the foam makes arranging easier because it holds the pieces in place.

Arrange an assortment of similarly themed accent pieces at your front entry to set a welcoming stage for holiday visitors.

Rich in Tradition

Nothing shows off the deep colors of a fresh evergreen garland and wreath better than a pristine white door. Tie on extra-wide red ribbons as accents, and you're all set. If you're in the mood for a bit more embellishment, add twinkling lights to the garland, and set a conifer surrounded by holly berries in a pretty container.

*Big lanterns and
wrapped boxes
welcome the season.*

Wreath of Good Fortune

Bells are thought to attract good luck and bring prosperity, and what better way to greet the season? This temple-bell wreath starts with a green extruded craft foam wreath form, which is more dense than the usual craft foam and better supports the bells.

here's how

Use U-shaped floral pins to attach reindeer moss to the top and sides of the wreath form. Cut enough short lengths of ribbon to encircle the wreath. Fold lengths in half and pin around the outside edge of the wreath. Loop long ribbons around the bottom of the wreath. Tie bells at the ends of the ribbons.

Natural materials make beautiful and inexpensive Christmas decorations. Combine them with potted plants, ribbons, and other holiday accessories, such as candles and ornaments, to enjoy all season long.

Evergreen Greetings

Top off a square mailbox with an
abundant bouquet of winter plants.
This mailbox has a convenient planting
space at the top, but the idea translates
well for any flat surface. Fill a wide,
shallow planter with a mix of winter-
hardy plants. Tuck in ornaments and
oversized pinecones to add color and fill
in gaps. Center the container on the top
of the mailbox.

A Little Extra

Let an existing mailbox planting be the starting point for a festive presentation. For a
mailbox with a post that extends above the
box, loosely wrap sheer ribbon around a
pine garland and drape the garland around
the mailbox. Use wire to hold the garland in
place. Wire clusters of bright nandina berries
to the top of the post and finish with a big
bow for an eye-catching flourish.

Wrapped and Ready

Encircle a traditional mailbox/lamppost with
a pine garland, securing it to the post with
wire. Wire magnolia leaves and apples to the
garland. Use floral picks with wires to secure
the apples. Wire or tie loopy bows beneath the
lantern to form an ornate collar.

decorate with WREATHS

Nothing says Christmas like a wreath. Hang one on the front door and another above the mantel to fill your home with holiday magic. On these pages, you'll find lots of fresh ideas for this seasonal favorite.

Magnolia leaves make perfect holiday wreaths. They dry beautifully, transitioning from green to a lovely bronzy gold.

To make a magnolia wreath, start with a florist foam wreath, which can be found at most crafts and discount stores. Soak the wreath in water. Insert individual magnolia leaves into the foam so they are perpendicular to the form, covering the entire wreath. To hang the wreath, loop ribbon around the top of the wreath, and secure the ribbon with a tack or small finishing nail. Use florist wire to attach a bow.

Fresh magnolia wreaths will last two to three weeks. You can refresh the greenery by soaking the entire wreath in a tub of water for a few minutes.

Personalize your wreath with a variety of nontraditional trims. Strands of Spanish moss add unexpected flair to a pine wreath (left), while a small owl and bird's nest seem comfortably at home on a shaggy cypress wreath (right).

Versatile grapevine wreaths make ideal bases for berries. For the trio of wreaths shown below, stems of nandina, popcorn (Chinese tallow), and privet berries are simply wedged into the wreaths.

The scent of fresh citrus blends beautifully with aromatic evergreens, and the contrast of brilliant orange against dark green provides a stunning seasonal display.

To attach fruit to a greenery wreath or garland, insert a wired florist pick into the fruit, and then wire in place. Use loose oranges (as seen in the galvanized buckets shown at right) to carry pops of color throughout the decoration.

super citrusy scents

■ To maximize the release of citrusy fragrance, use a sharp knife to make vertical slits in the rind.
■ Allow the slit oranges to air-dry for a few hours before attaching them to allow time for the juice to begin to dry.
■ Using wired florist picks, attach the oranges to a wreath (as shown on the seeded eucalyptus wreath below), or arrange several in a glass bowl for a festive potpourri. The lovely aroma will linger for days.
■ Dress up arrangements of oranges and greenery with gold- or copper-colored ribbons to boost the festive mood.

Wreaths that break the round barrier garner even more attention than their circular cousins. Add to that an unusual hanging technique, such as two ribbon hangers instead of one (left), or unique embellishments, such as flattened flatware stamped with seasonal sentiments (opposite and below), and your holiday decorating takes a giant ornamental leap. To make a square wreath, tape blocks of florist foam to a wooden picture frame, then insert flowers or evergreen sprigs.

Use sheer ribbons to tie decorations to wreaths, trees, and garlands for a more decorative punch.

Coordinate wreath colors to suit your room's decor. Tie brightly colored ribbons into bows and wire them to an evergreen wreath to complement the room's color scheme (above and right). For added interest, use a mix of ribbon textures, widths, and compatible colors.

Take advantage of a bright wall color, such as the red wall shown on the opposite page, to showcase a frosty white pinecone wreath. Hang wreaths in front of mirrors to double their impact.

Nostalgic Noel

The simple joy of gumdrops makes this wreath a favorite with all ages. Jumbo red, white, and green candies and a jaunty polka-dot bow distinguish its charm.

To make the wreath, you'll need a plastic craft foam wreath form, masking tape, wire, wooden picks, gumdrops, and ribbon—the quantities needed will depend on the size of the wreath form. Begin by wrapping masking tape around what will be the top of the wreath. The tape reinforces the wreath for hanging. Wrap wire around the wreath over the tape, bending the wire into a hanging loop at the back of the wreath. Break wooden picks in half, inserting the broken ends into the gumdrops. Cover the top and sides of the wreath with gumdrops. Tie a bow at the top of the wreath, hiding the wire.

A Plate Full of Cheer

Give a favorite holiday plate the star treatment by framing it with a fluffy evergreen wreath (facing page). Attach a wire plate hanger to the plate, and place the plate in the center of the wreath. Wire the wreath to the plate hanger. Wire or tie a bow at the top.

Pretty Ribbons

A satiny ribbon wreath feels right at home in the bedroom (above). Select ribbons in colors that coordinate with your room's colors, and you may be tempted to leave the wreath hanging year-round. Using pins to attach the ribbons, rather than tying them around the wreath, means you use less ribbon and offers the perfect opportunity to use all those snippets you couldn't bear to throw away.

here's how

To make the wreath, you'll need a plastic craft foam wreath form, ribbons, U-shaped florist pins, and straight pins (for narrow ribbon). Start by tying a ribbon hanger at the top of the wreath (photo 1). Fold lengths of ribbon into big loops and pin them to the wreath form, covering the top and sides (photo 2).

Bunches of Berries

Create a dramatic decoration—times four! Use gardening clippers to make a cut in the side of a vine wreath.
Hook another vine wreath through the cut; repeat two
more times. Use wire to make a hanging loop on the
back of each wreath. Tuck berries and greenery into the
wreaths. Finish with a bow at the top of each wreath.

Mist evergreen wreaths every couple of days to keep them fresh and green throughout the season.

Back to Nature

Trim a plain grapevine wreath for the holidays with materials in keeping with its casual rustic look (facing page). Randomly tuck reindeer moss between the vines. Wind a velvety ribbon around the wreath, and dangle leaf ornaments from the top of the wreath to fill the center. Look for moss at crafts and hobby stores.

Personal Statement

Make your wreath uniquely yours by using it to frame your initial (top right). Decide whether a rectangular or circular wreath is best suited for the letter you want to use. A wreath that's made on a florist foam form that has a sturdy plastic base works best because it gives you a solid surface for attaching the letter. Use adhesive putty on the back side of the letter to attach the letter to the wreath. As an alternative, hang the letter on the door; then hang the wreath so it surrounds the letter. Look for materials, including letters, at crafts and hobby stores.

Send a Message

Attach a small chalkboard to your wreath to convey a merry greeting to passersby (bottom right). Use the board to write best wishes for the holidays, an invitation to a neighborhood open house, or even reminders to the family.

great GARLANDS

Whether fragrant festoons of evergreens or swags of popcorn and cranberries, garlands are mainstays of Christmas decorating. Take a look at these enchanting interpretations to spark your imagination for your own creative designs.

Trendy Blend

Pair a Christmas classic—a grand holly garland—with fashionable accents for an updated mantel style. Let citrus fruits spark the color scheme for flowers and candles in shades of red, orange, and green. Stack a pyramid of oranges in a large container to enhance the hearth. Use florist picks to hold the oranges in place.

Easy Does It

Don't you love it when the most simple idea results in a fabulous finish? Create a dazzling stairway decoration simply by adding ornaments to an evergreen garland (left). Embellishing the garland with anything else would take away from the simple charm. Just place the garland, and hang the ornaments. You'll be finished in minutes! If necessary, use more than one ornament hanger so the entire ornament hangs beneath the garland.

All in a Row

If you don't have a mantel or you just want to do something different this year, hang your stockings in a window (below). Trim the display with beaded garlands for a double-duty decoration that looks good both indoors and out. Tie fluffy bows at the ends of the garland for a pretty finish.

Cute Countdown

String this whimsical advent garland for a fun way to tick off the days 'til Christmas. Recruit the kids to help cut out designs from decorative papers and recycled holiday cards to glue on tiny gift bags. Fill the bags with small surprises that lead right up to the big day. Look for materials at crafts and discount stores.

here's how

To make the Advent garland, decorate small gift bags with paper cutouts and stickers. Number the bags from 1 to 25, using numbers cut from paper or rub-on transfers. Fill the bags with small treats, and then use ribbons and clothespins to attach the bags to twine.

To All a Good Night

Cozy-up the bedroom with a lighthearted garland made by stringing together ornaments and small stockings on a ribbon. Tie the garland to the footboard of the bed (facing page). Enhance the garland decoration with a coordinating wreath (below). The ornaments and wreath shown here are made from recycled fabric scraps and are so cuddly you'll be tempted to snuggle up with them for a long winter's nap, making them perfect accessories for the bedroom.

kitchen ACCENTS

It's the heart of the home and the favorite gathering spot when friends and family get together, so give the kitchen the attention it deserves when it's time to decorate for the holiday season. Here are some fresh ideas.

Tool Time

Search the kitchen cupboard for cute cooking implements, and arrange them on the counter-top for a seasonal decoration. Add a touch of green with potted plants, such as rosemary, parsley, and tiny cedar trees. Fill in with fruits and flowers in shades of red, green, and white.

Hang It Up

Deck the walls with a tree-shaped display of Christmas plates. Use wire plate hangers, or, for invisible hangers, use adhesive-backed plate hangers that stick to the backs of the plates. The adhesive hangers are less likely to scratch or chip the plates and are easily removed by soaking the plates in warm water.

Dress the kitchen window with a jaunty garland made by stringing petite packages on a shiny cord.

Flame On

Beautiful soup ladles are naturals for trimming the kitchen mantel. Use long ribbons to tie the ladles to stocking holders. Add a warm glow by placing flameless tea lights in the ladles.

Flameless candles are the key to this glowing arrangement. They're widely available at crafts and discount stores.

Herbal Essence

A bay leaf wreath and garland are ideal holiday decorations for the kitchen. Bay leaves are long lasting, dry beautifully, and can be harvested for cooking.

Pump up the charm by adding a fragrant herb swag to the wreath. To make an herb swag, clip stems of a variety of herbs that dry well, such as rosemary, bay, and lavender. Tie stems together with raffia, then tie or wire to the bay wreath.

Drape a kitchen doorway with a bay leaf garland to carry the theme into an adjoining room.

Metric Equivalents

The recipes that appear in this cookbook use the standard U.S. method for measuring liquid and dry or solid ingredients (teaspoons, tablespoons, and cups). The information on this chart is provided to help cooks outside the United States successfully use these recipes. All equivalents are approximate.

Metric Equivalents for Different Types of Ingredients

A standard cup measure of a dry or solid ingredient will vary in weight depending on the type of ingredient. A standard cup of liquid is the same volume for any type of liquid. Use the following chart when converting standard cup measures to grams (weight) or milliliters (volume).

Standard Cup	Fine Powder (ex. flour)	Grain (ex. rice)	Granular (ex. sugar)	Liquid Solids (ex. butter)	Liquid (ex. milk)
1	140 g	150 g	190 g	200 g	240 ml
¾	105 g	113 g	143 g	150 g	180 ml
⅔	93 g	100 g	125 g	133 g	160 ml
½	70 g	75 g	95 g	100 g	120 ml
⅓	47 g	50 g	63 g	67 g	80 ml
¼	35 g	38 g	48 g	50 g	60 ml
⅛	18 g	19 g	24 g	25 g	30 ml

Useful Equivalents for Liquid Ingredients by Volume

¼ tsp	=						1 ml
½ tsp	=						2 ml
1 tsp	=						5 ml
3 tsp	=	1 Tbsp	=			½ fl oz	=	15 ml
	=	2 Tbsp	=	⅛ cup	=	1 fl oz	=	30 ml
	=	4 Tbsp	=	¼ cup	=	2 fl oz	=	60 ml
	=	5⅓ Tbsp	=	⅓ cup	=	3 fl oz	=	80 ml
	=	8 Tbsp	=	½ cup	=	4 fl oz	=	120 ml
	=	10⅔ Tbsp	=	⅔ cup	=	5 fl oz	=	160 ml
	=	12 Tbsp	=	¾ cup	=	6 fl oz	=	180 ml
	=	16 Tbsp	=	1 cup	=	8 fl oz	=	240 ml
	=	1 pt	=	2 cups	=	16 fl oz	=	480 ml
	=	1 qt	=	4 cups	=	32 fl oz	=	960 ml
						33 fl oz	=	1000 ml	=	1 l

Useful Equivalents for Dry Ingredients by Weight

(To convert ounces to grams, multiply the number of ounces by 30.)

1 oz	=	¹⁄₁₆ lb	=	30 g
4 oz	=	¼ lb	=	120 g
8 oz	=	½ lb	=	240 g
12 oz	=	¾ lb	=	360 g
16 oz	=	1 lb	=	480 g

Useful Equivalents for Length

(To convert inches to centimeters, multiply the number of inches by 2.5.)

1 in			=	2.5 cm		
6 in	=	½ ft	=	15 cm		
12 in	=	1 ft	=	30 cm		
36 in	=	3 ft	= 1 yd	=	90 cm	
40 in			=	100 cm	=	1 m

Useful Equivalents for Cooking/Oven Temperatures

	Fahrenheit	Celsius	Gas Mark
Freeze Water	32° F	0° C	
Room Temperature	68° F	20° C	
Boil Water	212° F	100° C	
Bake	325° F	160° C	3
	350° F	180° C	4
	375° F	190° C	5
	400° F	200° C	6
	425° F	220° C	7
	450° F	230° C	8
Broil			Grill

Recipe Index

General Index